28 = 11/17/2004
3 copies
30 = 11/2010/2

CRIME AND CRIMINALS

OPPOSING VIEWPOINTS®

Other Books of Related Interest in the Opposing Viewpoints Series:

America's Prisons
Civil Liberties
Criminal Justice
The Death Penalty
Drug Abuse
Social Justice
War and Human Nature

Additional Books in the Opposing Viewpoints Series:

Abortion
AIDS
American Foreign Policy
American Government
American Values
America's Elections
Animal Rights
Biomedical Ethics
Censorship
Central America
Chemical Dependency
China
Constructing a Life Philosophy
Death and Dying
Economics in America
The Environmental Crisis
Euthanasia
The Health Crisis
Israel
Japan
Latin America and U.S. Foreign Policy
Male/Female Roles
The Mass Media
The Middle East
Nuclear War
The Political Spectrum
Poverty
Problems of Africa
Religion in America
Science & Religion
Sexual Values
The Soviet Union
The Superpowers
Teenage Sexuality
Terrorism
The Third World
The Vietnam War

CRIME AND CRIMINALS

OPPOSING VIEWPOINTS®

David L. Bender and Bruno Leone, *Series Editors*

William Dudley, *Book Editor*

OPPOSING VIEWPOINTS SERIES ®

Greenhaven Press, Inc.   PO Box 289009   San Diego, CA 92128-9009

Library of Congress Cataloging-in-Publication Data

Crime & criminals : opposing viewpoints / William Dudley,
                                                    book editor.
    p.   cm. — (Opposing viewpoints series)
    Includes bibliographies and index.
    Summary: Presents opposing viewpoints on various issues involving crime and criminals, including the causes of crime, treatment of criminals, and gun control.
    ISBN 0-89908-416-8 (pbk.) : $7.95 — ISBN 0-89908-441-9 (lib. bdg.) : $13.95
    1. Crime and criminals—United States. 2. Crime prevention—United States. 3. Corrections—United States. 4. White collar crimes—United States. 5. Gun control—United States. [1. Crime and criminals.] I. Dudley, William, 1964-   . II. Title: Crime and criminals. III. Series.
HV6777.C75   1989
364'.973—dc20   89-2155
                                                        CIP
                                                         AC

"Congress shall make no law . . . abridging the freedom of speech, or of the press."

First Amendment to the US Constitution

The basic foundation of our democracy is the first amendment guarantee of freedom of expression. The *Opposing Viewpoints Series* is dedicated to the concept of this basic freedom and the idea that it is more important to practice it than to enshrine it.

Contents

Chapter 5: Would Gun Control Reduce Crime?

Why Consider Opposing Viewpoints?

"It is better to debate a question without settling it than to settle a question without debating it."
Joseph Joubert (1754-1824)

The Importance of Examining Opposing Viewpoints

The purpose of the Opposing Viewpoints Series, and this book in particular, is to present balanced, and often difficult to find, opposing points of view on complex and sensitive issues.

Probably the best way to become informed is to analyze the positions of those who are regarded as experts and well studied on issues. It is important to consider every variety of opinion in an attempt to determine the truth. Opinions from the mainstream of society should be examined. But also important are opinions that are considered radical, reactionary, or minority as well as those stigmatized by some other uncomplimentary label. An important lesson of history is the eventual acceptance of many unpopular and even despised opinions. The ideas of Socrates, Jesus, and Galileo are good examples of this.

Readers will approach this book with their own opinions on the issues debated within it. However, to have a good grasp of one's own viewpoint, it is necessary to understand the arguments of those with whom one disagrees. It can be said that those who do not completely understand their adversary's point of view do not fully understand their own.

A persuasive case for considering opposing viewpoints has been presented by John Stuart Mill in his work *On Liberty*. When examining controversial issues it may be helpful to reflect on this suggestion:

> The only way in which a human being can make some approach to knowing the whole of a subject, is by hearing what can be said about it by persons of every variety of opinion, and studying all modes in which it can be looked at by every character of mind. No wise man ever acquired his wisdom in any mode but this.

Analyzing Sources of Information

The Opposing Viewpoints Series includes diverse materials taken from magazines, journals, books, and newspapers, as well as statements and position papers from a wide range of individuals, organizations and governments. This broad spectrum of sources helps to develop patterns of thinking which are open to the consideration of a variety of opinions.

Pitfalls To Avoid

A pitfall to avoid in considering opposing points of view is that of regarding one's own opinion as being common sense and the most rational stance and the point of view of others as being only opinion and naturally wrong. It may be that another's opinion is correct and one's own is in error.

Another pitfall to avoid is that of closing one's mind to the opinions of those with whom one disagrees. The best way to approach a dialogue is to make one's primary purpose that of understanding the mind and arguments of the other person and not that of enlightening him or her with one's own solutions. More can be learned by listening than speaking.

It is my hope that after reading this book the reader will have a deeper understanding of the issues debated and will appreciate the complexity of even seemingly simple issues on which good and honest people disagree. This awareness is particularly important in a democratic society such as ours where people enter into public debate to determine the common good. Those with whom one disagrees should not necessarily be regarded as enemies, but perhaps simply as people who suggest different paths to a common goal.

Developing Basic Reading and Thinking Skills

In this book, carefully edited opposing viewpoints are purposely placed back to back to create a running debate; each viewpoint is preceded by a short quotation that best expresses the author's main argument. This format instantly plunges the reader into the midst of a controversial issue and greatly aids that reader in mastering the basic skill of recognizing an author's point of view.

A number of basic skills for critical thinking are practiced in the activities that appear throughout the books in the series. Some of the skills are:

Evaluating Sources of Information   The ability to choose from among alternative sources the most reliable and accurate source in relation to a given subject.

Separating Fact from Opinion   The ability to make the basic distinction between factual statements (those that can be demonstrated or verified empirically) and statements of opinion (those that are beliefs or attitudes that cannot be proved).

Identifying Stereotypes   The ability to identify oversimplified, exaggerated descriptions (favorable or unfavorable) about people and insulting statements about racial, religious or national groups, based upon misinformation or lack of information.

Recognizing Ethnocentrism   The ability to recognize attitudes or opinions that express the view that one's own race, culture, or group is inherently superior, or those attitudes that judge another culture or group in terms of one's own.

It is important to consider opposing viewpoints and equally important to be able to critically analyze those viewpoints. The activities in this book are designed to help the reader master these thinking skills. Statements are taken from the book's viewpoints and the reader is asked to analyze them. This technique aids the reader in developing skills that not only can be applied to the viewpoints in this book, but also to situations where opinionated spokespersons comment on controversial issues. Although the activities are helpful to the solitary reader, they are most useful when the reader can benefit from the interaction of group discussion.

Using this book and others in the series should help readers develop basic reading and thinking skills. These skills should improve the reader's ability to understand what they read. Readers should be better able to separate fact from opinion, substance from rhetoric and become better consumers of information in our media-centered culture.

This volume of the Opposing Viewpoints Series does not advocate a particular point of view. Quite the contrary! The very nature of the book leaves it to the reader to formulate the opinions he or she finds most suitable. My purpose as publisher is to see that this is made possible by offering a wide range of viewpoints which are fairly presented.

David L. Bender
Publisher

Introduction

"The streets are safe in Philadelphia, it's only the people who make them unsafe."

Frank Rizzo

In many respects, the United States is a country obsessed with crime. Newspaper articles detailing criminal incidents appear every day, and television news programs frequently begin with the latest crime story. Television police series remain popular, as do shows which reenact actual crimes in lurid detail and invite viewers with information on the suspect to call the police. Hollywood motion pictures often feature criminals and frequently romanticize them.

The prevalence of crime in the media raises the question of how much the media's portrayal of crime is based on reality. How does crime affect Americans in daily life? Kevin N. Wright, a crime researcher, argues that while the number of crimes committed in the US is high (averaging 35 million incidents a year), the probability of being victimized by a violent crime is smaller than many people think. He writes that the odds of an individual being murdered each year are about one in ten thousand, and that the chance of being injured by a criminal is less than being injured in accidents around the home. Wright concludes, "The American news media and the criminal justice establishment exploit the public by sensationalizing crime."

Yet crime affects people in serious ways even when they are not direct victims. Consumers pay higher prices in stores because of shoplifting. Burglary and auto theft result in higher security and insurance costs. The total costs of embezzlement, fraud, and other white-collar crimes run in the billions of dollars. Taxpayers pay additional billions of dollars to house criminals in prisons.

Another more insidious cost of crime is fear. Fear is a feature of many high-crime neighborhoods, where residents live in terror of muggers, drug traffickers, and gangs. Yet crime and the fear of crime are not confined to these communities. If you routinely lock the doors of your car or residence, if you plan your schedule to avoid certain places at certain times, or if you refrain from walking outside at night, you have been touched by America's crime problem. David C. Anderson, a crime reporter and editor

13

for *The New York Times,* described crime in middle-class neighborhoods as "an annoying preoccupation that never went away. . . . And if one thought about it long enough, the preoccupation turned to outrage."

Crime & Criminals: Opposing Viewpoints, replaces the 1984 edition with all new viewpoints. It presents viewpoints from criminologists, social workers, former prisoners, and psychologists. Topics debated are What Causes Crime? How Should Criminals Be Treated? How Can Crime Be Reduced? How Can White-Collar Crime Be Controlled? and Would Gun Control Reduce Crime? As the viewpoints in this book reveal, many important questions concerning the problem of crime remain unresolved.

What Causes Crime?

CRIME AND CRIMINALS

Chapter Preface

Why do some people commit crimes while others abide by society's laws? People have answered this question from many different perspectives.

One perspective on criminality is that biological traits are responsible. This idea has its scientific roots in the work of nineteenth-century criminologist Cesare Lombrosco. Lombrosco believed that criminals could be recognized by certain physical features such as crooked noses and handle-shaped ears. Although his theories aobut recognizing criminals by their appearance have been discredited, research continues today as scientists attempt to determine if genetic tendencies are involved in criminal behavior. In one study, psychologist Sarnoff Mednick surveyed children of criminals who were adopted and raised by noncriminal parents, and found that they were more likely to become criminals than other children.

Others argue that the causes of crime are environmental. Childhood experiences of family abuse and poverty are two reasons often used to explain why people become criminals. Those who believe crime results from environmental factors often advocate job programs, housing programs, and redistributing wealth as ways to stop crime.

The viewpoints in this chapter examine several ideas on the causes of crime.

"Growing inequality . . . will increase the risks of crime and violence."

Poverty Causes Crime

Elliott Currie

Elliott Currie is a sociologist with the Institute for the Study of Social Change at the University of California at Berkeley. He has written articles and the book *Confronting Crime: An American Challenge.* In the following viewpoint, Currie discusses several economic and social trends that he believes contribute to America's crime problem. These trends include growing poverty and inequality, a lack of jobs with adequate pay, and cuts in government programs that support families.

As you read, consider the following questions:

1. What are some of the economic trends Currie labels as ominous?
2. How does Currie connect international economics with the problem of crime?
3. Why is it important to have social programs that support families, according to Currie?

Elliott Currie, *What Kind of Future?* San Francisco, CA: The National Council on Crime and Delinquency, 1987. Reprinted with permission.

Unless we act swiftly and soon, the United States may be a more crime-ridden society in the year 2000 than it is today.

America has already achieved unfortunate distinction as the leader in criminal violence among the world's industrial societies. Barring substantial changes in our current social policies, that unenviable record will not only continue, but may well worsen— with grim and pervasive effects on the quality of American life.

No one, of course, can predict the future with anything like scientific precision; we do not pretend to have a crystal ball. But we *can* observe a number of important trends that will have a profound effect on our chances for security or insecurity, violence or social peace, social alienation or cooperation and productivity. Among them are trends in economic opportunity and equality; in the nature and distribution of work; in the pressures on American families; and in the composition of our population. . . .

Growing Inequality

By every measure we have, the United States is becoming a more unequal society. Without concerted efforts to halt the forces underlying this trend, it promises to continue into the future. Growing inequality will bring many negative consequences for the quality of American life; from increased risks of disease and infant mortality to escalating homelessness to increased threats to family stability. And it will increase the risks of crime and violence.

Inequality breeds violence and crime in many deeply interrelated ways. It creates bitterness, resentment, and alienation among those who see themselves excluded from rewards others share—not just material goods or income alone, but also self-esteem and the chance to participate as full members of their society on an equal footing with others.

Inequality and its usual companion, harsh economic deprivation, weaken and stress the social institutions that make for the healthy growth and development of individuals. They put powerful pressures on families, too often leading to poor parenting, neglect, domestic violence and child abuse. They increase the risks of alcoholism, drug abuse, and inadequate health care—all of which, in turn, put children and youth at a higher risk of delinquency and crime. Inequality and severe poverty sharply limit access to high-quality education and training. They increase the risks of teen-age pregnancy and unwanted children, helping to perpetuate new generations of impoverished and ill-prepared families.

So it is especially ominous that the last several years have brought a wider spread of inequality than since the federal government began gathering statistics on the distribution of income shortly after World War II.

This trend is particularly troubling because it is striking hardest at younger families with children. According to a recent study sponsored by the Joint Economic Committee of Congress, low-income families with young children saw their income drop by more than 25 percent, on average, from 1973 to 1984.

The most dramatic expression of this trend is the rising rate of poverty among America's children. The chance of living in a family below the poverty line, for a child under 18, has risen an astonishing 26 percent since 1979 alone. About one out of every four American children under age six is poor; two out of five are poor if they are Hispanic, and nearly half are poor if they are Black.

For many of these children, especially if they are Black or Hispanic, there is a disturbingly large chance that they will remain in poverty for much of their childhood and perhaps into adulthood. For most families who experience it, poverty is a temporary state they will occupy only briefly. But a Black child born into a poor family can expect to remain in poverty for an *average* of 10 years. It is the children of this sharply rising American poverty who will arrive at the high-crime teenage and young adult years by the turn of the century.

No Mystery

Nobody questions that street criminals typically come from the bottom of the socioeconomic ladder. Unemployment leads to higher arrest rates. Current get-tough programs are aimed at offenders who come from an underclass of brutal social and economic deprivation.

The circumstances that lead some of these people to crime are no mystery. They are born into families struggling to survive—if they have families at all. They are raised in deteriorating, overcrowded housing. They lack adequate nutrition and health care. They are subjected to prejudice and educated in unresponsive schools. They are denied the sense of order, purpose, and self-esteem that makes law-abiding citizens. With nothing to preserve and nothing to lose, they turn to crime for economic survival, a sense of excitement and accomplishment, and an outlet for frustration, desperation, and rage.

David L. Bazelon, *Questioning Authority*, 1988.

Behind these trends lie several complex and interrelated factors. One is the high unemployment of the 1980s which has struck hardest at younger and lower-income workers. This is not just the result of cyclical changes in the fortunes of the economy as a whole. More disturbingly, after each recession since the 1970s we have been left with a higher rate of joblessness than before. In turn, this helps account for the growing proportion of families who are dependent on public assistance to keep them above, or even near, the poverty level. The number of such families, often called "pretransfer" poor in economic language, has risen even faster than the poverty rate as a whole since the beginning of the 1970s.

But widening inequality and deepening poverty also reflect a growing gap in the earnings of people who *do* work. Until the mid-1970s, American workers' wages were becoming slowly but steadily more equal. In the late 1970s, they began to move farther and farther apart. This is partly the result of an influx of younger people into the labor force, the grown-up children of the "baby boom" of the 1950s and 1960s. But this is only part of the story, for even when we take account of the lower age of the work force, the widening wage gap remains."

At the bottom, millions of family heads who work full-time, year-round, do not earn enough money to pull their families out of poverty without public assistance; and their numbers have increased dramatically in the 1980s. The proportion of heads of households whose earnings from year-round work would not bring a family of four above the poverty line jumped by about *one-third* between 1979 and 1984 alone.

In short, one of the most startling trends in the United States today is that a growing proportion of Americans cannot make an adequate living—even as measured by the minimal poverty standard of the federal government—by legitimate work. Adding to the effect of this trend are sharp reductions in cash benefits for low-income people since the mid-1970s. Adjusted for inflation, the average value of benefits under the Aid to Families with Dependent Children (AFDC) program has fallen by a third since 1970; the number of children actually receiving benefits has also fallen significantly, though the number of children poor enough to be eligible for them has risen sharply. There were two million more poor children in 1984 than in 1980, but half a million *fewer* children receiving welfare.

The Changing Shape of Work

Meanwhile, at the other end of the scale, many Americans are doing better and better—enjoying rising earnings, increased discretionary income, and growing power to consume goods and services. We have long understood that this paradox of growing poverty and deprivation amidst growing affluence and plenty is one of the most fertile seedbeds for criminal violence. In the 1950s, observers called it "social dynamite" and predicted—correctly— that it would explode before long. Today, it is a ticking time bomb in the heart of America's cities.

These deepening social divisions are, in part, the result of some of the most far-reaching changes in our history in the ways Americans make a living, or fail to—changes that may have profound effects on crime and violence in the future.

20

We have not yet gotten over the effects of an earlier massive change in the world of work—the transformation of agriculture from an employer of millions of Americans (especially poor Americans) to one that today employs less than 3 percent of the labor force. This transformation threw millions of rural Americans into an urban-industrial economy that was not prepared to absorb them. It was a major contributor to the "urban crisis" that struck American cities from the 1960s onward, with symptoms of rising crime, inner-city joblessness and poverty, drug abuse, and family disruption. The casualties of that transformation, and their descendants, today make up a substantial part of what we have come to call the urban "underclass."

Poverty and Gangs

The gangs, the drugs, the senseless violence are attractive only because children of the black community—and children of poverty, regardless of race—have been made to feel like nothing, like worthless objects, like dirt staked on top of other generations of dirt. Through no fault of their own, these questions nag them from deep within the soul, and the gangs at least give them something to which they can belong, something that gives a meaning to existence.

Herb Cawthorne, *San Diego Tribune*, November 3, 1988.

New economic and technological shifts threaten to aggravate this still-unresolved crisis. In the past, blue-collar employment in traditional industries like steel and automobile manufacturing brought many of the unskilled poor—and their children—into jobs which could provide something close to a "middle-class" income and lifestyle. This was especially important in raising the economic status of Black and Hispanic Americans, accounting for a good part of these groups' economic gains up through the 1960s.

There is much debate over just how much of "smokestack America" has been lost in recent years, and how much will remain in the future. Some argue that America is undergoing rapid "deindustrialization"; others that only a few traditional industries have been declining and that, overall, the share of manufacturing industry in the American economy has remained roughly stable for decades. But few deny that the prospects for *employment* in these industries have dimmed—whether or not the industries themselves survive or even prosper.

Behind this shift lies a fundamental change in America's economic position in the wider world. The United States has faced increasing international competition in the past decade—a trend that can only accelerate in the remaining years of the 20th century, especially because of the growing economic power of some of the newly industrializing countries such as Korea and Taiwan. No one today can pick the "winners" and "losers" in that competition. But we can be sure that sharpened international competition will lead to continued changes in the labor market at home, some of which have been visible for years: more use of automation in place of costly human labor, more transferring of jobs to low-wage countries overseas, and more attempts to cut wages in jobs that remain.

The Limits of Service Jobs

Some observers point to the economy's recent record of job creation as evidence that the outlook for jobs is bright, especially in the emerging "service" economy, that sprawling category that includes everything from doctors, lawyers and psychotherapists, to hamburger cooks and hospital floor-sweepers. But three stubborn problems cloud this hope.

First, far too many of the new jobs created in the service economy are poor-paying, low-quality jobs that cannot support a family and offer few chances for advancement into jobs that can. It is true that many jobs have been created in the 1980s. But the proportion of newly created jobs that pay very low wages has also risen sharply. Between 1963 and 1973, a period of strong expansion in the American economy, less than one new job in every five paid poverty-level wages. But between 1979 and 1985, almost half the new jobs offered only poverty-level wages.

The trend is striking—and ominous. Studies of employment and crime have consistently shown that the kinds of low-paid, unstable jobs we are now creating in such profusion can offer young people no solid stake in their communities, no reliable hope for the future, and no strong shield against the attractions of illegal work—especially the illicit drug trade. Parents locked into these jobs are the ones most likely to abuse or neglect their children; husbands locked into these jobs are the ones most likely to abuse their wives.

Second, many have looked to the growth of "high-tech" industries—computers, electronics, and others—to provide more rewarding job opportunities. Good new jobs *have* opened up in these industries; but not enough of them. High-technology industries represent only a small fraction of current jobs in the U.S. and, despite faster growth, are expected to provide only between one-sixteenth and one-tenth of new jobs created in the next decade. More disturbingly, many of the same forces that are undermining employment in traditional industries are now at work, with troubling speed, in high-technology industries themselves. Such forces include rapid automation, loss of jobs to low-wage havens overseas, and workforce reductions in the face of intensifying competition.

22

Too few good jobs are being created in the American economy; and too many of those we *are* creating are vulnerable to being displaced in the future.

There is a third ominous trend: Those high-level jobs that have been created by the emerging economy have rarely gone to the people most disadvantaged by economic change and most at risk of crime and other social pathologies by the turn of the century.

Some areas of the country have seen strong job growth in the 1980s, based on a booming service economy. But most of the *good* new jobs require more skills and education than the urban poor possess, thereby creating a growing mismatch between jobs and people in the cities. Between 1970 and 1984, New York City gained almost a quarter of a million jobs requiring some college, but *lost* almost half a million requiring less than a high school diploma. The result is what some have called the "dual city"—a city increasingly split between those with the skills and connections that enable access to good jobs, and those whose lack of requisite skills and connections will increasingly cause them to be left behind in the economy of the 21st century. . . .

CRIME ROOTS U.S.A.

To the disturbing trends we've outlined so far—rising inequality, growing deprivation combined with growing affluence, diminishing opportunities for stable, rewarding work—must be added the negative consequences of current social policies in income support, family planning and health care.

Families and Social Policy

What is especially troubling is that these policies have hit hardest at programs designed to support families and children. The family is the single most important institution shaping the chances that individuals will be carefully nurtured and brought up—or not; taught to treat others with compassion and respect—or not; prepared adequately for the requirements of a demanding educational system and a complex economy—or not. Policies that undermine the capacity of families to nurture and to socialize may have long-range consequences which will only become fully apparent when today's children become tomorrow's teenagers and young adults. . . .

When combined with the disturbing trends in the labor market and in income distribution, these policies threaten to give us something close to the worst of all possible worlds for poor families in the coming years. They will have diminished services and supports just when larger social and economic forces are sharply increasing the need for them. If these trends are allowed to continue, we may expect to see a worsening of the disaster which already afflicts low-income families in the United States:

—More families headed by parents who are too young;
—More families headed by parents who are too poor;
—More families with children they cannot afford;
—More children who are saddled with more physical and psychological deficits; and
—More children whose parents have inadequate training in bringing them up and inadequate supports to help them do so.

In turn, we can confidently predict that this will lead to more abused and neglected children and more children entering school burdened by health and learning disabilities—more children, in short, who will not only face potentially diminished opportunities, but also diminished personal resources to enable them to take advantage of those opportunities that do exist. They will be a generation made both volatile and handicapped—in a world itself grown increasingly precarious and difficult even for those best-prepared.

24

"Poverty doesn't cause crime. Crime causes poverty."

Poverty Does Not Cause Crime

James K. Stewart

James K. Stewart is director of the National Institute of Justice. In the following viewpoint, he asserts that crime is the cause, not the result of poverty. Not only are poor inner-city residents directly victimized by criminals, he argues, but crime also causes indirect harm by driving away businesses and fostering community decay. Efforts to fight poverty, Stewart concludes, must begin by combating crime.

As you read, consider the following questions:

1. In what ways has crime harmed poor communities, according to Stewart?
2. According to the author, how does the criminal justice system make the crime problem worse?
3. Why does Stewart believe that crime is more of a problem for the poor than for the wealthy or middle-class?

"The Urban Strangler," by James K. Stewart is reprinted from *Policy Review* Issue No. 37, Summer 1986. *Policy Review* is a publication of The Heritage Foundation, 214 Massachusetts Avenue, NE, Washington, DC 20002.

The idea that poverty causes crime goes back at least as far as Aristotle, who called poverty "the parent of revolution and crime." But in the American inner city, the relationship is exactly the reverse. Poverty doesn't cause crime. Crime causes poverty—or more precisely, crime makes it harder to break out of poverty. The vast majority of poor people are honest, law-abiding citizens whose opportunities for advancement are stunted by the drug dealers, muggers, thieves, rapists, and murderers who terrorize their neighborhoods. These predators are not Robin Hoods of some 1960s ideal; they are career criminals who are destroying the labor and hopes of the poor and they are as oppressive as the most avaricious totalitarian regime.

The most obvious way that criminals prey upon the poor is by robbing them of their property—and sometimes their lives. According to the Bureau of Justice Statistics, 9.6 percent of households with incomes of less than $7,500 were burglarized in 1984. This was the highest victimization rate in the country, nearly twice as high as for households in the $25,000 to $30,000 range, and the poorest also suffer the highest victimization rates for violent crimes. Households with incomes in the $7,500 to $14,999 range suffer the highest median economic losses from personal crimes, including robbery, assault, and theft. Since poor people often cannot afford insurance, and since personal property accounts for almost all of their capital, the theft of a TV, furniture, or car can be devastating. Robberies of cash or checks—for rent, welfare, or Social Security—may at one stroke eliminate a family's ability to pay for home, food, or future.

The typical criminal does not rob from the rich to aid the poor; he steals from the helpless to help himself. There's a routine on "Mother's Day"—the day every week when welfare checks arrive in the mail—of criminals extorting or stealing checks from welfare recipients or looting them from their mailboxes. Automatic deposits or safe deposit boxes aren't necessarily safer, since a criminal who knows your weekly income can collect on penalty of physical assault.

Indirect Costs

The less direct costs of crime to the poor may be even more destructive. The traditional means by which poor people have advanced themselves—overtime, moonlighting, or education to improve future opportunities—can easily be obstructed by crime and fear. Why risk a late job or night school if the return home means waiting at deserted bus stops and walking past crowds of threatening teenagers? A secretary declines overtime opportunities if they extend into the evening because she fears being robbed between the taxi and her front door. A husband gives up night school rather than leave his wife and young children alone at home.

Crime lowers property values in inner cities, making it harder for poor people to accumulate capital and borrow money. Studies in Chicago by Mario Rizzo and Barton A. Smith have shown that for every rise of one percent in the crime rate, rents and home values drop by 0.2 to 0.3 percent. The result is disastrous for families saving and scrimping to build up some modest capital; only by moving can they improve their lot. . . .

Criminals Cause Crime

Criminals cause crime—not bad neighborhoods, inadequate parents, television, schools, drugs, or unemployment. Crime resides within the minds of human beings and is not caused by social conditions. Once we as a society recognize this simple fact, we shall take measures radically different from current ones. To be sure, we shall continue to remedy intolerable social conditions for this is worthwhile in and of itself. But we shall not expect criminals to change because of such efforts.

Stanton E. Samenow, *Inside the Criminal Mind*, 1984.

Similarly, crime can destroy even the most attractive public housing projects, turning them into catastrophes for their tenants. With their long hallways, lonely elevators and stairwells, and absence of street life, public housing high-rises trap and deliver victims to their criminal predators; often they are more treacherous breeding grounds of crime than the squalid tenements they replaced. It was largely because of crime that the Pruitt-Igoe housing complex in St. Louis became uninhabitable and had to be demolished. The Cabrini-Green apartments in Chicago remain in use, but they are ridden with fear.

Crime and Business

Crime strangles commerce and industry in the inner city, and therefore makes it harder for poor people to get jobs. Wherever people are afraid, the market cannot be free. And the high crime rates of poor neighborhoods prevent their residents from taking full advantage of the employment opportunities offered by America's market economy.

A number of economic features ought to attract capital to revive inner cities. Most poor neighborhoods are located in or near the center of our cities and therefore should be prime locations for commerce. The inner city usually provides easy access to railheads, highways, water, and power, as well as to a ready labor supply. It already has the infrastructure that is often missing from the suburbs and exurbs.

But crime in these neighborhoods builds a hurdle to economic development that investors cannot leap. As one recent National

Institute of Justice study reports, crime and the *fear* of crime can influence entrepreneurs' investment decisions more than high taxes or labor costs. Crime is one of the major reasons why businesses restrict operations, relocate, sell, or close down. The Bronx was once an industrial center for injection molders in the plastics industry; crime was one of two main pressures (the other was energy costs) that drove the industry out. . . .

Criminal Recycling Centers

Criminals can tyrannize poor neighborhoods because they are not significantly threatened by the criminal justice system. Only 20 percent of reported crimes are ever solved. And a large proportion of crimes—especially in poor neighborhoods—are never reported. Among households with incomes of less than $7,500, only 40 percent of burglaries and fewer than one-third of all household crimes are ever reported. In poor neighborhoods, people are usually reluctant to turn someone in, call the police, or testify in court. Their reticence is understandable, for local justice policy quickly releases criminal suspects and then delays their trials for months. Victims and key witnesses are therefore exposed to opportunities for intimidation by criminals or their confederates.

In addition, many inner city residents lack confidence in a criminal justice system that recycles convicted felons back into the community where they continue to prey upon victims. Fewer than 30 percent of those convicted of violent crimes and serious property crimes are sentenced to prison. Seventy percent are sent back into the community on "felony probation," a status which leaves them virtually without supervision. The majority of those on felony probation (65 percent) are rearrested for similar crimes within three years.

Because the poor have little or no mobility, there is no escape from these predators or from the totalitarianism of crime. Where criminal enterprises such as narcotics dealing, prostitution, and numbers are the chief income-producing activities, they choke off the growth of legal enterprises, while generating even greater numbers of related crimes in the community. And the street crime typical of poor neighborhoods—robbery, assault, larceny, burglary, drug dealing and use—has a profoundly debilitating effect on the economy.

Neighborhood Deterioration

A recent joint report by the Citizens' Crime Commission of New York City and the Regional Plan Association noted that the two "primary fears of pedestrians in urban public spaces" are "the fear of being suddenly and violently attacked by a stranger and the fear of being bothered by panhandlers, drunks, addicts, rowdy teenagers, loiterers, the mentally disturbed, and other disorderly people." The latter fear—the fear of what James Q. Wilson has termed "incivilities"—may be as powerful as the fear of more serious crime. Abusive or insulting language, harassment, drug use and sale, public drinking, and loitering teenagers are often interpreted as signs of more serious potential crime.

Of course, a panhandler who stands in front of the same store every day, a mentally ill person shouting at passersby, or a group of teenagers hanging out on a street corner are probably not plotting a crime. But when disorderly behavior reaches a certain density on the street, there is less of a deterrent to antisocial behavior. People feel insecure about working, shopping, eating, or strolling in the area. In Jamaica Center, in Queens, New York, a survey of office workers found that 60 percent left their buildings at lunchtime no more than once a week. Fifty-four percent avoided going through the local park during the day, even though it would have been more convenient to do so.

People React Differently

Poverty does not automatically turn people to crime. Poor people all react differently to their situation. Many of the black poor are the hardest working people in society, often working two and three jobs at once.

What defeats these efforts is the continual cycle of insecurity and violence that pervades these neighborhoods. When hardworking black people cannot be protected by the larger society, there is little hope that their decent, law-abiding efforts can lead their communities to much economic progress.

Poverty does not cause crime. It is just the opposite. Crime causes and perpetuates poverty.

William Tucker, *Vigilante*, 1985.

Such acts of avoidance eventually isolate people and empty out public places. They suggest how predatory crime and fear can damage the community in a way that extends far beyond personal injury and loss. As James Q. Wilson has observed:

Predatory crime does not merely victimize individuals, it impedes and in the extreme case, even prevents the formation and maintenance of community. [It disrupts] the delicate nexus of ties, formal and informal, by which we are linked with our neighbors.

Neighborhood deterioration usually starts with an increased sense of fear and vulnerability. Commerce slows; people go elsewhere to shop and stay off the streets in the evening; stores put in alarms and bars in the windows; going-out-of-business sales increase, and as businesses change hands, the quality of merchandise declines and prices rise. Buildings get shabbier and some are abandoned. Disorderly street behavior increases. Investments and loans dry up. People who can afford to move out of the area do; schools deteriorate; and the whole community slides down the spiral of economic and social decline.

No urban redevelopment program can arrest the decline of inner city neighborhoods unless it is accompanied by a sharp reduction in crime. Billions of federal anti-poverty dollars have been poured into depressed inner cities without reviving them economically. The reason is that the people who live and work there are afraid and cannot make the most of the opportunities offered them. The natural dynamic of the marketplace cannot assert itself when a local economy is regulated by crime.

Enterprise zones will be no more successful in reviving inner cities unless they make security a top priority. Tax breaks can influence business locations, but they are of no avail to the company that cannot make a profit because its employees won't work overtime and its customers are afraid to visit. Crime is the ultimate tax on enterprise. It must be reduced or eliminated before poor people can fully share in the American dream.

Eradicating the Parasite

The best anti-poverty policy is a vigorous attack on crime in poor communities. Yellow fever was finally cured when attention was shifted from treating the dying patients to controlling the mosquito that carried the disease. Likewise, inner cities can be restored to economic health if we eradicate the parasite that infects them—crime.

A number of experiments around the country show that the spiral of commercial decline in a crime-ridden neighborhood can be stopped. The key is a dramatic reduction in crime.

In the early 1970s, a 40-block area in the East Brooklyn neighborhood of New York was home to about 200 businesses employing 3,000 people. But the area was deteriorating. By 1979, the number of businesses had fallen to 45, and they employed 1,500 people. The overwhelming reason given by businesses for leaving the neighborhood was fear of crime.

This is a familiar story of decline. A similar one could be told of neighborhoods in virtually every major American city. But in East Brooklyn Industrial Park, there is a surprising sequel. Between 1980 and 1982, the number of burglaries in the 40-block area fell from 134 to 12, the number of street robberies from 208 to 62. Signs of commercial vitality appeared. Twenty new firms have moved into the area and at least 40 others have expressed interest. A new office building of 60,000 square feet is under construction and other buildings are being renovated.

These and other changes were the fruit of a project by a private development company to increase security in the neighborhood.

Working in collaboration with the New York City Public Development Corporation and the police and fire departments, the Local Development Corporation of East New York tore down abandoned buildings, fenced properties, put in burglar alarms, trained private security guards, patrolled the area, provided escort services for residents and businesses—and succeeded in persuading local businesses and residents to help pay for the project. The city contributed by repairing streets and putting in new lighting. . . .

Success in Los Angeles

Improved security is also the key to a remarkably successful urban project in Watts. The riots that destroyed parts of the Los Angeles community 20 years ago wiped out marginal businesses and appeared to have killed off new business growth. New enterprises could not take root because crime made people unwilling to work, shop, or make deliveries in the area. Investors wouldn't touch the neighborhood, even with the prospect of capturing the market, because of the low customer traffic and risks of high losses.

Unemployment and Crime

Though the rise and fall in crime rates may have some connection with changes in the unemployment rate, that connection is hard to detect. . . .

A person who has lost his job may vent his anger and frustration by hitting or killing a spouse or friend, or he may become so moody and depressed as to be incapable of any action, including an assault. A family afflicted by the economic loss consequent on unemployment may be torn asunder or drawn together. There is no good reason in advance for assuming one reaction or another.

James Q. Wilson and Philip J. Cook, *The Public Interest*, Spring 1985.

The first commercial enterprise of any kind to be built since the riots was the Martin Luther King, Jr. Shopping Center, which opened in 1984 at a location formerly called "Charcoal Alley" as a result of its fiery devastation in the riots. Estimated first-year sales were about $45 million, or about $350 per leasable square foot—more than three times the average revenues of first-year shopping centers. Though it was built in one of the most violent and crime-ridden areas of the city, no major acts of violence or vandalism have occurred there. "The success of the shopping center shows that you can make money and create jobs here without fear of the stereotype that says you can't do business in the ghetto because of crime," said Dr. Clyde Oden, a Watts physician who is president of the Watts Health Foundation.

Built by Alexander Haagen Development, the shopping center is designed to be an oasis of security where businesses can function and customers can do their banking and shopping without fear. The entire facility is surrounded by a wrought-iron fence like the one surrounding the White House. Inside there is a control center with closed circuit TV monitors. Private security guards trained by the developer patrol the shopping center 24 hours a day, and the center also has a Los Angeles Police field office.

The center has created jobs for local residents through its private security program as well as its stores. In the words of Grace Payne, executive director of a neighborhood job training and community counseling center, construction of the mall is "the greatest move that has been made for the people in this community to have jobs." Four smaller shopping centers have subsequently opened in the area. . . .

The programs in Brooklyn . . . and Watts show that, if security is provided, businesses can take root in even the most hostile environment. Reducing crime and its disruptive effect on community ties eliminates the largest and most devastating obstacle to development in many poor neighborhoods. And where businesses can develop, they encourage further growth and help create a community's cohesiveness and identity.

Crime is a hazard to everyone in our society, but it hurts the poor the most; the wealthy and the middle class can call upon private and community resources to cushion them from some of its dangers. The first step in any urban anti-poverty program must therefore begin with the reduction of crime. This means more vigorous prosecution of predatory criminals and more vigorous protection of people in poor neighborhoods. America is beginning to take the steps necessary to fight terrorism overseas; the time has come to fight the even more threatening terrorism in our own cities.

"Criminality is an unfortunate by-product of the American way of life."

American Values Cause Crime

Kevin N. Wright

The United States has a much higher violent crime rate than many other industrialized countries. In the following viewpoint, Kevin N. Wright explains this difference by citing American cultural values of autonomy, materialism, and distrust of authority. These values, combined with a lack of family and neighborhood social controls, all contribute to crime in the US, Wright argues. Wright is an assistant professor at the criminal justice program of the State University of New York at Binghamton.

As you read, consider the following questions:

1. According to the author, what prevents people from committing crimes?
2. What examples does Wright use to show that exploitation is an integral part of American life? Do you agree or disagree?

Kevin N. Wright, THE GREAT AMERICAN CRIME MYTH (Contributions in Criminology and Penology, No. 9, Greenwood Press, Inc., Westport, CT, 1985), pp. 182-192. Copyright © 1985 by Kevin N. Wright. Reprinted with permission of author and publisher.

Social order is not and can never be obtained or maintained by coercion. Law-abiding behavior is acquired primarily through socialization. Think about the last time you were extremely angry with someone, so enraged that you could have struck or even killed that person. What prevented you from going ahead and doing it? Something within you, some unidentified force, kept you from physically injuring your adversary. But you probably never considered that you might be punished for your action. The threat of criminal sanction is simply not a strong or important determinant of behavior. Rather, through a process of learning and socialization you came to know that hurting others is unacceptable. . . .

Exploitation and American Society

The problem with social control within American society is demonstrated not only by criminality but also by widespread exploitive behavior. Not all exploitive acts are considered criminal, but almost all criminal acts are exploitive. Where interpersonal exploitation is common, the distinction between criminal and noncriminal varieties is not important when considering its causes and controls. Criminality and other forms of exploitation occur because they are culturally prescribed and permitted, and because informal prohibitions and sanctions are inadequate within that culture.

Let us begin by considering the vast amount of such behavior in the United States. If exploitation is broadly defined as "taking unfair advantage of another person for personal gain," examples from all aspects of American life become apparent. For example, dishonest students exploit their peers by taking unfair academic advantage. Recent studies indicate that cheating is common to all levels of education. It is widespread in secondary schools and is described as epidemic in universities. . . .

Another example is the widespread occurrence of consumer fraud, where companies market products or services that are not what they are supposed to be. The product may not be genuine or safe or exactly as advertised, or it may break within the first few days after it is purchased. Such practices are exploitive because business is acquired by selling a product that does not exist. Many consider such acts good business and are quick to trot out the old admonition "Let the buyer beware." Whether acceptable or not—a question of value—consumer fraud involves selfish utilization of others. . . .

Even the medical profession, which has traditionally been regarded as more altruistically than monetarily motivated, has recently been accused of exploiting patients for economic gain. Doctors order unneeded medical tests or schedule surgeries—particularly appendectomies, tonsillectomies and hysterectomies—

when the medical benefits of such measures are not always evident. Investigations of the federal Medicare program revealed this practice, as well as outright fraud involving doctors, hospitals, and other health care providers.

Other subtle forms of exploitation also crept through the practice of health care. Few dentists will fill a cavity without an initial visit and a thorough cleaning of all your teeth. The profession argues that this is preventive dentistry, but the larger fees involved are inescapable. . . .

What Is Acceptable?

If Daddy can pull one over on his boss and stay home sick when he is not really sick, why can't I cheat on an exam? If a company forces me to work in an unsafe plant, why can't I take tools from it? Other examples could be given, but the point is that in a society where exploitation is common, it becomes difficult to discern what is acceptable and what is not acceptable. Legal definitions are insufficient. Whether people even consider the effects of their activities on others, and whether they care, is determined by how they have been socialized. In a society where one is often reminded that the other guy is likely to take advantage, it is difficult to instill the belief that exploitation is bad. . . .

Crime is determined within the dominant culture of a particular society. As long as people are socialized to accept and practice various forms of exploitation because of the value placed on achievement, particularly material achievement, and not to concern themselves too much with the means of achievement, then crime will be prevalent.

Kevin N. Wright, *The Great American Crime Myth*, 1985.

Some forms of American interpersonal exploitation are considerably more seedy than those discussed so far. Pornography, for example, exploits the human body and the act of love by reducing each to an object of lust from the complex beings and human events they actually are. It is demeaning and cheapens life. This is clearest in child pornography, where a young model is taken advantage of for profit and where in the end childhood and children in general suffer degradation from abject portrayal. But look at the popularity of pornography, both soft-core and hardcore. People spend billions of dollars for it—in print, in film and videotape, and for live showings.

And the American news media and the criminal-justice establishment exploit the public by sensationalizing crime. Each profits from the consumption of horrible crime stories either in increased sales or in bigger budgets. It is yet another form of the use of others for one's own ends. . . .

It should be clear that exploitation is part of American life. In fact, in reading these examples you have probably been reminded of other forms of exploitation with which you personally are familiar.

Exploitation and Crime

The proposition that exploitation is a common theme in American social life should not surprise anyone. This is a nation that values achievement and prides itself on the ability to overcome obstacles in order to solve major problems and achieve great things. But achievement is a difficult motivation to control and can easily take the form of overachievement when the ends are considered to justify any means and when the act of achieving becomes more important than what one does to reach that outcome. To the degree that this happens within society, achievement will be more highly regarded than honesty, integrity, self-restraint and control, and respect for other people. But is this not the way it is in the United States? People are often evaluated by their possessions—status is determined by wealth—not by the way they live their lives.

As an expedient and effective method of achievement, taking unfair advantage of others is one way, and perhaps a common way, of getting ahead, of gaining the competitive edge, and in the end of acquiring wealth, status, and power in American society. Given the Americanization of exploitation, is it any wonder that criminality is so prevalent? People constantly receive the message that exploitation is acceptable. Examine these common admonitions: "I don't care what it takes to get the job done," "Show them who's boss," "You owe it to yourself," "You deserve it," "Win at all costs." The motivations, the rationalizations, and even the methods of utilization are all present in American culture. Criminality merely surfaces as one method of expressing this popular theme.

You may object to this assertion. You may argue that criminality is a form of exploitation but that compared with other forms, it is qualitatively more reprehensible and the offender is more culpable. You may not be as frightened or angered by other forms as you are by blatant destruction and theft of property and violent confrontation. But some forms of exploitation are as dangerous as those defined as criminal, and the step from some exploitation to worse exploitation is shorter than from no exploitation to worse. Any number of factors may contribute to the selection of one form of exploitation over another. The fact that exploitation is common makes it more difficult for the inhibitors—self-restraint and control—to be effective. Despite any degree of reprehensibility or culpability, the presence of exploitation and the diminution of important inhibitors creates an environment conducive to crime. Attacking criminality alone is illogical. It is analogous to an attempt to extinguish the flames of a fire fed by an open gas jet: the flames are the major problem, but the cause is the gas. . . .

This explanation of crime control raises an interesting and important question. Can a modern, achievement-oriented society be well controlled, or are such societies doomed to experience high levels of crime? The answer is that a well-contained, controlled, complex, and modern society is possible. Japan is the best example. It is an achievement-oriented nation that recently outstepped American productivity. Yet the crime rate in Japan is only a fraction of that in the United States. For every crime of any sort in Japan, four *serious* crimes take place in the United States. A person is ten times more likely to be murdered in America, six times more likely to be the victim of theft, and 208 times more likely to be robbed. A woman is thirteen times more likely to be raped. The differences are real, but why?

The Social Context

As long as we think of crime and other social problems as consequences of individual or isolated social causes, our vision is, by necessity, limited and distorted. We cannot blame heredity, family upbringing, poverty, urban living, and so on as the ultimate or exclusive causes of criminality. All these factors, even inherited qualities of the individual, become effective only in the context of the larger society, which operates under a particular socioeconomic setup and its corresponding ideologies. These ideologies are both the historic result and the actual support of a particular social system. It is time we realized that the curse of crime, drug addiction, impersonal relationships, prostitution, separated families, child abuse, various venereal disease epidemics, as well as the many superlative achievements of the American society, are explainable not as individual aberrations or malfunctions of certain social institutions, but in terms of the overall American value system, which, as we have seen, is rooted in the concepts of free enterprise, individual achievement, personal pursuit of happiness, relative indifference to the problems of other human beings, permissiveness, and almost total lack of discipline in child rearing and educational practices.

Parviz Saney, *Crime and Culture in America*, 1986.

The key is in effective social discipline resulting from viable informal controls. Most Japanese people live within stable networks of people they know and who know them, so their social environments are more personal than those found in the United States and consist of friends and family with whom long ties and traditions exist. Because such relationships are valued, Japanese people refrain from activities that might jeopardize their acceptance in the social network. A much stronger sense of social responsibility and an appreciation for the dire consequences of deviant behavior results. Social constraints are tied to personal attachments, and people obey the law not because of some external threat from government but because the risks of dishonor within the informal group are too great.

For individuals in Japan, the sense of personal integrity and moral obligation is stronger than that found in the United States. In Japan, just as in this nation, status is associated with achievement and determined by employment and wealth, but people are also judged by their honorableness. An individual without great material achievement can be considered a worthy and respected person. This system works well because known people who are socially important understand what you are like, know whether you are honorable, trustworthy, and considerate. Outward symbols to strangers are less important than meaningful opinions about integrity. Informal social groups serve two important functions: to educate children in proper and respectable behavior through effective socialization, and to reinforce that discipline by their group pressure and importance.

Authority is also regarded differently by the Japanese. In contrast to the assertive, suspicious, and often resentful attitudes Americans have, the typical response in Japan is one of subservience and compliance. The act of pleading guilty by accused criminals provides an illustration of this difference. In the United States somewhere around 90 to 95 percent of all people convicted plead guilty—because they are plea-bargaining, receiving a lesser charge or sentence for cooperating with law enforcement authorities. Approximately the same proportion of Japanese criminals also plead guilty, but in Japan plea-bargaining is illegal. To Americans, who challenge authority and resist intervention, this is inconceivable. But the Japanese offender throws himself on the mercy of the court; to regain his honor, he admits wrongdoing and accepts his punishment. This tells us a great deal about the utility of formal sanctions. As one author suggests, in Japan "rather than official action prompting compliance with social norms, compliant attitudes toward authority enhance the efficiency of official action." . . .

Crime in Switzerland

Switzerland is a modern Western nation with Western customs, but it too has little crime. . . . Just as in Japan, social atomization has been avoided, and there are informal groups that are capable of applying pressure to assure conformity. Familial stability and strength has remained largely intact in Switzerland, and this allows families to exercise significant influence on their members. Until recently a distinctive youth culture was not present in Swiss society and greater intergenerational integration occurred, allowing for closer supervision and more complete socialization of young people. . . .

It could be argued that the low level of crime in Japan is attributable to the high social homogeneity within the population. To a degree this is true and irrefutable. But social heterogeneity and a low incidence of crime are found in Switzerland. This would suggest that social homogeneity, while helpful, is not necessary for the maintenance of a restrained society. It might also be suggested that the absence of poverty in Switzerland accounts for its lower crime rate, but in Japan there is considerable poverty yet little crime. The feature the two nations hold in common is clearly the effective informal controls. . . .

Conclusions

Criminality is culturally prescribed by the acceptance and practice of exploitive behavior within American society. The distinction between criminality and other forms of exploitation, while perhaps qualitatively different, is predominantly one of legal definition which often becomes muddled.

Low incidence of criminality is attributable to the inculcation of self-control within a population. If there is a strong sense of interpersonal responsibility, and if individual worth is defined by honor and integrity as well as by achievement, criminality is unlikely to be a significant problem. Cultural assimilation of these values occurs not because of formal dictates by the state but within small, informal groups of known people who can effectively socialize and supervise one another. This is possible within a society only when cellular, tribelike groups survive the social atomization that occurs as society and state are differentiated.

Such cellular configurations are not found in American society. In fact, specific characteristics of the United States work directly against the development of such stable networks. Americans prize individualism, social and geographic mobility, privacy, and autonomy. They are suspicious of authority and believe in the separation of public and private responsibilities. These attributes work directly to preclude effective use of informal controls.

So the United States finds itself in an unfortunate situation. It experiences high levels of criminality, and many citizens are injured and robbed each year. People wish the problem could be reduced, if not resolved, and as a nation accustomed to accomplishing its goals, this objective does not appear to be unreasonable. But punitive formal controls will simply not work. And given the social characteristics of American society, neither will informal constraints. Criminality is an unfortunate by-product of the American way of life.

"The causes of crime lie in a combination of predisposing biological traits channeled by social circumstance into criminal behavior."

Biological Factors Cause Crime

James Q. Wilson and Richard J. Herrnstein

James Q. Wilson is a professor of management at the University of California at Los Angeles. Richard J. Herrnstein is professor of psychology at Harvard. Together they wrote *Crime and Human Nature*, from which this viewpoint is taken. Wilson and Herrnstein assert that crime is not caused solely by social forces. They argue that some people are more likely to become criminals than others because of physical and psychological traits that can be traced to heredity and early childhood development.

As you read, consider the following questions:

1. According to the authors, are criminals born or made?
2. What are two heritable factors Wilson and Herrnstein believe can contribute to crime?
3. Does biology explain differences in crime rates between races, according to the authors?

A revolution in our understanding of crime is quietly over-throwing some established doctrines. Until recently, criminologists looked for the causes of crime almost entirely in the offenders' social circumstances. There seemed to be no shortage of circumstances to blame: weakened, chaotic or broken families, ineffective schools, antisocial gangs, racism, poverty, unemployment. Criminologists took seriously, more so than many other students of social behavior, the famous dictum of the French sociologist Emile Durkheim: Social facts must have social explanations. The sociological theory of crime had the unquestioned support of prominent editorialists, commentators, politicians, and most thoughtful people.

Today, many learned journals and scholarly works draw a different picture. Sociological factors have not been abandoned, but increasingly it is becoming clear to many scholars that crime is the outcome of an interaction between social factors and certain biological factors, particularly for the offenders who, by repeated crimes, have made public places dangerous. The idea is still controversial, but increasingly, to the old question "Are criminals born or made?" the answer seems to be: both. The causes of crime lie in a combination of predisposing biological traits channeled by social circumstance into criminal behavior. The traits alone do not inevitably lead to crime; the circumstances do not make criminals of everyone; but together they create a population responsible for a large fraction of America's problem of crime in the streets. . . .

Identical Twins

The most compelling evidence of biological factors for criminality comes from two studies—one of twins, the other of adopted boys. Since the 1920's it has been understood that twins may develop from a single fertilized egg, resulting in identical genetic endowments—identical twins—or from a pair of separately fertilized eggs that have about half their genes in common—fraternal twins. A standard procedure for estimating how important genes are to a trait is to compare the similarity between identical twins with that between fraternal twins. When identical twins are clearly more similar in a trait than fraternal twins, the trait probably has high heritability.

There have been about a dozen studies of criminality using twins. More than 1,500 pairs of twins have been studied in the United States, the Scandinavian countries, Japan, West Germany, Britain and elsewhere, and the result is qualitatively the same everywhere. Identical twins are more likely to have similar criminal records than fraternal twins. For example, the late Karl O. Christiansen, a Danish criminologist, using the Danish Twin Register, searched police, court and prison records for entries regarding twins born in a certain region of Denmark between 1881 and 1910. When an identical twin had a criminal record, Christiansen found, his or her co-twin was more than twice as likely to have one also than when a fraternal twin had a criminal record.

In the United States, a similar result has recently been reported by David Rowe, a psychologist at the University of Oklahoma, using questionnaires instead of official records to measure criminality. Twins in high school in almost all the school districts of Ohio received questionnaires by mail, with a promise of confidentiality as well as a small payment if the questionnaires were filled out and returned. The twins were asked about their activities, including their delinquent behavior, about their friends and about their co-twins. The identical twins were more similar in delinquency than the fraternal twins. In addition, the twins who shared more activities with each other were no more likely to be similar in delinquency than those who shared fewer activities.

Family Studies

No single method of inquiry should be regarded as conclusive. But essentially the same results are found in studies of adopted children. The idea behind such studies is to find a sample of children adopted early in life, cases in which the criminal histories of both adopting and biological parents are known. Then, as the children grow up, researchers can discover how predictive of their criminality are the family histories of their adopting and biological parents. Recent studies show that the biological family history contributes substantially to the adoptees' likelihood of breaking the law.

Genetics Do Influence Criminality

Our study, like others, strongly suggests that genetic influences can lead to the development of criminal behavior. And because genetic transmission can involve only biological factors, we conclude that biological characteristics must be responsible for some criminal behavior, especially that of multiple offenders.

Sarnoff Mednick, *Psychology Today*, March 1985.

For example, Sarnoff Mednick, a psychologist at the University of Southern California, and his associates in the United States and Denmark have followed a sample of several thousand boys adopted in Denmark between 1927 and 1947. Boys with criminal biological parents and noncriminal adopting parents were more likely to have criminal records than those with noncriminal biological parents and criminal adopting parents. The more criminal convictions a boy's natural parents had, the greater the risk of criminality for boys being raised by adopting parents who had no records. The risk was unrelated to whether the boy or his adopting parents knew about the natural parents' criminal records, whether the natural parents committed their crimes before or after the boy was given up for adoption, or whether the boy was adopted immediately after birth or a year or two later. The results of this study have been confirmed in Swedish and American samples of adopted children.

Genetic Factors

Because of studies like these, many sociologists and criminologists now accept the existence of genetic factors contributing to criminality. When there is disagreement, it is about how large the genetic contribution to crime is and about how the criminality of biological parents is transmitted to their children.

Both the twin and adoption studies show that genetic contributions are not alone responsible for crime—there is, for example, some increase in criminality among boys if their adopted fathers are criminal even when their biological parents are not, and not every co-twin of a criminal identical twin becomes criminal himself. Although it appears, on average, to be substantial, the precise size of the genetic contribution to crime is probably unknowable, particularly since the measures of criminality itself are now so crude.

We have a bit more to go on with respect to the link that transmits a predisposition toward crime from parents to children. No one believes there are "crime genes," but there are two major attributes that have, to some degree, a heritable base and that appear to influence criminal behavior. These are intelligence and temperament. Hundreds of studies have found that the more genes people share, the more likely they are to resemble each other intellectually and temperamentally.

Crime and Intelligence

Starting with studies in the 1930's, the average offender in broad samples has consistently scored 91 to 93 on I.Q. tests for which the general population's average is 100. The typical offender does worse on the verbal items of intelligence tests than on the nonverbal items but is usually below average on both.

Criminologists have long known about the correlation between criminal behavior and I.Q., but many of them have discounted it for various reasons. Some have suggested that the correlation can be explained away by the association between low socioeconomic status and crime, on the one hand, and that between low I.Q. and low socioeconomic status, on the other. These criminologists say it is low socioeconomic status, rather than low I.Q., that fosters crime. Others have questioned whether I.Q. tests really measure intelligence for the populations that are at greater risk for breaking the law. The low scores of offenders, the argument goes, betray a culturally deprived background or alienation from our society's values rather than low intelligence. Finally, it is often noted that the offenders in some studies have been caught for their crimes. Perhaps the ones who got away have higher I.Q.s.

But these objections have proved to be less telling than they once seemed to be. There are, for example, many poor law-abiding people living in deprived environments, and one of their more salient characteristics is that they have higher I.Q. scores than those in the same environment who break the law.

The Average Criminal

The average offender tends to be constitutionally distinctive, though not extremely or abnormally so. The biological factors whose traces we see in faces, physiques, and correlations with the behavior of parents and siblings are predispositions toward crime that are expressed as psychological traits and activated by circumstances. It is likely that the psychological traits involve intelligence and personality, and that the activating events include certain experiences within the family, in school, and in the community at large.

James Q. Wilson and Richard J. Herrnstein, *Crime and Human Nature*, 1985.

Then, too, it is a common misconception that I.Q. tests are invalid for people from disadvantaged backgrounds. If what is implied by this criticism is that scores predict academic potential or job performance differently for different groups, then the criticism is wrong. A comprehensive recent survey sponsored by the National Academy of Sciences concluded that "tests predict about as well for one group as for another." And that some highly intelligent criminals may well be good at eluding capture is fully consistent with the belief that offenders, in general, have lower scores than nonoffenders.

If I.Q. and criminality are linked, what may explain the link? There are several possibilities. One is that low scores on I.Q. tests signify greater difficulty in grasping the likely consequences of action or in learning the meaning and significance of moral codes. Another is that low scores, especially on the verbal component of the tests, mean trouble in school, which leads to frustration, thence to resentment, anger and delinquency. Still another is that persons who are not as skillful as others in expressing themselves verbally may find it more rewarding to express themselves in ways in which they will do better, such as physical threat or force.

Crime and Temperament

For some repeat offenders, the predisposition to criminality may be more a matter of temperament than intelligence. Impulsiveness, insensitivity to social mores, a lack of deep and enduring emotional attachments to others and an appetite for danger are among the temperamental characteristics of high-rate offenders. Temperament is, to a degree, heritable, though not as much so as intelligence. All parents know that their children, shortly after birth, begin to exhibit certain characteristic ways of behaving—they are placid or fussy, shy or bold. Some of the traits endure, among them aggressiveness and hyperactivity, although they change in form as the child develops. As the child grows up, these traits, among others, may gradually unfold into a disposition toward unconventional, defiant or antisocial behavior.

Lee Robins, a sociologist at Washington University School of Medicine in St. Louis, reconstructed 30 years of the lives of more than 500 children who were patients in the 1920's at a child guidance clinic in St. Louis. She was interested in the early precursors of chronic sociopathy, a condition of antisocial personality that often includes criminal behavior as one of its symptoms. Adult sociopaths in her sample who did not suffer from psychosis, mental retardation or addiction, were, without exception, antisocial before they were 18. More than half of the male sociopaths had serious symptoms before they were 11. The main childhood precursors were truancy, poor school performance, theft, running away, recklessness, slovenliness, impulsiveness and guiltlessness. The more symptoms in childhood, the greater the risk of sociopathy in adulthood.

Other studies confirm and extend Dr. Robins's conclusions. For example, two psychologists, John J. Conger of the University of Colorado and Wilbur Miller of Drake University in Des Moines, searching back over the histories of a sample of delinquent boys in Denver, found that "by the end of the third grade, future delinquents were already seen by their teachers as more poorly adapted than their classmates. They appeared to have less regard for the rights and feelings of their peers; less awareness of the need to accept responsibility for their obligations, both as individuals and as members of a group, and poorer attitudes toward authority."

Childhood Problems

Traits that foreshadow serious, recurrent criminal behavior have been traced all the way back to behavior patterns such as hyperactivity and unusual fussiness, and neurological signs such as atypical brain waves or reflexes. In at least a minority of cases, these are detectable in the first few years of life. . . .

Premature infants or those born with low birth weights have a special problem. These children are vulnerable to any adverse circumstances in their environment—including child abuse—that may foster crime. Although nurturing parents can compensate for adversity, cold or inconsistent parents may exacerbate it. Prematurity and low birth weight may result from poor prenatal care, a bad diet or excessive use of alcohol or drugs. Whether the bad care is due to poverty, ignorance or anything else, here we see criminality arising from biological, though not necessarily genetic, factors. It is now known that these babies are more likely than normal babies to be the victims of child abuse.

The Ancient Debate

Few questions stir more passion than the ancient debate over the relative importance of heredity and the environment. The debate is often stated in extreme form: genes are destiny and environment does not matter, or vice versa. Yet there is no organism without both genes and environment. Heredity affects traits and behavior and the evidence is strong that many individual characteristics have a genetic basis, no matter how slight. The possibility that the tendency toward law-abidingness or criminality has a genetic basis cannot be dismissed out of hand.

Morgan O. Reynolds, *Crime by Choice*, 1985.

We do not mean to blame child abuse on the victim by saying that premature and low-birth-weight infants are more difficult to care for and thus place a great strain on the parents. But unless parents are emotionally prepared for the task of caring for such children, they may vent their frustration at the infant's unresponsiveness by hitting or neglecting it. Whatever it is in parent and child that leads to prematurity or low birth weight is compounded by the subsequent interaction between them. Similarly, children with low I.Q.s may have difficulty in understanding rules, but if their parents also have poor verbal skills, they may have difficulty in communicating rules, and so each party to the conflict exacerbates the defects of the other.

Political Reactions

The statement that biology plays a role in explaining human behavior, especially criminal behavior, sometimes elicits a powerful political or ideological reaction. Fearful that what is being proposed is a crude biological determinism, some critics deny the evidence while others wish the evidence to be confined to scientific journals. Scientists who have merely proposed studying the possible effects of chromosomal abnormalities on behavior have been ruthlessly attacked by other scientists, as have those who have made public the voluminous data showing the heritability of intelligence and temperament.

Some people worry that any claim that biological factors influence criminality is tantamount to saying that the higher crime rate of black compared to white Americans has a genetic basis. But no responsible work in the field leads to any such conclusion. The data show that of all the reasons people vary in their crime rates, race is far less important than age, sex, intelligence and the other individual factors that vary within races. Any study of the causes of crime must therefore first consider the individual factors. Differences among races may have many explanations, most of them having nothing to do with biology.

The intense reaction to the study of biological factors in crime, we believe, is utterly misguided. In fact, these discoveries, far from implying that "criminals are born" and should be locked up forever, suggest new and imaginative ways of reducing criminality by benign treatment. The opportunity we have is precisely analogous to that which we had when the biological bases of other disorders were established. Mental as well as physical illness— alcoholism, learning disabilities of various sorts, and perhaps even susceptibilities to drug addiction—now seem to have genetic components. In each case, new understanding energized the search for treatment and gave it new direction. Now we know that many forms of depression can be successfully treated with drugs; in time we may learn the same of Alzheimer's disease. Alcoholics are helped when they understand that some persons, because of their predisposition toward addiction to alcohol, should probably never consume it at all. A chemical treatment of the predisposition is a realistic possibility. Certain types of slow learners can already be helped by special programs. In time, others will be also. . . .

It took years of patiently following the life histories of many men and women to establish the linkages between smoking or diet and disease; it will also take years to unravel the complex and subtle ways in which intelligence, temperament, hormonal levels and other traits combine with family circumstances and later experiences in school and elsewhere to produce human character.

"The primary cause of crime is . . . the failure of individuals to develop right values and to resist evil."

Lack of Moral Character Causes Crime

Donald D. Schroeder

Many people believe that searching for the causes of crime in poverty or other social ills misses the point. In the following viewpoint, Donald D. Schroeder states that crime is caused by the moral failure of criminals to distinguish between right and wrong. He argues that families and the criminal justice system should treat wrongdoing with punishment. Schroeder is a senior writer for *The Plain Truth*, a magazine published and distributed by the Worldwide Church of God.

As you read, consider the following questions:

1. How might the author's experiences described at the beginning of the viewpoint affect his attitudes towards crime?
2. What arguments does Schroeder give in explaining why poverty does not cause crime?
3. According to the author, how is character established?

Donald D. Schroeder, "Crime: The Causes and the Cure," *The Plain Truth*, August 1988.

I know how upsetting it can be to be a crime victim. During a recent year I was a victim of crime three times within a period of only a few months.

First, while on an outing in the mountains with my family, I had my car battery stolen.

Shortly after this exasperating experience, I walked right into the middle of a store robbery. The person behind the counter I thought was the clerk wasn't a clerk but a robber in the process of his day's activity. One of his partners suddenly came out from behind a display, pointed a gun at me and forced me to lie face down in a back room with a trembling employee until the robbery was finished.

A few months after this I had my car stolen, which I fortunately recovered intact.

Fear of Crime

It's no wonder citizens in more and more places are frightened. Rising crime now plagues rural and well-to-do suburban areas as well as inner-city ghettos. Fear of crime has made many people feel they are virtual prisoners within their own homes or neighborhoods. They are afraid to be alone, afraid of straying from short familiar paths to travel or shop, afraid to change neighborhoods, afraid of strangers.

Why the increasing crescendo of crime and violence in our world? Why worsening juvenile and criminal gang behavior and senseless crimes against total strangers or innocent passersby?

There are causes of these frightening problems. No society will ever effectively conquer crime unless it correctly identifies and eliminates the *causes* of crime.

The tragedy of our age is this: Though law enforcement and government officials today identify some major causes of crime, they still find themselves able to do little or nothing about them.

False Causes

Most criminologists, sociologists and other officials are forced to fight crime at the wrong end of the problem. Many people blame rising crime on the lack of police, or the easy availability of guns or drugs, or on an overburdened and often crippled criminal justice system, or on underemployment, violent entertainment or poverty. These conditions do contribute to the crime problem, but they do not deal with the most fundamental causes.

The chief cause of criminal behavior is not poverty. It is true, poverty-stricken ghettos concentrate and aggravate the social conditions that encourage criminal behavior. But such factors don't automatically produce a criminal mentality. The majority of individuals living in poverty areas in both developed and developing nations are not criminals or violent. Only a minority are—though their numbers are growing for discernible reasons.

We must also answer why senseless crime, theft, dishonesty and violence are growing in middle- and upper-class families, businesses, communities and schools.

The Primary Cause

The primary cause of crime is the lack of right character!

It is the failure of individuals to develop right values and to resist evil, whatever its source. When children or adults—rich, poor or middle class—allow themselves, or are encouraged, to develop criminal attitudes in their character, the results will be quite obvious. They *become* criminals!

Criminal thinking and behavior come from wrong spiritual attitudes and values of mind. They spring from a willingness to take and get things at harm or loss to others. They usually result from unwillingness to work legitimately and patiently to achieve what one needs or wants. Or from impatience or unwillingness to solve problems peaceably. . . .

The Need for Discipline

More than two decades ago, Herbert T. Jenkins, chief of police of Atlanta, Georgia, clearly answered the question of why so much crime and why so many children become delinquents. Listen to his words:

"In my 30 years of experience, I have come to the conclusion that the lack of discipline and self-discipline are the major roots of all crime. If the family fails to discipline a youngster, thereby instilling in him a sense of self-discipline, then it later becomes the almost hopeless job of the courts to try to do it. For that is where this type of youngster always ends up."

The Real Dividing Line

I suggest that it is time we all—black, white, brown, what have you—get one thing straight. The real dividing line in society isn't between blacks and whites. It's between good people and bad ones, between those who accept their responsibilities as citizens and those who don't know the meaning of such words.

William Murchison, *Conservative Chronicle*, February 10, 1988.

Children must be taught by parents and other responsible adults in society to recognize, resist and overcome emotional feelings of instability, destructiveness, defiance of authority or lying, in their character. They must be taught to value and respect other humans and their property. If a society doesn't train its youths in such attitudes in early years of life, it is certain to have a horrendous crime problem.

Moral and stable family life is necessary to cure crime. Tragically, the stable family unit is being rapidly broken down through divorce, separation and desertion. Proper rearing of children is often undermined because parents frequently are too busy with other interests, activities or pleasures.

Moral Relativism

For several decades now, moral relativism—the lack of judgment or discernment of what's right and wrong—has been in fashion in many homes, schools and even in religious institutions. The evil fruits that moral relativism has engendered are many and bitter.

Vicious criminal behavior occurs in all classes but is mostly concentrated in inner-city ghettos of the United States and other nations where the family structure is most greatly fragmented.

Often there is no father figure whom young men and women can look up to and emulate. Street toughs are their only models of "success."

As a result, each generation comprehends less and less what decency, goodness and proper affection mean. Eventually, more and more youths have little or no compassion, no caring feelings for others but themselves. They feel they become somebody only if they dehumanize another human being.

Parents, how many of you strive to set a right example and train your children in right character? The personalities of some children, maybe yours, demand more attention, guidance and discipline—coupled with affection and love—than others.

The Hidden Enemy

Another critical cause of criminal thinking is totally overlooked in many homes and virtually neglected in modern education. Millions are utterly unaware of the existence of evil spirit beings that work to induce damaging attitudes in humans—attitudes that, if responded to, lead to harmful or criminal actions.

Millions simply don't believe in the existence of spirits that rebelled against their Creator and that must be resisted—Satan the devil and his demons. If not resisted, these evil spirits can temporarily possess one and lead one into unexpected crime!

The general influence of evil spirits is the primary impulse of many sinful and criminal attitudes, which most crime fighters simply are not dealing with. . . .

But not every person responds precisely the same way to Satan's efforts to influence human beings, or to other harmful or criminal influences within society. How humans respond depends on family experiences and character training, on prevailing social or cultural values, on deterrents to criminal behavior, and also on individual personality and temperament qualities. Some personalities and temperaments are clearly more responsive to criminal thinking than others.

Yet, more than the teaching of right morality and values alone within the family unit, schools or churches is needed to deter criminality worldwide. Some persons need stronger deterrents.

The Need for Punishment

Character is a product of free moral agency. Even in homes where parents may set a right example and do their best to teach right values, some children still choose to do things that are criminally wrong. They may allow themselves to engage in criminal activities because they think they can get away with it, or think they won't be caught, or be seriously punished if they are. . . .

Crime will be deterred only when would-be criminals know punishment for their crimes will be swift and sure. But today it is not. Criminal youths are often caught for serious crimes only to be spewed right back onto the streets by juvenile justice systems not set up to handle large numbers of hardened vicious criminals. What deterrent is there for a young lawbreaker if he is considered a hero by peers for "beating the system"? . . .

Something is seriously wrong with any nation's values and system of justice when criminals develop the arrogant idea that crime pays.

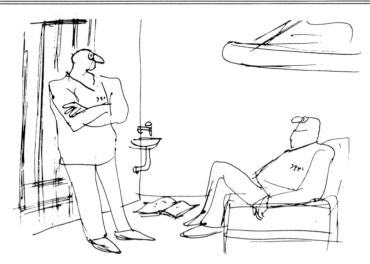

"Who was it said 'Laws were made to be broken'?"

Drawing by Ross; © 1986 The New Yorker Magazine, Inc.

That tragic condition means there are vast numbers of outwardly "good" citizens who are willing to profit from illicit or illegal activity in their own lives, even though they don't like to think of themselves as criminal.

Why aren't the vast majority of criminals quickly spotted, turned in and given swift and sure justice? Too often, because sizable numbers in the populace, or friends or associates, are willing to look the other way when wrongdoing is going on, or are willing to excuse or cover up for them, or hide them, or buy the services of their illegal activities.

Supporting Crime

Organized crime can be stopped by citizens not patronizing their services—gambling, loansharking, prostitution—or succumbing to graft or corruption.

Illicit drug pushers and the horrendous health problems and corruption they engender all over the world exist because millions of citizens are willing to use the drug culture's services.

White-collar crime, on-the-job theft and petty thievery are often justified because "everybody's doing it." Employee theft and dishonesty feed the climate of criminality and corruption within a society and add their own costly price. Many stores and businesses lose 10 times more to pilfering employees than they do to shoplifters; many banks lose more to embezzlers than to bank robbers.

If a society is to cure crime, the vast, overwhelming majority of members of society, especially its leaders and honored role models, must hold to high moral standards of behavior and not be corrupt or hypocrites. Crime will be deterred when criminals know that the dishonest, violent, deceitful and corrupt simply will not be tolerated and honored by those wielding power and authority. Rather they will be quickly exposed and punished.

That, unfortunately, isn't what we see in many areas of the world today.

"Follow vandals and amateur shoplifters as they duck into alleys and dressing rooms and you will be moved by their delight in deviance."

Thrill-Seeking Causes Crime

Jack Katz

Many theories on the causes of crime focus on how the criminals' family upbringing or economic status contributes to their illegal behavior. In the following viewpoint, Jack Katz argues that the focus should instead be on the attractiveness of the criminal act itself. He argues that many people commit crimes for psychological satisfaction, rather than for material gain. Katz is a sociology professor at the University of California at Los Angeles.

As you read, consider the following questions:

1. What does a person find when examining crime, according to Katz?
2. What theory by Robert Merton does Katz criticize?
3. Why does the author dispute the theory that racism causes crime?

The closer one looks at crime, at least at the varieties examined here, the more vividly relevant become the moral emotions. Follow vandals and amateur shoplifters as they duck into alleys and dressing rooms and you will be moved by their delight in deviance; observe them under arrest and you may be stunned by their shame. Watch their strutting street display and you will be struck by the awesome fascination that symbols of evil hold for the young men who are linked in the groups we often call gangs. If we specify the opening moves in muggings and stickups, we describe an array of "games" or tricks that turn victims into fools before their pockets are turned out. The careers of persistent robbers show us, not the increasingly precise calculations and hedged risks of "professionals," but men for whom gambling and other vices are a way of life, who are "wise" in the cynical sense of the term, and who take pride in a defiant reputation as "bad." And if we examine the lived sensuality behind events of cold-blooded "senseless" murder, we are compelled to acknowledge the power that may still be created in the modern world through the sensualities of defilement, spiritual chaos, and the apprehension of vengeance.

Running across these experiences of criminality is a process juxtaposed in one manner or another against humiliation. In committing a righteous slaughter, the impassioned assailant takes humiliation and turns it into rage; through laying claim to a moral status of transcendent significance, he tries to burn humiliation up. The badass, with searing purposiveness, tries to scare humiliation off; as one ex-punk explained to me, after years of adolescent anxiety about the ugliness of his complexion and the stupidity of his every word, he found a wonderful calm in making "them" anxious about *his* perceptions and understandings. Young vandals and shoplifters innovate games with the risks of humiliation, running along the edge of shame for its exciting reverberations. Fashioned as street elites, young men square off against the increasingly humiliating social restrictions of childhood by mythologizing differences with other groups of young men who might be their mirror image. Against the historical background of a collective insistence on the moral nonexistence of their people, "bad niggers" exploit ethnically unique possibilities for celebrating assertive conduct as "bad.". . .

Sentimental Materialism

Just fifty years ago, Robert K. Merton published his "Social Structure and Anomie," an article once counted as the single most frequently cited and reprinted paper in the history of American sociology. Arguing against Freud and psychological analysis in general, Merton attributed deviance to a contradiction in the structure of modern society: "Americans are bombarded on all sides" by the goal of monetary success, but the means or opportunities for achieving it are not as uniformly distributed. A generation later, Richard Cloward and Lloyd Ohlin, with a revised version of "opportunity" theory, hit perhaps the pinnacle of academic and political success in the history of criminology, winning professional awards and finding their work adopted by the Kennedy administration as part of the intellectual foundations of what later became the War on Poverty. After a hiatus during much of the Republican 1970s and 1980s, materialist theory—the Mertonian ideas now bolstered by rational-economic models of social action that had become academically attractive in the interim—is again promoting the lack of opportunity (unemployment, underemployment, and low "opportunity cost") to explain crime.

Crime Can Be Fun

The frustrations and deferred gratification of the "square's world" are usually too much for a criminal. He can't stand "the square life, with all its loneliness and no fun," as one criminal put it. The high-risk, high-excitement life of crime—with its obvious payoffs for sheer prowess and cunning—offers an almost irresistible alternative.

The thing that much of contemporary criminology seems to miss is that *crime can be fun.* There seem to be few criminals who will not admit in their candid moments that they enjoy what they are doing.

William Tucker, *Vigilante,* 1985.

That this materialist perspective is twentieth-century sentimentality about crime is indicated by its overwhelming inadequacy for grasping the experiential facts of crime. . . .

Consider the many sensually explosive, diabolically creative, realities of crime that the materialist sentiment cannot appreciate. Where is the materialism in the experience of the *barrio* "homeboy," the night before the first day of high school?

Although I was not going to be alone, I still felt insecure. . . . my mother, with an accentuated voice, ordered me to go to sleep. Nevertheless, my anxiety did not let my consciousness rest; instead, what I did was look in the mirror, and began practicing the traditional steps that would show my machismo. . . . Furthermore, I was nervously thinking about taking a weapon to the school grounds just to show Vatos from other barrios the answer of my holy clique. All kinds of evil thoughts were stirring in me.

The problem for Merton and materialist theory is not simply with some youthful "gang" activity. There is now strong evidence

56

that a high proportion of those who go on to especially "serious," "heavy," "career" involvements in criminality start in early adolescence, long before job opportunities could or, in a free social order, should become meaningful considerations. Actually, when Albert Cohen pointed out, long ago, the "'versatility' and the 'zest' with which some boys are observed to pursue their group-supported deviations," Merton was willing to concede that much of youth crime was beyond his theory of deviance. It was enough if, as Cohen had offered in a conciliatory gesture, Merton's materialism applied to "professional" or serious adult property criminals.

Money Not Important

But if we look at persistent criminals, we see a life of action in which materialism is by no means the god. Instead, material goods are treated more like offerings to be burnt, quickly, lest retention become sacrilege. As suggested by "dead presidents," a black street term for U.S. cash, there is an aggressive attack on materialism as a potentially misleading, false deity. Robby Wideman seemed to have Merton in mind when he told his brother:

> Straight people don't understand. I mean, they think dudes is after the things straight people got. It ain't that at all. People in the life ain't looking for no home and grass in the yard and shit like that. We the show people. The glamour people. Come on the set with the finest car, the finest woman, the finest vines. Hear people talking about you. Hear the bar get quiet when you walk in the door. Throw down a yard and tell everybody drink up. . . . You make something out of nothing.

The aspiration is not to what is advertised on television. Robby Wideman was not incapable of identifying what drove him; it was to be a star—something literally, distinctively transcendent. Street people are not inarticulate when they say that "the endgame is to *get over*, to *get across*, to *make it*, to *step fast*." This language is only a "poetic" indirect reference to aspirations for material status if we refuse to recognize that it directly captures the objective of transcendence.

Different Aims

So, a lot of juvenile forms of violent crime and an important segment of serious adult crime do not fit the sentimentality of materialism. Neither does the central thrust that guides men and women to righteous slaughters, nor the project of primordial evil that makes "senseless killings" compellingly sensible to their killers, nor the tactics and reverberations of sneaky thrills. None of these fits, in the Mertonian scheme, the actions of "innovators" who accept the conventional aims but use deviant means. The aims are specifically unconventional: to go beyond the established moral definitions of the situation as it visibly obtains here and now. Nor can we categorize these deviants as "retreatists" who reject conventional means and ends. For Merton, retreatists were a spiritually dead, socially isolated, lot of psychotics, drunkards, and vagrants; today's "bag ladies" would fit that category. And, surely, these deviants are not "rebels" with revolutionary ideas to implement new goals and means.

None of this argument denies the validity of the recurrent correlations between low socioeconomic status or relative lack of economic opportunity, on the one hand, and violent and personal property crime on the other. The issue is the causal significance of this background for deviance. A person's material background will not determine his intent to commit acquisitive crime, but a person, whether or not he is intent on acquisitive crime, is not likely to be unaware of his circumstances.

Instead of reading into ghetto poverty an unusually strong motivation to become deviant, we may understand the concentration of robbery among ghetto residents as being due to the fact that for people in economically more promising circumstances, it would literally make no sense—it would virtually be crazy—to commit robbery. Merton had no basis but the sentiments stirred by his theory to assume that crime, even materially acquisitive crime, was more common in the "lower strata." In part, the appeal of his theory was promoted by the obvious significance of material circumstance in the shaping of crime. We need fear only a few exceptions if we claim that lawyers will not stick up banks, "frequent-flyer" executives will not kill their spouses in passionate rages, and physicians will not punch out their colleagues or that the unemployed will not embezzle, the indigent will not fix prices, and the politically powerless will not commit perjury in congressional testimony. But this is a different matter from claiming that crime or deviance is distributed in the social structure according to the relative lack of opportunity for material gain.

Recognizing Stereotypes

A stereotype is an oversimplified or exaggerated description of people or things. Stereotyping can be favorable. However, most stereotyping tends to be highly uncomplimentary and, at times, degrading.

Stereotyping grows out of our prejudices. When we stereotype someone, we are prejudging him or her. Consider the cartoon below: it exemplifies several common stereotypes in the way it pictures criminals as subhuman, defense lawyers as greedy, and judges as misguidedly soft-hearted.

Jim Morin, © 1980 *The Miami Herald*. Reprinted with permission.

The following statements relate to the subject matter in this chapter. Consider each statement carefully. *Mark S for any statement which you feel is an example of stereotyping. Mark N for any statement which you feel is not an example of stereotyping. Mark U if you are unsure.*

If you are doing this activity as a member of a class or group, compare your answers with those of other class or group members. Be able to defend your answers. You may discover that others will come to different conclusions than you. Listening to the reasons others present for their answers may give you valuable insights in recognizing stereotypes.

> S = *stereotype*
> N = *not a stereotype*
> U = *unsure or undecided*

1. Crime is caused by soft-headed judges and prison administrators who let convicted criminals go free.

2. Most of the nation's crime occurs in poverty-stricken areas where there are few jobs.

3. Poor people become criminals because they are too uneducated and lazy to work in legitimate jobs.

4. Poor people become criminals in order to provide food for their starving children.

5. People in prison generally score lower on IQ tests than the general population.

6. Criminals are generally not as smart as normal people.

7. Most crimes committed by blacks victimize other blacks.

8. Criminals have no concept of delayed gratification—they want everything now.

9. Many drug addicts turn to crime.

10. Criminals are victims of society.

11. Many criminals were abused as children by their parents.

12. More Americans become criminals because they are products of a culture that glorifies violence and greed.

13. Most people know a crime victim or have been victims themselves.

14. Bad parenting causes crime—small children should be kept in line or they will turn into criminals.

15. Most poor people are not criminals.

Periodical Bibliography

The following articles have been selected to supplement the diverse views presented in this chapter.

Gary Abrams	"Portrait of a Mass Killer," *Los Angeles Times*, January 12, 1988.
Charles Colson	"Criminals Are Made, Not Born," *Christianity Today*, January 16, 1987.
Elliott Currie	"Crime and the Conservatives," *Dissent*, Fall 1985.
James Fallows	"Born To Rob: Why Do Criminals Do It?" *The Washington Monthly*, December 1985.
Randy Frame	"Violence for Fun," *Christianity Today*, February 21, 1986.
Jeffrey Hart	"Family: Root of Black Crime," *Conservative Chronicle*, September 16, 1987. Available from Box 29, Hampton, IA 50441.
Sherrye Henry	"Women in Prison: Why and How They Got There," *Parade Magazine*, April 10, 1988.
Alex Kotlowitz	"Urban Wastelands," *The Wall Street Journal*, June 22, 1988.
Jeff Meer	"Murder in Mind," *Psychology Today*, March 1987.
Thomas Moore	"The Black-on-Black Crime Plague," *U.S. News & World Report*, August 22, 1988.
William Murchison	"Racial Dividing Line Is Between Good and Bad," *Conservative Chronicle*, February 10, 1988.
Alex Poinsett	"Why Our Children Are Killing One Another," *Ebony*, December 1987.
Joseph Sobran	"Understanding Willie Horton," *National Review*, December 9, 1988.
Jarvis Tyner	"Crime Is in the Genes of Capitalism, Not People," *People's Daily World*, March 20, 1987. Available from USPS 146920, 239 W. 23rd Street, New York, NY 10011.

How Should Criminals Be Treated?

CRIME AND CRIMINALS

Chapter Preface

The development of the science of psychology in the early twentieth century gave rise to the idea that criminals are not evil, but rather are sick or socially deprived, and therefore should be treated, not punished. Advocates such as psychiatrist Karl Menninger believed that this new scientific knowledge made the very concept of punishment obsolete. Belief in rehabilitation led to many programs and prison reforms designed to help criminals become lawful members of society.

Since the 1970s the goal of rehabilitating criminals has been sharply criticized. Continued high crime rates made many people disillusioned about the effectiveness of psychology. Studies failed to establish any consistently successful method of rehabilitating criminals, and in fact, one study by Robert Martinson became well-known for its conclusion that "nothing works."

The conflicts between the goals of punishment and rehabilitation form the basis for the debates in this chapter.

"People can live decent, civilized lives in prison and graduate to decent, civilized lives in the free world."

Criminals Should Be Sentenced to Prison

Robert Johnson and Jackson Tory

In the United States, the preferred method of punishment for criminals has always been prison. However, prisons are constantly under attack as being unsanitary, overcrowded, violent, and counterproductive. In the following viewpoint, Robert Johnson and Jackson Tory argue that this criticism is exaggerated and should not prevent society from using prisons as the primary punishment for criminals. Johnson, the author of Part I, is a professor of justice at American University in Washington, DC. Tory is the author of Part II and a professor of sociology and director of the Institute for Criminological Research at Rutgers University in New Jersey.

As you read, consider the following questions:

1. What does Johnson believe is the benefit of prison?
2. Why does Tory believe that prisons are as humane as they possibly can be?

I

Rehabilitation used to be a respectable and even popular penological goal, but little is heard about it these days. Today, we seek to inflict a just measure of pain on offenders and let the matter of punishment go at that. But a just punishment, as the philosopher Plato long ago made clear, must always hold out to the offender the prospect of moral education and, hence, personal reform.

Plato said a person subjected to punishment should emerge "a better man, or failing that, less of a wretch." His point was that punishment should mete out redeeming pain, not debilitating harm. If prisons are to be settings of just punishment, then the pain wrought by imprisonment must be a source of rehabilitation.

Hard Time

Inmates serve hard time, and it is the nature of prison that they should do so. Though few inmates are damaged in any lasting way by the pains of imprisonment, not many of them are rehabilitated by their suffering either. Most inmates learn little of value during their stint behind bars, mostly because they adapt to prison in immature and often self-defeating ways. As a result, they leave prison no better—and sometimes considerably worse—than when they went in. But people can live decent, civilized lives in prison and graduate to decent, civilized lives in the free world. Imprisonment, in other words, can be a constructively painful experience. It is my contention that we can ask no more of our prisons, and should settle for no less.

Inmates can learn something worthwhile during their confinement. The most valuable lessons that inmates can learn are those that enable them to cope maturely with the pains of imprisonment. Mature coping means dealing directly with one's problems using the resources legitimately at one's disposal; refusing to employ deceit or violence (other than in self defense); and building mutual and supportive relationships with others.

Offenders who cope maturely come to grips with problems in prison living; they try to solve problems rather than simply endure them. They tackle their problems without violating the rights of others to be safe in their person and in their property. More generally, they treat others, staff and inmates alike, as fellow human beings who possess dignity and worth. These inmates are the solid citizens of the prison community and are likely to become solid citizens of the free community as well.

Mature Coping

Admittedly, only a minority of inmates cope maturely with the pressures of prison life. Most of the other inmates who do not, however, could be helped to do so. Inmates who adjust well are able to carve out niches or sanctuaries that serve as supportive neighborhoods in the larger impersonal city that is the prison. Niches serve as shelters from the worst of prison life and provide arenas in which inmates can rehearse new ways of solving problems. They are spawning grounds for citizens, first in prison, later in the free world.

Prisons Are Reality

The cold, hard, grim realities are inescapable: Prisons are not the total answer or even the ultimate solution, but adequate prisons are more than just options—prisons are unavoidable realities. Moreover, it is perilous to avoid, not just the necessity of additional prison space, but the urgency of providing that additional prison space now!

Ronald L. Powell, *Manchester Union Leader*, March 18, 1987.

Niches can be made more readily available to inmates. To achieve this goal, inmates must be classified not merely in terms of custody level or even remedial program requirements but also in terms of adjustment needs. They must be placed in responsive settings, oriented to the pressures of prison living, and monitored in their reactions to confinement. Although this is a big job, the tools to accomplish it are readily available. We have classification systems that group inmates reliably; we know enough about prison life to develop decent orientation modules; our staff, particularly the correctional officers, can observe inmates and help them adjust. We have it in our power to put in place a classification and management process that, in effect, makes the typical prison environment a niche.

To the extent that budgets permit, we must also enrich these niches with educational, vocational, and therapeutic programs. Ideally, all prison environments should serve meaningful functions for meaningfully related groups of inmates. Specific environments can be organized to deal with specific problems. An overriding function of all prison environments, however, should be to provide a rehearsal for citizenship in other harsh settings, most notably the low-income, high-crime, and distinctly prison-like milieus from which most inmates are drawn and to which the vast majority of them will one day return.

The pains of imprisonment can indeed be a source of rehabilitation. The challenge is to arrange our correctional resources to promote growth through adversity. This is a challenge worth meeting. For the men and women who are helped to cope maturely with the pressures of prison living, hard time is constructive time, and prison life is both just and good.

II

American prisons get terrible publicity. Stories of rape, murder, hostage-taking and overcrowding abound, as do those of judicial orders to release prisoners or close prisons because of conditions of "cruel and unusual punishment."

Is there a pattern of official brutality in prisons? *Official* brutality, no. Nowadays incarcerated offenders are responsible for nearly all the violence in American prisons. Officials generally are businesslike with their unpleasant clients. Until the 18th century, however, prisons were rare, but official brutality *was* the rule. Perpetrators of serious crimes were enslaved, executed (often as painfully as possible), maimed, flogged, branded or publicly mutilated while in the pillory. Harsh punishments were not reserved only for what would today be regarded as serious offenses. As recently as 1868, the state of North Carolina allowed capital punishment for 30 offenses, including adultery.

Prisons Substitute for Harsher Punishment

Prisons were devised only 200 years ago as a substitute for harsher punishments. True, dungeons existed for at least 1,000 years to incarcerate persons whom ruling monarchs perceived as troublesome. However, dungeons were not prisons, and *jails* weren't prisons either. Accused people were detained in jails to ensure their presence at trials, as were debtors to make them pay up. But the idea of deprivation of freedom as *punishment* for violators of serious rules did not attract support until Benjamin Franklin's time.

Dr. Benjamin Rush, one of the signers of the Declaration of Independence and a prominent physician, read a paper about crime and punishment to a group of intellectual Quakers in Franklin's home on March 9, 1787. Rush advocated replacing traditional physical punishments with deprivation of freedom (through solitary confinement) and the opportunity for penitence (through Bible study and work in the cells). The Pennsylvania Prison Society was formed to carry out this program, and soon Pennsylvania had a "penitentiary," intended to rehabilitate offenders.

Nineteenth-century American prisons did not live up to Rush's humane intentions. Many of them—Auburn, for example, in New York state—inflicted severe punishments on inmates to enforce arbitrary rules. In Auburn, inmates were forbidden to speak to one another. Violators of "the silent system" were flogged, chained to the floor and "stretched" with ropes attached to a pulley in the ceiling, confined in an unventilated "sweat box," and, while shackled naked to a wall, targeted with a high-pressure water hose. Prisoners were "slaves of the state."

By comparison with 19th-century American prisons and with contemporary prisons in all but a couple of dozen democratic

67

countries (out of 167 independent nations), prison conditions today in the U.S. are almost luxurious: beds and mattresses rather than a floor, flush toilets instead of a pot, uninspired but wholesome food, heated cells and workshops, access to counselors, to telephones, to a library, to legal aid, and to procedures for adjudicating grievances concerning prison policies.

Contemporary American prisons also provide inmates with recreation, with vocational training, and with education programs, including day release in order to attend local colleges. Taxpayers pay about $15,000 a year per inmate for these amenities in maximum-security prisons and somewhat less in medium- and minimum-security prisons. But the most important amenity is safety from official brutality: American prisoners need not fear beatings by their guards. Although assault from other inmates is all too common, the guards try to protect prisoners from one another.

A Necessary Choice

Prisons need not and should not be human warehouses, nor ugly and brutalizing. Nor should they be used to chill political dissent or sincere efforts to change our social order in the direction of a more equitable, just and crime-free culture. Neither should they be used cosmetically, to remove "nuisances" from our streets, to hold the inept, unpleasant or unemployed who present no real physical danger to others. But until the millennium when the crime-producing factors in our world will have been eliminated, incarceration of the dangerous and the deliberate—the violent, the professional, the organized and the willful, persistent offender—is not only necessary but is itself an alternative to worse choices.

Donald J. Newman, *Psychiatric Annals*, March 1974.

American prisons today cannot have arbitrary rules nor can they enforce reasonable rules arbitrarily, because both state and federal courts are constantly intervening to protect the human rights of inmates. The civil-rights revolution that accelerated in the 1960s meant that prisons could not be run according to the whims of wardens or guards. By 1978, the last year for which I could locate statistics, 9,730 civil-rights cases on behalf of inmates of state prisons were filed in the *federal* courts alone. Prison officials spend an appreciable amount of their time in court defending themselves against charges that their administrative acts have deprived inmates of rights protected by the First, Fourth, Eighth, 13th and 14th amendments to the Constitution.

The threat of judicial intervention has resulted in fewer restrictions on mail privileges, on press interviews, and on religious worship, and has liberalized visits with friends and relatives. American prisons constantly reexamine the reasonableness of security measures like cell searches and body-cavity searches, as well as disciplinary transfers to other institutions. They have established minimum standards for medical and dental care, exercise, food, privacy, shower privileges, heat, work, and other amenities whose absence judges might construe as constituting "cruel and unusual punishment."

Operating civilized prisons is expensive—as Americans imprisoned for violating the laws of Third World countries learn to their sorrow. The 43 countries with a gross national product per capita of $500 or less—Pakistan and Nepal, for example—cannot afford the creature comforts and the programs available in U.S. prisons. In poor countries, the family of a prisoner often is expected to provide him with his food. An imprisoned individual without friends or relatives risks starvation. As for medical and dental services, prisoners in Third World countries had better avoid illness and toothaches.

But a high gross national product does not guarantee civilized imprisonment. The labor camps and psychiatric prisons of the Soviet Union are notorious for beatings and brainwashing. Murderers and robbers are treated less cruelly than political prisoners in Soviet prisons but callously by American standards.

If American prisons are so decent, why the constant criticisms from prisoners, journalists, judges, even criminologists? Because the critics respond not only to current realities but to what they think prisons should be like. Americans have high standards for the treatment of human beings.

Nothing To Be Ashamed Of

In terms of expectations, liberals deny that there can be a good prison. They are right. But the worst feature of American prisons is the other prisoners. As a means of coping with serious misbehavior, the American prison is a good try in an imperfect world. The U.S. has made its prisons increasingly civilized. In comparison with the historical alternatives to imprisonment—as well as with the ghastly prisons in some Third World and Marxist societies—American prisons are nothing to be ashamed of.

"*Alternative programs cost less; they seem to do a better job of controlling crime.*"

Criminals Should Be Given Alternatives to Prison

Joan Petersilia

More than a half-million people are in prison and ten billion dollars is spent each year on prisons in the United States. In spite of these statistics, many people believe society is no closer to reducing crime and thus conclude that prisons are not effective. In the following viewpoint, Joan Petersilia agrees with this view and argues that alternative sentences like community service should be employed. Petersilia is a senior researcher for RAND Corporation's criminal justice program. The RAND Corporation is a San Francisco-based think tank.

As you read, consider the following questions:

1. What prevents Americans from endorsing widespread use of prison alternatives, according to Petersilia?
2. What does the author believe are the benefits of prison alternatives?
3. Why does the author argue that prison sentencing does not work?

Joan Petersilia, "Alternatives to Prison: Cutting Costs—and Crime," *Los Angeles Times*, January 31, 1988. Reprinted with permission.

More than a half-million people are locked up in this country; that total grows by more than 1,000 inmates each week. In 1989 Americans will spend close to $10 billion operating the nation's prisons.

Using prison sentences so extensively has put a serious strain on state resources. For most states, prison outlays mean drawdowns in other public services. For example, in California, a $300-million state expenditure deficit caused in part by the rising costs of the prison system resulted in a cutback in funds for public education and medical services for the poor.

Despite this enormous investment, our prisons are operating at a national 110% of capacity, and we are far from controlling crime. The prison population doubled over the past 15 years, yet the violent crime rate is now substantially higher. Further, the number of probationers has increased even faster than the number of prisoners, and more than half the probationers are now felons— many convicted of violent crime.

No Prison Space for Murderers

There is a major irony here: By giving judges no options but prison or probation, most states no longer have enough prison space to accept or to keep some serious criminals for very long. These criminals wind up on probation or early parole, and caseloads have gotten so large that probation and parole officers cannot effectively supervise them. The average "supervision" probably consists of seeing the average offender once a month or less. Furthermore, the time served in prison has grown shorter now than in the past. The average time prisoners served in 1970 was 18 months; now it is 13 months, a decrease partly resulting from prison overcrowding.

Most Americans agree that something must be done.

More and more states have been experimenting with programs that provide alternatives to prison sentences. Not long ago, public demands to "get tough on crime" would have made such experiments politically unthinkable. But that was before crime rates and mandatory sentencing laws combined to make prison conditions themselves unlawful in many states.

Although spending on prisons has increased about 10% every year since the mid-1970s, 37 states are now under court order to do something about prison overcrowding. Because building prisons puts a terrible strain on most states' budgets, taxpayers have been more willing to consider programs that might cost less—as long as they also control and punish criminals appropriately.

These programs may herald a fundamental change in sentencing concepts and options, or they may simply be quick fixes to prison overcrowding. The country is long overdue for such a fundamental change, and even if these programs begin as stopgap measures, they provide a singular opportunity to start reshaping the nation's corrections philosophy.

Most of these programs are "community-based," but they differ from traditional probation in important ways. The convicted criminal remains in the community but under strict surveillance and conditions intended both to punish and to prevent the offender from committing any more crimes. Programs range from intensively supervised probation to electronically monitored house arrest to short term "shock" imprisonment, followed by strict probation regimens. But most require that offenders have a job (or go to school), perform some kind of public service and pay monetary compensation to their victims. Offenders are also subject to frequent, unannounced visits from program officers and police and to random drug testing.

Restoration

Frances Ellen, who served three months in prison and 1,500 hours community service for income tax and securities violations, spent her time designing and leading support groups for other offenders.

"It's sort of like having a major heart attack," she said. "How do you restore yourself? We showed them how to deal with guilt, shame, embarrassment, the sense of self-esteem that had been destroyed."

Larry Margasak, *The San Diego Union*, December 18, 1988.

National interest in developing such "intermediate" sanctions has been phenomenal—and understandable. There were only two electronically monitored house-arrest programs in 1985; today there are more than 50. Such programs are much cheaper than prison. For example, house arrest costs about $5,000 to $8,000 a year—or about $10,000 a year less than the cost of keeping an inmate in prison. Further, since program participants work, they pay state and local taxes and states do not have to pay the welfare payments that prison inmates' families often collect.

Despite their stringency and lower cost, these programs have their critics. The bulk of "correcting" has always been done in the community by probation and parole agencies. Yet the public has traditionally felt that any sentence other than prison is too lenient for "serious" offenders (although the definition of "serious" differs radically in different parts of the country). Victims' rights groups, such as Mothers Against Drunk Driving, are especially concerned that these programs, however stringent, do not match the seriousness of the crime. Their criticisms must be carefully considered. However, they cannot be used to justify the historical situation in sentencing and corrections.

Ultimately, alternatives must be judged by their effectiveness in protecting the public. And so far, fewer than 10% of the offenders in the alternative programs have committed new crimes (and most were misdemeanors), compared with about 50% of regular probationers and released prisoners. Not only do these alternative programs cost less; they seem to do a better job of controlling crime. However, we must be careful in interpreting this effect.

Property Offenses

Because these programs are still experimental, judges are exercising great caution in sentencing offenders to them. Most programs limit participation to property offenders with minor criminal records, which undoubtedly helps explain the low arrest rates. Consequently, we have no evidence that the bulk of prisoners—and certainly not violent offenders—could be safely put in these programs. However, the results do suggest that some states have an identifiable subset of prisoners who could be. And more than half of all prison admissions nationwide are for property or public-order offenses. Many of these offenders are much like the people in the alternative programs.

By putting more of this type in alternative programs, the states could cut their corrections costs directly and ease the pressure to build more prison space. They might also lower crime rates. First, the programs might free up prison space for more serious, violent offenders. Second, they might be more successful than traditional probation has been in controlling property criminals. The evidence to date suggests that the alternative programs may have something to offer such offenders that neither prison nor probation has. . . .

Cheaper and Better

In short, these programs are cheaper than imprisonment, seem to control crime better than traditional probation does and prepare offenders for re-entry into society better than either one. Yet, there is still the concern about "just deserts." Because these programs don't lock criminals up, critics believe the punishment is not fitting the crime.

Ironically, this belief may reflect the law-abiding citizen's perceptions of harsh punishment more than it does the serious criminal's. Some of the programs have encountered surprising resistance from offenders. Given a choice between intensive surveillance in the community or a shorter term in prison, many choose prison. In an Oregon experimental program, for example, half of the eligible offenders chose prison over the alternative. From this response, it seems clear that at least some offenders see the conditions imposed by the alternative programs as extremely punitive.

The incarceration rate continues to climb

Year	US population (in millions)	Numbers of Prisoners	Prisoners per 100,000 population
1988	246	582,000	237
1987	244	546,000	224
1983	235	420,000	180
1980	227	321,000	142
1970	203	196,000	97
1960	179	213,000	119
1950	151	166,000	110
1940	132	174,000	132
1930	123	148,000	121
1925	106	93,000	88
1918	92	75,000	82
1900	76	57,000	75
1890	63	45,000	71
1870	40	33,000	83
1860	31	19,000	60
1850	23	7,000	30
1840	17	4,000	24

Source: American Correctional Association

Experience has amply demonstrated that there are no quick fixes or easy answers to the problems of crime or punishment. However, we have learned the hard way that simply building more prisons is not the answer. In a recent opinion survey, the non-profit Public Agenda Foundation found that Americans strongly support increased use of alternatives to imprisonment. Much of this support is based on the belief that society must try new approaches because, besides being too expensive, the current system is a failure at reducing crime.

It is much too soon for definitive answers about how the alternative programs will affect long-term criminal behavior. But if the programs fulfill their early promise, we will have found more than a short-term response to prison crowding. We will have begun to shape a new, less costly, more humane and more effective approach to reducing crime.

"The certainty of restitution, by requiring payment, takes the profit out of crime."

Criminals Should Make Restitution for Their Crimes

Charles Colson

In the following viewpoint, Charles Colson advocates a policy of forcing criminals to make direct payments to the victims of their crimes. He argues that such punishment is more effective than prison. Colson was special counsel to President Richard Nixon from 1969 to 1973 and served seven months in jail for his role in the Watergate scandal. He is currently chairman of Prison Fellowship, a Christian ministry organization.

As you read, consider the following questions:

1. What problems does Colson see with US prisons?
2. What are some of the benefits of restitution, according to Colson?
3. Why does Colson believe restitution can be a more effective deterrent to crime?

"Crime and Restitution," by Charles Colson is excerpted from an article in the Winter 1988 issue of *Policy Review*, a publication of The Heritage Foundation, 214 Massachusetts Avenue, NE, Washington, DC 20002.

America's prisons have been called "graduate schools for crime." It stands to reason: Take a group of people, strip them of possessions and privacy, expose them to constant threats of violence, overcrowd their cellblock, deprive them of meaningful work—and the result is an embittered underclass more intent on getting even with society than on contributing to it. Prisons take the nonviolent offender and make him live by violence. They take the violent offender and make him a hardened killer.

I saw this process firsthand when I served time in prison for a Watergate-related offense. My life was threatened during my first week behind bars—and I watched bitter men around me become more bitter and angry as the long months went by. I have seen the same dynamic at work in the hundreds of prisons I have visited in the years since. . . .

An Expensive Failure

We pay a great deal for prisons to fail so badly. Like all big government solutions, they are expensive. It costs approximately $80,000 to build one cell and $17,000 per year to keep a person locked up. That's about the same as the cost of sending a student to Harvard. Because of overcrowding it is estimated that more than $10 billion in construction is needed to create sufficient space for just the *current* prison population.

The plain truth is that the very nature of prison, no matter how humane society attempts to make it, produces an environment that is inevitably devastating to its residents. Even if their release is delayed by longer sentences, those residents inevitably return to damage the community. And we are paying top dollar to make this possible. . . .

The Restitution Alternative

Why should taxpayers be forced to pay exorbitant amounts to keep nonviolent criminals sitting in prison cells, where they become bitter and more likely to repeat their offenses when they are released? Instead, why not put them to work outside prison, where they could pay back the victims of their crimes? Why not initiate work programs—restitution, that is—making a criminal in some manner pay back a victim for his loss? Examples of this approach to punishment can be found as far back as Old Testament law. The thief who stole an ox was required to pay his victim five head of cattle; innovative judges, on a small scale, are beginning to make use of this principle once again today.

The most obvious benefit of this approach is that it takes care of the victim, the forgotten person in the current system. Those who experience property crime deserve more than just the satisfaction of seeing the offender go to prison. As my colleague Daniel Van Ness, president of Justice Fellowship, has put it,

. . . All the legal systems which helped form western law emphasize the need for offenders to settle with victims. The offense was seen as primarily a violation against the victim. While the common welfare had been violated and the community therefore had an interest and responsibility in seeing that the wrong was addressed and the offender punished, the offense was not considered primarily a crime against the state as it is today.

A Real Change

Second, restitution offers the criminal a means to restore himself—to undergo a real change of character. Mere imprisonment cannot do this, for nothing can destroy a man's soul more surely than living without useful work and purpose. Feodor Dostoevsky, himself a prisoner for 10 years during czarist repression, wrote, "If one wanted to crush, to annihilate a man utterly, to inflict on him the most terrible of punishments . . . one need only give him work of an absolutely, completely useless and irrational character." This is exactly what goes on in the "make work" approach of our prisons. And it is one of the contributing factors to prison violence.

A Sense of Justice

The idea that a burglar should return stolen goods, pay for damage to the house he broke into and pay his victims for the time lost from work to appear at a trial meets with universal support from the American people. Many are surprised to learn that this is not already the case in all property crimes. There is, of course, a reason that the concept of restitution appeals to America's sense of justice. It is based on our Judeo-Christian heritage, as well as the rule of reason. In both the New and Old Testaments those who have stolen from their neighbors are required to restore the stolen property and repay them twice or four times over to compensate for the loss. Restitution also provides an alternative to imprisonment for non-violent criminals, reducing the need for taxpayers to continue building prisons (at the cost of $70,000 for a new jail cell) and paying $16,000 to keep *one* prisoner incarcerated for a year.

Jack Kemp, *Crime and Punishment in Modern America*, 1986.

But working with the purpose of paying back someone you have wronged allows a criminal to understand and deal with the real consequences of his actions. The psychologist Albert Eglash argues that "restitution is something an inmate does, not something done for or to him. . . . Being reparative, restitution can alleviate guilt and anxiety, which can otherwise precipitate further offenses."

Third, restitution would be far less expensive than the current system. Experience shows that the cost per prisoner can be as low as 10 percent of that of incarceration, depending on the degree of supervision necessary. Removing nonviolent offenders from prison would also relieve overcrowding, eliminating the necessity of appropriating billions more public dollars for prison construction.

But would restitution deter crime with the same effectiveness as prison? Prisons themselves have not done much of a job when it comes to deterrence. Nations with the highest incarceration rates often have the highest crime rates. But studies of model restitution programs demonstrate that they greatly reduce the incidence of further crime, since they restore a sense of individual responsibility, thus making the offender more likely to be able to adjust to society. Reducing recidivism is the most direct way to reduce crime.

Criminal justice authorities also tell us that it is not so much the type of punishment that deters crime, but rather the certainty of punishment. Van Ness comments, "With respect to deterrence, virtually any sanction, imposed swiftly and surely, has a deterrent effect. An effectively run restitution program, therefore, will deter."

A Greater Deterrent

I believe that in many cases, aggressive restitution programs would be a greater deterrent than the threat of prison. I remember talking in prison with a hardened convict who had spent 19 of his 38 years locked up. He was in for a heavy narcotics offense that drew a mandatory life sentence. "How in the world could you have done it?" I asked.

"I used to be a rod carrier," he answered, "on the World Trade Center building—80 floors up, getting $18 an hour. One misstep and I was dead. With hash I could make $300,000 a week. One misstep and I was in prison. Better odds."

The immediate payoff of crime is so great that many are willing to risk prison. But the certainty of restitution, by requiring payment, takes the profit out of crime. I would advocate restitution far beyond the money gained by a particular crime; the assets of organized crime members and heavy narcotics dealers, for example, could be seized at arrest and confiscated on conviction, with the offender ordered to make further restitution through work programs. That is real punishment. . . .

Conclusion

Crime is the result of morally responsible people making wrong moral decisions, for which they must be held accountable. The just and necessary response to such behavior is punishment, which may include restitution for community service, stiff fines, or, in cases where the offender is dangerous, prison. But let's not kid ourselves any longer. Prison isn't to cure the individual. It's to lock him up.

"Locking up one high-rate burglar for a year will prevent as many crimes as locking up 40 of the intermittent burglars."

Career Criminals Should Be Incarcerated

Eugene H. Methvin

Some studies have indicated that a relatively small group of criminals is responsible for a large number of crimes. These findings have led some people to urge the criminal justice system to focus on catching and imprisoning these repeat offenders. In the following viewpoint, Eugene H. Methvin advocates using prison to isolate hard-core criminals from the rest of society. Methvin was a senior editor for *Reader's Digest*.

As you read, consider the following questions:

1. According to Methvin, why is the crime rate so high?
2. What are some of the characteristics of hard-core criminals, according to the author?
3. What changes does Methvin recommend for the juvenile justice system?

Eugene H. Methvin, "The Proven Key to Crime Control." Reprinted with permission from the May 1986 Reader's Digest. Copyright © 1986 by The Reader's Digest Assn., Inc.

New York City Deputy Police Inspector John J. Hill was fuming as he studied the map of his new command, a two-square-mile, 130,000-population precinct in Brooklyn. He saw hundreds of red pins, each one denoting a robbery.

In October 1981, Hill ordered 90th Precinct officers to collect photographs and records of everyone arrested in the previous two years for robbery, or any other serious felony, who was now back "on the street." To focus more effectively on these criminals, the officers divided their rogues' gallery into seven neighborhood albums and added indexes of physical characteristics, aliases and residences.

Analyzing these data, officers realized they were arresting the same offenders repeatedly, usually in the same neighborhoods. Soon robbery victims, instead of waiting days to view thousands of photos at the central police headquarters, were whisked to the 90th Precinct to study a few dozen pictures. Almost overnight, the precinct's officers were making arrests in an astounding *half* of all reported robberies, 2 1/2 times the New York Police Department's average.

Within six months, the 90th Precinct's robberies dropped over 40 percent. The plunge has now continued for four straight years, from 2223 in 1981 to 1187 in 1985. Burglaries and rapes have also declined sharply.

New Methods

Nationwide, America experienced an 11.5-percent drop in serious crime reported in the three years 1982–84—believed to be the largest decrease since FBI uniform crime reporting began more than 50 years ago. Several factors are involved in this decline. One is the Neighborhood Watch program in which citizens throughout the country are helping police fight crime. Another is that the crime-prone population of 15- to 19-year-olds has declined in the last decade. Most important, however, is our increasing attention to career criminals—identifying them as early as possible and locking them up. We have almost doubled our prison population in the last ten years.

But crime is still outrageously high. The rate per 100,000 people is nearly 50-percent greater than it was 20 years ago. Why? Because our legislators and law-enforcement officials have been slow to respond to new and proven methods of crime control. The nation has learned a number of strategic lessons about coping with lawlessness, and evidence suggests that we can achieve even greater reductions if we act vigorously.

Hard-Core Criminals

Ten years ago, little was known about the rates at which individual criminals commit crimes. Since then, research has revealed that far more crime is committed by a smaller fraction of offenders than anyone had suspected. This knowledge has helped police, prosecutors and judges sharpen methods for nailing these violent predators.

In 1978, University of Pennsylvania criminologist Marvin Wolfgang completed a first-of-a-kind study of virtually the entire population of 9945 males born in 1945 and raised in Philadelphia. Wolfgang's findings electrified the law-enforcement world: 627 of these young men, just under seven percent of the group, had collected at least five arrests before age 18, and they accounted for nearly two-thirds of all the violent crimes committed by the "Class of '45." Worse, these hard-core criminals admitted that, for each arrest, they got away with from 8 to 11 other serious crimes. Incredibly, even the 14 murderers among them averaged only four years behind bars.

When Wolfgang repeated the study on the 13,160 Philadelphia males born in 1958, the proportion of chronic offenders was virtually the same: 982 young men, 7.5-percent, collected five or more arrests before age 18. But there was a difference. The "Class of '58" was far more violent. Compared with the Class of '45, these youths had almost double the offense rate for rape and aggravated assault, triple for murder and a whopping five-fold for robbery. They are, says Wolfgang, "a very violent criminal population of a small number of nasty, brutal offenders. They begin early in life and should be controlled equally early."

A Promising Idea

The most promising new idea among law enforcement professionals is known as selective incapacitation. Once refined to a usable formula, it promises to predict high-rate offenders ("career criminals") early on so that the criminal justice system can effectively isolate these people from the society they prey upon. . . .

Sophisticated profiles of criminal behavior show that career criminals begin honing their craft young, usually by their early teens. If they could be recognized in their initial brushes with the law, the sentences they receive could better reflect the actual threat they pose. Such a tool would replace the largely arbitrary and subjective criteria used by judges, prosecutors, and prison officials in predicting future criminal behavior.

Lisa Schiffren, *Policy Review*, Spring 1985.

It would seem simple to say, "Lock 'em up," but the fact is that nation cannot afford to put them *all* away. If the Philadelphia ratios hold for the entire nation, we would have to keep 1.23 million young men in prison—more than double the present crowded population.

But research by the Rand Corporation indicates a way out of this dilemma, by providing a further breakdown of the crime-prone minority. Of 2190 prisoners questioned by Rand researchers, nearly all admitted to many more crimes than those for which they were convicted. But a tiny fraction of these career criminals proved to be *extraordinarily* high-rate offenders—superfelons. Half the burglars averaged fewer than six burglaries a year, while ten percent committed more than 230. Half the robbers committed five robberies a year, but ten percent averaged 87. Drug dealing was the most radically skewed: half the offenders averaged 100 deals a year; the upper tenth averaged 3251.

Thus, even chronic criminals are not a homogeneous lot; locking up one high-rate burglar for a year will prevent as many crimes as locking up 40 of the intermittent burglars.

Identifying Repeaters

Can we tell them apart? Experts say yes. The age at which offenders enter a life of crime and their use of drugs are two keys to identifying superfelons.

Males under age 18 commit perhaps as much as half of all serious crime in the United States. Arrest-record analyses and prisoner surveys demonstrate that high-rate predators begin by age 13 and hit their peak rates as robbers and burglars around 16. To Wolfgang, the factor that jumps out is the age at which these high-rate offenders commit their second serious offense. If they do it before 15, the probability is high they will commit dozens of offenses by age 30. He concludes: "After the third conviction, serious juvenile offenders should be considered adult criminals and treated accordingly."

Add Jan and Marcia Chaiken, who researched criminal behavior for Rand, "Offenders who support $50-a-day heroin addictions or who use both alcohol and barbiturates heavily are especially likely to be persistent, serious, high-rate criminals."

Criminologists from Temple and Maryland universities agree. They found that 243 Baltimore addicts committed about half a million crimes over 11 years, averaging 2058 apiece, 187 a year.

Criminal Profile

Using the inmate responses from the Rand survey, criminologist Peter W. Greenwood has refined the superfelon profile. He believes that a convicted robber or burglar should draw long-term imprisonment if he matches any four of these seven variables: 1. Convicted prior to age 16. 2. Committed to a juvenile facility. 3. Used heroin or barbiturates within two years before the current arrest. 4. Used heroin or barbiturates as a juvenile. 5. Held a job less than one of the two years before his current arrest. 6. Had a prior robbery or burglary conviction. 7. Spent more than half the preceding two years in jail.

Greenwood tested the validity of his seven-point profile against the sentences judges had given the 781 convicted robbers and burglars among Rand interviewees in California. His scale miscast as high-rate offenders only four percent of the intermittent offenders (who averaged five robberies a year) and mislabeled as low-rate offenders only three percent of the superfelons (who averaged 87 robberies a year).

The judges, however, gave many more low-rate offenders long terms and superfelons short terms. Greenwood argues that his strategy of "selective incapacitation" would have allowed California in 1981 to keep 700 fewer convicted robbers behind bars, while reducing street crime by 27,150 robberies and saving $10 million. . . .

Prison Works

City College of New York sociologist Robert Martinson tracked 400,000 criminals who went through special rehabilitation programs over a 25-year period. His stunning finding: seven out of ten who are convicted and then imprisoned or put on probation will never be arrested again; but none of the rehabilitation programs themselves curbed recidivism.

A century ago, Americans sent virtually every felon to prison. Today, even with our increasing use of imprisonment, only nine out of a hundred who are caught and convicted land behind bars. Declared Martinson: "That's where we went wrong. We abandoned a largely successful system of certain punishment in favor of all kinds of happy experiments where we told ourselves we did not have to be so nasty as to punish anybody."

More and more, studies like Martinson's are showing that while prisons may not rehabilitate, they do work as a deterrent. They also reduce crime by keeping the worst criminals away from society.

Concludes Alfred Regnery, administrator of the OJJDP [Office of Juvenile Justice and Delinquency Prevention]: "The criminologists have given us important knowledge about who commits crime. If police, prosecutors and judges put it to work, we can vastly improve the fairness and effectiveness of our criminal-justice system, ease prison crowding and enjoy safer streets and homes."

"The idea of selective incapacitation is a sound one in theory, but a nightmare in practice."

Imprisoning Career Criminals Will Not Work

David R. Struckhoff

Some people have argued that criminals who are likely to repeat their crimes should be kept imprisoned from the rest of society. In the following viewpoint, David R. Struckhoff questions whether this idea is practical. He argues that no one can safely predict which prisoners should be locked up and which can be safely released. The result might be that many people would be imprisoned needlessly. Struckhoff is a criminal justice professor at Loyola University in Chicago.

As you read, consider the following questions:

1. What important questions remain about imprisoning career criminals, according to Struckhoff?
2. Why would imprisoning repeat offenders be costly, according to the author?
3. Why does Struckhoff believe it might be unconstitutional to incarcerate offenders deemed dangerous to society?

Selective incapacitation, the process of assigning lengthy prison sentences or other types of freedom-restricting penalties to repeat criminal offenders to keep them out of the community or limit their circulation in it, has been a hot topic in criminal justice since 1975.

Past Studies

The history of selective incapacitation as it is currently being used may be traced to the work of Marvin Wolfgang, et al., at the University of Pennsylvania in 1972. Many scholars and practitioners consider this study to be the most important piece of research in criminal justice in the past two to three decades because of its influence on crime control policy. The study found that 6 percent of a sample of known delinquents born in Philadelphia in 1945 accounted for 52 percent of the known criminal offenses committed by the whole sample. A follow-up study of juveniles born in 1958 found that 7.5 percent of juveniles in a cohort of delinquents accounted for 68 percent of all index offense arrests. This research confirmed and documented what police, courts, and corrections professionals had long realized— there are a few offenders out there who account for a disproportionate amount of crime. The chronic recidivist, repeat offender, or career criminal had been found.

Within three years of Wolfgang's first publication, Shlomo and Reuel Shinnar produced a sophisticated formula for predicting the crime-reducing effect of varying lengths of incapacitation for chronic offenders. Assuming that each chronic offender committed 10 offenses per year in the free community, they estimated that the street robbery rate in New York City could be cut by 80 percent if every convicted street robber spent five years in prison.

The Shinnar estimates were challenged by the work of Stevens Clarke (1974), David Greenberg (1975), and Stephan Van Dine (1977), all of whom estimated a 4 percent reduction in crime under selective incapacitation. Other studies conducted were inconclusive, but all the researchers agreed the field needed better estimates of just how many crimes were being committed per year by repeat or chronic offenders freed in the community.

The Key Questions

The theory of selective incapacitation raises several questions and issues that must be addressed. Samuel Walker in *Sense and Nonsense About Crime* poses five questions about selective incapacitation:

• Can we correctly estimate the amount of crime reduction?

• Can we accurately identify chronic offenders and predict their future behavior?

- Can we afford the monetary costs of implementing selective incapacitation should it involve massive new detention center construction?
- Can we implement a policy of consistent selective incapacitation without violating constitutional rights?
- What will the side effects be?

To these, another question should be added: What penal or punitive sanctions might be included under the auspices of an expanded concept of selective incapacitation?

False Positives

No one has managed to develop a prognostic tool for identifying potential career criminals that does not also misidentify a large number of people as potential serious offenders. This "false positive" problem plagues most predictive ventures in criminal justice, whether of career criminals, violent people, or some other kind of lawbreaker. While it might be acceptable for a predictive scheme to generate a number of "false negatives," that is, individuals erroneously identified as unlikely aggressive offenders or career criminals, a system that puts people into prison who do not deserve to be there is another matter entirely. It is for reasons of this kind that enthusiasm for selective incapacitation has waned.

Don C. Gibbons, *The Limits of Punishment as Social Policy*, 1987.

The methodologies of estimating crime reduction under selective incapacitation rely on past behaviors of offenders or on predictions of offenders' future behavior. The higher the estimate of the number of annual crimes committed by recidivists or career criminals, the higher the models show the crime reduction rate achieved by locking those people up. One of the major problems in such prediction that has arisen is that it is almost meaningless to talk about the average number of offenses committed by chronic offenders. For example, the few offenders who are committing nearly 100 offenses per free year are sufficient to skew the estimates of the average number of offenses by all chronic offenders. Further, a definition of chronic offender has not been agreed on. These basic issues still need to be resolved.

The very heart of selective incapacitation policy involves finding chronic offenders and locking them up. Can these people be identified?

According to the Joliet, Illinois police department, the city has about 23 really high-rate offenders (how is high-rate defined?) out of a population of 80,000. But that's a guess, they say, and they don't know who's moving in and who's moving out. Additionally, the police aren't sure that some of these 23 aren't being blamed for crimes by some of their relatively slick informants and by other citizens for questionable reasons. So the police think they know the bad guys, but they're not positive.

Statistics

The judges look at the rap sheets of the accused brought to the bench. The rap sheet doesn't provide much of a guide to the reality of the offender's past. Statistically, the odds are that at least half of the things an offender has done haven't been reported, and that half of the reported ones aren't on the sheet because of processing and legal-technical restrictions and due process rights. So the judges don't know who the bad guys are either.

There are also those offenders with terrible reputations who haven't done much in actuality. These are the ones who can't commit crime well and are caught every time they try something.

In statistics, these two situations—missing cases that should be included and including cases that should be omitted—are referred to as false negatives and false positives, respectively. Even with the best predictive instruments, errors are made both ways. A prediction accuracy rate of 60 percent would be considered doing well. It's one thing to know there is a group out there that could be selectively incapacitated and yield a great reduction in crime; but it's an entirely different matter to select individuals out of that collectively with much precision. For some reason, people don't want to behave in a way that meets the criteria of actuarial tables. Some of them even change as they progress through life. Caution must be exercised in predicting from statistical trends candidates for selective incapacitation.

Monetary Costs

Walker argues that, while selective incapacitation is a politically attractive strategy in theory, it is a politically disastrous policy to implement due to staggering costs. For example, the Van Dine group estimated that a mandatory five-year sentence for all second-felony offenders in Ohio would result in a 500 percent to 600 percent increase in that state's inmate population, with the numbers jumping from 13,000 to 65,000 in five years. On the national scale, even a 400 percent increase would cause the inmate population to rise to more than 2 million people in five years. To build and operate correctional institutions on that scale would cost an estimated $75 billion to $120 billion—this to achieve a reduction of perhaps 25 percent to 28 percent in felony crime rates. At this point, the questions of how much society can afford for crime control and how to calculate cost-effectiveness arise.

There is also the issue of constitutional rights in selective incapacitation. Will offenders be sentenced for their crimes or for other reasons, such as lifestyle, race, job status, social class, and events in the offender's life history? Selective incapacitation involves making predictions of dangerousness to the community and frequency of future criminal acts. These predictions are made based on variables such as residential stability, marital status, employment history, family support, and other sociological variables that researchers have found to correlate positively or negatively with criminality. For example, should a chronic recidivist who commits a minor robbery and has "good" predictive variables not be incarcerated, while a first-time minor felony offender who has "bad" predictive variables be incarcerated? In other words, the question is, can predictions be made fairly and with any accuracy?

What effect will selective incapacitation have on the courts and the police? It may be argued that, in fact, the courts and police are already selectively incapacitating offenders based on their experience and knowledge of the cases they handle. In fact, the United States already does very well at incarcerating violent criminals, especially those who commit stranger-to-stranger crimes—when they are caught. The corrections community is already aware that the typical facility is filling up with violent inmates, and that most of the less dangerous types are being diverted elsewhere. A relatively rigid policy of selective incapacitation would force the courts to incarcerate many offenders who are currently being given alternative sentences, thus spreading the net of corrections even more widely than it is currently spread. While that bodes well for future corrections employment prospects, the cost factors as well as the social policy questions again become relevant.

Conclusion

The idea of selective incapacitation is a sound one in theory, but a nightmare in practice, mainly because of the problems of accurate scientific prediction of human behavior and the complex ethical and legal questions. The concept of selective incapacitation should not be expanded to include anything other than the limited notion of incapacitation.

"Lifers have always been an integral part of the furlough program and the lifers themselves . . . have had a positive impact on the success of the program."

Criminals Should Be Given Prison Furloughs

Robert Taliaferro

Prison furloughs are programs that allow prisoners, while still serving time, to leave prison to attend a job or to spend time with their families. Many people oppose these programs as allowing murderers to "run free." In the 1988 election campaign, Governor Michael Dukakis of Massachusetts was criticized for supporting his state's furlough program. In the following viewpoint, Robert Taliaferro uses this 1988 election debate as a basis to argue that prison furloughs are positive and necessary. He is serving a life sentence in Stillwater Prison in Stillwater, Minnesota.

As you read, consider the following questions:

1. What have furlough programs been used for, according to the author?
2. Why are attacks on furlough programs unfair and unjust, according to Taliaferro?

Robert Taliaferro, "What's all this about Lifer furloughs?" *The Prison Mirror*, November 4, 1988. Reprinted with permission.

As election 1988 ended one had to be amused at all the rhetoric which passed between the two parties regarding the Massachusetts furlough program.

It is rather strange that, with all the mud-slinging, someone did not take time to at least take a look at a position paper published by the Massachusetts Department of Corrections on the subject. . . .

The present law that everyone is up in arms about—due to a problem with one of the men on furlough (which just so happened in an election year)—has been in effect in the Commonwealth of Massachusetts since 1972.

Interestingly enough, the furlough concept is not something which has been thought of in the last few years—as the media would seem to project—it is a concept with a history which dates back to 1923.

Dr. Michael W. Forcier and Linda Holt put the research paper together and even though the Massachusetts program is bearing the brunt of the weight, similar programs—in 1987—existed in 45 states, the District of Columbia and the federal prison system. . . .

Furlough programs have existed through the presidential administrations of both parties—Democrat and Republican alike. . . .

Furloughs Are an Incentive

Furlough programs have been used as an incentive for progressive behavior in a prison; for job search, and residence search and for other reasons which facilitate a person's reintegration into the community.

The long-time prisoner finds this especially beneficial as he has been away from the community for such a long stretch of time, that he needs programs such as these to "come up to speed" with the rest of the world.

Releasing a long-timer into the community hot from prison does not allow him the cooling off period needed to keep him from becoming a statistical recidivist. Furlough programs, halfway houses and other programs are designed for this function. . . .

Interestingly enough, if one were to talk to correctional people about the long-timer and lifer, one would find that they are easier to manage; that they are more mature; and that they are less likely to recidivate—once released—than the short-term inmate.

In fact, during the 15 year span of the Massachusetts program the facts defining this are staggering.

According to the Forcier/Holt report, from 1972 to 1987 the Commonwealth logged 117,786 furloughs granted to 10,553 inmates. The statistics state that out of those furloughs granted, 426 resulted in escapes and 218 resulted in late returns which gave the program an escape rate of one-half of a percent.

In the same light, the escape rate declined over the years from 1.9 percent in 1972-73 to 0.2 percent in 1985.

Lifers have always been an integral part of the furlough program and the lifers themselves—and appropriate policy guidelines—have had a positive impact on the success of the program.

During the years 1981 to 1985, 1,824 furloughs were granted to lifers in the system, which resulted in 1 escape—or a rate of 0.05 percent.

The media blitz would have people believe that Massachusetts' furlough program helps promulgate the revolving door theory, but the statistics do not reflect this claim.

Furloughs Reduce Recidivism

In fact, the report credits the furlough program with being an "important variable in accounting for the systematic reduction in recidivism rates occurring in Massachusetts.

"The data revealed that those individuals who had experienced a furlough prior to release from prison had significantly lower rates of recidivism than did individuals who had not experienced a furlough prior to release."

The important fact is that the trend was consistent during the 11 successive years that the data was available, and that the people who had the lower rate of problems over any other class of prisoners, were those who were in for first or second degree murder.

Judging from the 1988 presidential race, it is obvious that solid party platform is no longer a prerequisite for gaining the White House. . . .

Furloughs Help Criminals

Dale Parent, a criminal justice analyst in Cambridge, Massachusetts, believes that allowing prisoners contact with the community enables them to seek employment and housing, as well as sustaining relationships with "significant others."

Parent terms furloughs as, "very helpful in encouraging reintegration into society."

David R. Brown, Stillwater *Mirror*, August 12, 1988.

To use one failure of the system to try and win an election is ludicrous at best . . . as a lifer one has to take personal offense to this; especially when one notes that the Pentagon buys 39 cent bolts for hundreds of dollars; or that billions can be sent overseas for foreign aid when thousands die in this country of exposure because they have to sleep on the streets regardless of the conditions.

One wonders, who takes responsibility for those actions? It would be interesting to see who would take responsibility if the International Court filed murder charges on the city which allowed a homeless person to die due to neglect, or lack of adequate funding for housing.

Criminals Are Responsible

Interestingly enough, most lifers and other long-timers take personal responsibility for their actions. It is not a furlough system which is at fault; it is not conjugal visits or the humane treatment of prisoners which is at fault.

What is at fault is the boiler-plate negative definitions of prisoners used for political gain, and the cutting of funds for programs in the community—and in prison—which have been proven as effective cutters of recidivist rates.

What is at fault is the use of one failure as a definitive example of a whole system failure . . . to use that failure as a personal vantage point to define why truth, justice and the American way would fail if one person or another would be elected as the *chief executive.*

The damnedest thing about it is that had the failure not occurred in an election year, no one would have paid any attention to it. . . .

The 1988 campaign evolved into a campaign of scapegoats, with the prisoner being the primary goat. Thus, for people in prison, it becomes a personal issue.

Prisoners, many of whom pay taxes—at least in Stillwater, MN— are not allowed to vote. But as taxpayers it appears that something seems wrong with a campaign which tries to cover its inadequacies by using a negative example of *any* group of people as its cornerstone.

From a prisoner's perspective, this is an act of cowardice . . . not strength, and right now this country needs strong dependable leadership more than ever.

The question is . . . when do we get it?

> *"I wish I could have a furlough—one weekend, or one hour, when my husband's death is not on my mind."*

Prison Furloughs Allow Criminals To Commit More Crimes

Robert James Bidinotto

Prison furloughs, in which prisoners are allowed to leave prison for brief periods of time, are highly controversial. In the following viewpoint, Robert James Bidinotto interviews several people whose family members were murdered by criminals on furloughs. Bidinotto describes these families' fight to end the prison furlough system. He is a former editor of *On Principle*, a monthly newsletter.

As you read, consider the following questions:

1. How does Bidinotto's definition of the furlough system differ from Taliaferro's, the author of the opposing view?
2. Why does the author quote victims' relatives to make his point?

Robert James Bidinotto, "Getting Away With Murder," *Reader's Digest*, July 1988. Copyright © 1988 by The Reader's Digest Assn., Inc. Excerpted with permission of the author.

On the night of October 26, 1974, Joey Fournier, age 17, was working alone at the Marston Street Mobil service station in Lawrence, Mass. Three men drove up, and two entered the gas station, brandishing knives and demanding money. Joey gave them $276.37 and pleaded for his life.

Minutes later, Michael Byron, one of Joey's friends, stopped by. The office floor was covered with blood. Horrified, Michael found Joey's body stuffed in a trash barrel, his feet jammed up near his chin. He had been stabbed 19 times.

Three men—Alvin Wideman, Roosevelt Pickett and William R. Horton, Jr.—were soon apprehended. All confessed to the robbery, but not to Joey's murder. Prosecutors were convinced, however, that the actual killer was Horton. He had previously served three years in South Carolina for assault with intent to murder.

In May 1975, the trio was convicted of armed robbery and first-degree murder. In many states, they could have forfeited their lives. But a few weeks earlier, Gov. Michael Dukakis had vetoed a death-penalty bill.

Still, a first-degree murder conviction in Massachusetts was supposed to mean a mandatory sentence of life in prison, with no possibility of parole. The Fournier family, devastated by their loss, took comfort in the prosecutor's assurance that Joey's killers would never again walk the streets.

Under a little-known state law, however, such first-degree killers were eligible for unguarded, 48-hour furloughs from prison. On June 6, 1986, William Horton was released from the Northeastern Correctional Center in Concord. He never came back.

He Heard Footsteps

About 7:30 P.M. on April 3, 1987, Clifford Barnes, 28, heard footsteps in his house in Oxon Hill, Md. He called out, thinking Angela Miller, his fiancée, had returned early from a wedding party. Instead, a man suddenly loomed before him, pointing a gun. It was William Horton.

For the next seven hours, a laughing Horton punched, pistol-whipped and kicked him. Horton also cut him 22 times across his midsection.

Later that night, Angela returned. Bound and gagged, Cliff listened in helpless horror to Angi's screams as Horton savagely attacked her. For four hours, she was assaulted, tied up, and twice raped.

Finally Cliff broke free and staggered to a neighbor's home for help. When Horton went to check on him, Angi cut herself loose and escaped through a window. Now panicked, Horton stole Cliff's car and fled. After a high-speed police chase, he was wounded in a shoot-out and captured.

In Lawrence, Susan Forrest, a young reporter for the *Eagle-Tribune*, was covering Horton's rampage and recapture. But one chilling detail puzzled her. "The question everyone wants answered," she wrote, "is how a cold-blooded murderer ever got out in the first place."

Forrest's editor, Dan Warner, encouraged her to find out. But she ran into a bureaucratic stone wall. Michael Fair, commissioner of the Massachusetts Department of Correction, at first refused to talk to her. Then he cited the state's 1972 Criminal Offender Record Information Act, which strictly limits public access to court and prison records of convicted criminals. The law granted convicted killers a right to privacy that made their crimes virtually a state secret.

Warner and Forrest were outraged. They could not find out why Horton had been released—or how many other Hortons were walking the streets. Forrest appealed to the governor for an interview, but was rebuffed.

Still, Susan Forrest's hard-hitting front-page stories provoked public wrath. And two state representatives—former police officer Larry Giordano and Joseph Hermann—introduced a bill to ban furloughs for first-degree murderers.

Releasing a Murderer

At the public hearing on Giordano's bill on May 27, 1987, members of Joey Fournier's family listened as his sister, Donna Fournier Cuomo, and father, Ronald, begged lawmakers to end the furloughs. Another witness, George Chaffee of Derry, N.H., told a harrowing tale. His 44-year-old mother had been brutally beaten and murdered in 1970 by confessed Massachusetts rapist John Zukoski. Even after being convicted for second-degree murder, Zukoski became eligible for furloughs; and in September 1986 he was paroled. A few months later, Zukoski was arrested and indicted yet again for beating and raping a woman.

THE WIZARD OF ID By Parker and Hart

"How many times," Chaffee demanded, "does a person have to rape and murder before he is locked up for good?"

The victims' families made a powerful impact on everyone present.

An "Honor System" for Murderers

The Massachusetts inmate-furlough program was enacted in 1972 under Gov. Francis W. Sargent, and a killer soon escaped. This stirred up a legal controversy, but in 1976 Governor Dukakis pocket-vetoed a bill to ban furloughs for first-degree murderers. It would, he said, "cut the heart out of efforts at inmate rehabilitation."

The furlough program, in essence, released killers on an "honor system" to see if they would stay out of trouble. This trial-and-error approach helped the governor decide when to commute, or reduce, a first-degree murder sentence, thus making a lifer eligible for parole. On average, in Massachusetts, prisoners whose sentences are commuted from life without parole spend fewer than 19 years in prison. Governor Dukakis, in fact, had already commuted the life sentences of 28 first-degree murderers by March 1987.

When Donna Fournier Cuomo learned that Horton had been repeatedly granted furloughs, all the nightmares of her brother's death returned. At the May 27 hearing, she met other concerned women: Maureen Donovan, Joan Bamford, Joanne Pekarski and Gertrude Lavigne. They had learned that the weekend Horton fled, he'd been spotted only two blocks from Donovan's home. "It could have been my family he went after," she said.

The women circulated a petition to support Representative Giordano's furlough-ban bill. But the bill was stalled in committee by legislative allies of Governor Dukakis.

In the face of growing public opposition, the Dukakis administration made some revisions in the furlough guidelines (eligibility became 12½ years in prison rather than ten), but defended the program relentlessly. At a news conference, bureaucrats trotted out figures showing that relatively few killers on furlough had escaped. Human Services Secretary Philip Johnston told astonished reporters, "Don't forget that Mr. Horton had nine previous successful furloughs."

To Commissioner Fair, furloughs were a prison "management tool." Unless a lifer has hope of parole, he argued, "we would have a very dangerous population in an already dangerous system." But, critics wondered, if armed guards can't control "very dangerous" killers inside locked cells, how are unarmed citizens supposed to deal with them? . . .

Later, a meeting with Dukakis convinced the women that their best option was to put a referendum about furloughs on the

November 1988 ballot. Within weeks, they formed CAUS—
Citizens Against Unsafe Society.

Susan Forrest had still been unable to get Horton's records. Fed
up, Dan Warner invited every newspaper editor in the state to a
meeting in May 1987. There he and Forrest denounced the
prisoner-privacy statute and asked for support to open Horton's
files. The result was a flood of articles and indignant editorials.
Finally, under pressure, the state released Horton's records. These
confirmed that while in prison he had a record of 11 disciplinary
infractions, three drug-related. Yet prison officials eventually gave
Horton "excellent" evaluations and said "he projects a quiet sense
of responsibility."...

Families Tell Their Stories

A Massachusetts House committee held further hearings.
Families of other victims told their stories, including Vivianne
Ruggiero, whose 27-year-old husband, John, a police officer, had
been shot in the head five times without provocation. John left
his widow with two small children. Meanwhile, Vivianne testified,
John's convicted killer, Daniel Ferreira, sentenced to life without
parole, had married while on one of 33 furloughs. "Isn't he lucky
that he can go on with his life?" Vivianne said bitterly. "I wish
I could have a furlough—one weekend, or one hour, when my husband's death is not on my mind."

Cliff and Angi Barnes, Horton's victims, also testified. "I'm tired
of hearing about the rights of prisoners," Angi said. "As far as I'm
concerned, they gave up their rights when they took another person's life." Cliff was asked about statistics touting the success rate
of the furlough program. "So we're expendable," he retorted. "Is
that what they're saying?"

After the hearings, CAUS members worked feverishly to collect and deliver signed petitions to city halls across the state. Late
at night on December 1, 1987, nine bone-weary volunteers
crowded into Joan Bamford's living room to tally the results. They
needed 50,525 signatures. They had 52,407....

Although the CAUS referendum was virtually assured of voter
approval in November, Representative Giordano reintroduced his
furlough-ban bill to halt the program even sooner....

On March 22, 1988, at a packed news conference, the governor
promised not to veto Giordano's bill.... On April 28, after the
legislature passed the furlough ban by a wide margin, the governor signed it into law....

For Donna Fournier Cuomo, the issue remains hauntingly,
harshly personal. On the 13th anniversary of her brother's murder,
she visited the now-deserted gas station in Lawrence. She cried
softly as she stared at the weeds and empty windows, symbols
of a terrible waste. *Joey,* she thought, *would have been 30 years old.*

Evaluating Concerns in Sentencing Criminals

Once a person is found guilty of a crime, the next step in the criminal-justice system is sentencing. It is here that judges make the decision on how society should treat the criminal.

Judges must consider a variety of concerns when they sentence the criminal. Some of these concerns are listed below:

1. punishing the criminal in proportion to the severity of the crime
2. rehabilitating the criminal
3. exacting revenge on behalf of the crime victims
4. having the criminal make restitution
5. deterring other people from committing similar crimes
6. isolating the criminal from the public to insure public safety
7. keeping sentences short to prevent prison overcrowding
8. avoiding cruel and inhumane punishment

This activity will allow you to assess how criminals should be treated and to explore some of the concerns judges and other criminal-justice personnel must consider when sentencing criminals.

Step 1. Imagine that you are a judge, and have the following criminals to sentence. For each case, decide which of the eight concerns listed above you must consider when determining the severity of the sentence.

_____ a fourteen-year-old boy found guilty of purse snatching for the second time

_____ a teenage gang member who shot a bystander during a drive-by shooting

_____ a man convicted of sexually abusing his daughter

_____ a woman found guilty of embezzling money from her employer

_____ a man convicted of murdering a hitchhiker; he has also confessed to killing others

_____ a woman who poisoned her husband to collect money from his life insurance policy

_____ a computer programmer who electronically stole one million dollars from a bank

_____ a man who stole three thousand dollars from a bank by threatening to kill people at gunpoint

_____ a person found guilty of selling marijuana to high school students

Step 2. Students should compare their choices in small groups.

Step 3. The class should discuss the following questions:

1. What differences exist between the concerns you found most relevant for the different criminals? Justify your reasons.

2. Are there other concerns not mentioned in this activity that you believe are important in treating criminals?

Periodical Bibliography

The following articles have been selected to supplement the diverse views presented in this chapter.

George M. Anderson	"Prison Violence: Victims Behind Bars," *America*, November 26, 1988.
Donald R. Bailey	"Serving a Self-Imposed Life Sentence . . ." *Christian Social Action*, January 1989.
Jack Eckerd	"Responsibility, Love, and Privatization," *Policy Review*, Summer 1988.
Bernard Farbar	"My Life Inside," *Esquire*, September 1988.
Richard Greene	"America's Prisons: Who's Punishing Whom?" *Forbes*, March 21, 1988.
John Irwin and James Austin	"It's About Time," *The Angolite*, November/December 1988. Available from the Louisiana State Penitentiary, Angola, LA 70712.
Kim A. Lawton	"So What *Should* We Do with Prisoners?" *Christianity Today*, November 4, 1988.
Thomas Orsagh and Mary Ellen Marsden	"Inmates = Appropriate Programs = Effective Rehabilitation," *Corrections Today*, August 1987.
Keenen Peck	"High-Tech House Arrest," *The Progressive*, July 1988.
Linda Rocawich	"Lock 'Em Up," *The Progressive*, August 1987.
Fred Scaglione	"You're Under Arrest—At Home," *USA Today*, November 1988.
Denny Smith	"How To Keep the Criminals in Jail," *Conservative Digest*, July 1988.
Patricia van Voorhis	"Correctional Effectiveness: The High Cost of Ignoring Success," *Federal Probation Quarterly*, March 1987. Available from Probation Division, Administrative Office of the United States Courts. Washington, DC 20544.
Andrew von Hirsch	"Punishment To Fit the Criminal," *The Nation*, June 25, 1988.

How Can Crime Be Reduced?

CRIME AND
CRIMINALS

Chapter Preface

The criminologist James Q. Wilson once responded rather cynically to a massive government study on crime. He stated that although it contained much interesting information, it did not provide any answers to a very important question: "What do we do tomorrow morning that will reduce the chance of my wife having her purse snatched by some punk on the way to the supermarket?" Wilson's question sums up the feelings of many people who are frustrated by the lack of a simple solution to the problem of reducing crime in the US.

Communities and individuals have fought crime in a number of ways. Proposals to reduce crime can be divided into two categories: those aimed at potential criminals and those aimed at potential victims of crime.

Solutions aimed at potential criminals attempt to make crime less attractive by increasing the penalties for it. These solutions include longer prison terms for criminals and spending more money on law enforcement so that the chances of criminals being caught and punished are greater. A quite different approach is to fund inner-city youth employment training programs, which try to help people develop opportunities to succeed without crime.

Others argue that no matter what is done, there will always be people willing to break the law. To discourage crime, citizens should change their behavior and environment to make crime more difficult. One example of an effective crime prevention program is the national Neighborhood Watch. Neighbors organize to keep watch over each other's homes and notify police of any suspicious activity.

The viewpoints in this chapter debate a variety of suggestions on what can be done to reduce crime.

"The sanctions of the criminal justice system are the only realistic hope we have for controlling the crime rate."

Imprisoning More Criminals Will Reduce Crime

Ernest van den Haag

Ernest van den Haag is the John M. Olin Professor of Jurisprudence and Public Policy at Fordham University in New York and a well-known scholar and author on criminal justice issues. In the following viewpoint, he argues that crime has risen in the US because the criminal justice system has allowed many guilty criminals to avoid punishment. By ensuring that crimes are firmly penalized, he concludes, potential criminals will be deterred from breaking the law.

As you read, consider the following questions:

1. What is the author's opinion about the search for the causes of crime?
2. What are the four purposes of punishment, according to van den Haag? Which does he stress?
3. According to van den Haag, how are legal sanctions and moral restraints connected?

Ernest van den Haag, "Must the American Criminal Justice System Be Impotent?" *Pace Law Review*, Spring 1986. Reprinted with permission.

Crime rates have long been much higher in America than in Europe. Many causes have been alleged. Perhaps heterogeneity, pluralism, federalism, liberty, or demographic factors explain part of the difference. But learning as much is not helpful because we cannot or will not give up any of these features of our society. Similarly, genetic, social and psychological causes of crime such as low intelligence, broken families, or parental mistreatment are not likely to be greatly affected by any remedies which society can devise. Although still favored by presidential commissions, poverty, inequality and bad housing have also been discredited as causes of crime.

Consider poverty. America is the world's wealthiest major country; yet it also has one of the world's highest crime rates—a crime rate higher in prosperity than in depression, and which rises "with increases in median family income." There is inequality. However, no correlation has ever been demonstrated between crime rates and inequality or, for that matter, lack of public housing. Reducing inequality may be worthwhile per se; but even if, despite differences in effort and ability, we all received the same income—hardly a realistic prospect—there would still be inequality because some of us would spend our income on receipt (or even before) and others would save a portion. Enough inequality would remain to motivate robbers or burglars. Further, criminals may well victimize persons of equal wealth or even those who have less than they do.

Must Rely on Sanctions

Little can be done about these alleged causes of crime. They are of but academic interest to anyone who wants to reduce crime rather than use it as a pretext for social reform. Hence, the sanctions of the criminal justice system are the only realistic hope we have for controlling the crime rate.

Attempts by the criminal justice system to strengthen sanctions are costly. They require politically difficult reforms: more and better police, more prosecutors and better judges. In the short run, more prison space may be needed too. However, in the long run, the inmate population need not increase. If prospective criminals can be deterred by punishing actual criminals and punishing them more severely, ultimately fewer, rather than more, prison cells will be needed. There would be fewer criminals, although a greater proportion would be imprisoned. Reformers who try to discourage the public from strengthening penal sanctions by pointing to the additional prison space needed totally disregard the deterrent effect of imprisonment—that is, the ultimate reduction of the crime rate.

Textbooks usually give four purposes of punishment:
1. Justice

2. Deterrence
3. Incapacitation
4. Rehabilitation

Deterrence most directly addresses the crime rate. Crime is rewarding to the criminal only if its expected benefit exceeds its expected cost by more than other activities available to him. No cost is likely to be high enough to make crime unrewarding for everybody. Some persons enjoy risks, or underestimate actual costs. A few may even commit crimes for the pleasure of it, regardless of costs. Still, the cost which can be imposed on the criminals can suffice to make crime unrewarding for most people most of the time. The threat of punishment is the major disincentive available.

The Purpose of Punishment

Punishment and retribution *do* have a criminal justice function. Common sense and the studies demonstrate that crime *can* be reduced if we increase the certainty and severity of punishment, if we make the anticipated penalty outweigh the anticipated gain. Although we should, of course, continue our attack on poverty, unemployment, broken families, and the like, we must also apply the law's sanctions in a firm, fair way. Punishment resets the scales of justice. The threat of punishment deters criminal activity.

Ralph Adam Fine, *Escape of the Guilty*, 1986.

To help control high crime rates, the criminal justice system can increase the probability of punishment, the severity, or both. Probability is much costlier to increase than severity. It is easier to sentence criminals more severely than to catch and convict more of them. But, it should not matter whether we increase probability or severity. For a "career criminal" who commits numerous offenses every year, it does not matter materially whether, over a period of five years, he serves two years once (low probability, high severity) or one year twice (high probability, low severity). Either way, over five years, he serves two years in prison. However, there may be some differences in the psychological impact: the delayed punishment may be perceived as less probable. Furthermore, most offenders concentrate on the short term.

Punishment Creates Moral Restraints

Criminal opportunities obviously strike the eye of the career criminal. However, most people ignore them because they believe that "crime does not pay." They have internalized the moral restraints which form their law-abiding habits. In the words of James Fitzjames Stephen, "Some men, probably, abstain from murder because they fear that if they committed murder they

105

would be hanged. [They fear that murder does not pay.] Hundreds of thousands abstain from murder because they regard it with horror. [They abstain because of moral restraints.] One great reason why they regard murder with horror is that murderers are hanged. [The threat of punishment generates moral restraints which are internalized and form law-abiding habits.]"

Sir James' formulation explains why the criminal justice system mainly deals with two relatively small and marginal groups: those who did not sufficiently internalize most moral restraints and are committed to criminal careers, and those with almost normal moral restraints who are tempted by exceptional opportunities or needs. Once habitually committed to crime, criminals can seldom be deterred by feasible threats. The legal threat of punishment is important because it deters most people from *becoming*, rather than from being, criminals. The actual punishment of criminals is indispensable; first, to make the threats of the law credible and, second, to serve as a further threat to prospective offenders.

Reducing Crime's Advantages

Textbooks often give the erroneous impression that the crime rate depends on the psychological causes dwelled upon. However, these causes determine only *who* is capable of committing crimes. They do not determine the crime rate. Far more people are capable of committing crimes than actually do—just as far more people are capable of becoming dentists or delicatessen clerks than actually do. The important question is: why do no fewer and no more of the available individuals actually become dentists, delicatessen clerks, or criminals? What determines *the rate* of these activities at any given time?

The rate of crime depends on the comparative net benefit expected, as does the rate of dentistry or of delicatessen clerking. The net benefit equals the market value of the proceeds of crime, less the costs imposed on the criminal by the courts, that is, the risk of punishment which equals the threatened punishment divided by the probability of suffering it. The threatened punishment itself, which must be discounted by the improbability of suffering it, is only the legal list-price of crime.

While the gross benefit to the criminal in property crimes depends on the market price of the proceeds, the gross benefit of non-property crimes may be independent of any market. This is the case for rape, for the unlawful taking of money and, indeed, whenever the proceeds are directly consumed by the perpetrator. Many crimes are mixed. The rapist may rob the victim and take her money as well as her watch. Whatever the combination, an increase in the costs imposed by the courts will lead to a reduced net benefit for the criminal and, therefore, to less crime. There may well be a point of diminishing returns for such cost increases; there is no evidence to indicate we have reached it. . . .

In theory, one can increase the cost of crime by increasing moral restraints, by strengthening education or religion; in practice, the criminal sanction is indispensable. To illustrate, if we want to reduce littering, education and numerous strategically placed waste containers will help. However, neither will avail unless punishment is available as well. The punitive threat alone could accomplish the purpose although in less than optimal fashion. Education and the containers alone could not.

Don Hesse, *St. Louis Globe Democrat*. Reprinted with permission.

By trying to get what they want by illegal means, criminals act quite rationally if they can expect a comparative net advantage. It is society that acts irrationally by allowing crime to be profitable, yet objecting to it. Yet we are told *ad nauseam* by sociologists and psychologists that criminals are neither rational nor calculating and that, therefore, threats of punishment will not deter them; or, we are told that criminals do not expect to be caught, wherefore threats are idle.

The first part of both these propositions is irrelevant and the second untrue. Criminals indeed do not expect to be caught; if they did, they would not commit crimes. But, they are aware of the *risk* of being caught and are accordingly affected by the probability and severity of threatened punishments.

As we all do, criminals behave as though calculating. Calculation is embodied in our habits, though not necessarily in our awareness. When we choose cheap or expensive restaurants or shops, we do not engage in elaborate calculations each time. We have evolved an habitual life style based on what is available and profitable for us. So have criminals. Although not calculating, criminals, as do all sentient beings, respond to incentives and disincentives. Rationality is not needed for such responses which are equally characteristic of law-abiding citizens, criminals and rats. Calculations are needed only for predicting the responses of others.

To be sure, the same incentives or disincentives have different impacts on different individuals or on the same individuals in different situations. A disincentive sufficient for habitually law-abiding citizens does not suffice to deter habitual criminals. Disincentives strong enough to deter most people most of the time still do not suffice to deter all people all of the time. However, legal disincentives should suffice to deter from criminal conduct most young males. They are most often tempted. Yet, our sanctions have conspicuously failed to deter as many as could be deterred. . . .

Increasing Punishment

In the United States only a small proportion—less than three percent—of all those arrested for a felony are punished by imprisonment. Even in the best of circumstances, only a small percentage of all crimes is ever punished—so small that the activities of any criminal justice system mainly serve to stigmatize crime and vindicate the social order symbolically. Nonetheless, the criminal justice system is effective: most people avoid committing crimes. Perhaps sanctions and lotteries are effective for the same reason. Many people buy lottery tickets although the chances of winning are infinitesimal, far smaller than the chances of being punished for a crime. People irrationally hope to win in spite of low probability. Analogously, people may avoid crimes because of irrational fears of losing, in spite of low probability. Their anxieties about violating the laws lead most people to overestimate their chances of being caught and punished. Crime, we have all learned, will be followed by punishment. Anxieties are commingled with realistic fears. Even a three percent rate of punishment means taking a chance greater than appeals to most people most of the time. However, that chance is taken quite often by those who make crime their trade. Currently, the chance of severe punishment is not great enough to discourage as many as we wish. A five percent chance, which is quite feasible, may well halve the crime rate.

Criminals Are Rational

The evidence supports the idea that criminals are rational and responsible for their own behavior. They choose their crimes, and freely admit it in conversations. They respond to incentives. Crimes decrease as the severity of punishment and the risk of arrest and conviction increase.

Morgan O. Reynolds, *Crime by Choice*, 1985.

Withdrawal of the immunity in practice now granted juveniles, would by itself reduce the crime rate. The available data about juvenile crime and punishment do not permit a full analysis. However, in 1933, with forty-six percent of the population under age twenty-five, thirty-nine percent of all those arrested were less than twenty-five years old. In 1980, though comprising only forty-one percent of the population, fifty-six percent of all those arrested were under twenty-five. Other data confirm that there is currently more juvenile crime relative to adult crime than in the past. The explanation is quite simple. Since 1933 we have effectively given immunity to juveniles, a practice which ought to be stopped. Those charged with crime should be tried in adult courts and exposed to the same sanctions as adults. Insufficient competence should be presumed as a matter of law only when the suspect is less than twelve years of age. If incompetence is claimed by defendants over twelve years of age, it should be decided on by the courts in each case according to the evidence.

Imprisonment and Crime Rates

Crime rates declined in the United States during the nineteenth century and indeed up to the 1960's. However, between 1960 and 1975, there was a rapid rise—232%. Homicide rates increased to 10.2 per 100,000 by 1974, from 4.7 per 100,000 in 1961. Burglaries tripled in ten years; robberies more than tripled. Despite this rapid rise in crime, the number of persons in prison declined from 118 per 100,000 to 70 per 100,000. While crime rates rose, imprisonment rates declined. Indeed the probability that a felony "would result in imprisonment decreased *fivefold."* It takes no great acumen to conclude that crime rose *because* the risk of imprisonment declined. The judiciary, in charge of applying sanctions, became reluctant to convict and imprison. Just as punishment can control crime, nonpunishment can decontrol it. This is what happened in the 1960's. Criminals were spared and victims suffered. They still do. This seems as good an argument for mandatory and determinate sanctions and for reform of judicial procedures as can be imagined.

Judicial policies alone did not cause the rise of the crime rate in the 1960's. There was an increased number of young males in the crime-prone ages and other contributory factors during this prosperous period. But the added young males accounted for less than half of the rise in property crimes and no more than ten percent of the rise in violent crime. Clearly, crime rose rapidly between 1960 and 1980 because the severity and frequency of punishment declined. The cost of crime to the criminal was reduced by decreasing the severity and frequency of sanctions. Wherefore, the net benefit of crime to the criminal rose. . . .

Needed Changes

Many aspects of our current criminal justice system cause it to be less effective than it should be. Changes along the lines I have suggested are in the offing but will take a long time to implement. It took our courts quite some time to pull the teeth out of our criminal justice system. Perhaps, it will take less time to replace them.

"Instilling fear in offenders or potential lawbreakers through threats of imprisonment or other punitive measures cannot succeed."

Imprisoning More Criminals Will Not Reduce Crime

Don C. Gibbons

Don C. Gibbons is a sociology professor at Portland State University in Oregon. In the following viewpoint, he argues that severely punishing criminals has little effect on the crime rate. As proof, he shows that even though the US now has one of the highest incarceration rates in the world, crime rates have remained high. He concludes crime can be reduced only through major social reforms.

As you read, consider the following questions:

1. How does the author describe the present state of the criminal justice system?
2. What are the two basic types of formal crime control measures, according to Gibbons? Which one does he prefer?
3. How can crime be reduced, according to Gibbons?

Don C. Gibbons, *The Limits of Punishment as Social Policy.* San Francisco, CA: The National Council on Crime and Delinquency, 1987. Reprinted with permission.

For the past 15 years, American society has been pursuing crime control policies that reflect a central theme, "get tough with criminals." In particular, punitive measures have been urged as the way to deal with "garden-variety offenders" who commit offenses such as petty theft, burglary, or larceny, and who come most often from the underclass in American society. "Get tough" policies have been much less frequently urged for inside traders, physicians involved in Medicare fraud, or other upperworld criminals.

Have these punitive crime control policies produced a safer society? Is there less crime in the United States as a result of taking a hard line toward offenders? The answer is that the crime control policies of the past decade or so have produced few positive results. Starting in the early 1970s, markedly increased numbers of people have been warehoused in prisons, so that incarcerated offenders increased from about 200,000 per day to 500,000 per day in this period. But recent data would indicate that imprisonment has neither rehabilitated nor deterred most of those who have been sent to prisons. Most of those who have been imprisoned have been "low rate" offenders rather than "career criminals." We have purchased, at great cost, relatively little reduction in crime through imprisonment. . . .

Instilling fear in offenders or potential lawbreakers through threats of imprisonment or other punitive measures cannot succeed as the central strategy around which the criminal justice system is to operate. There is an urgent need for alternative and less harsh measures to be employed, along with sparing use of imprisonment, for violent offenders. The first line of defense against lawbreaking is a society that provides meaningful social and economic rewards for all of its citizens.

Getting Tough with Criminals

During the past two decades, opinion polls have repeatedly shown that American citizens perceive themselves to be under domestic siege from "barbarians from within" who threaten to rob them, burglarize their homes, assault them, or make their lives intolerable in other ways. In short, the belief is widespread that a "crime wave" has engulfed the United States. Many citizens also apparently think that the crime problem can be drastically reduced if our political leaders and those who run the correctional machinery exhibit the firmness and resolve that hard solutions require. Consistent and punitive actions are needed for those who offend against other citizens, so it has been said.

These punitive sentiments have been voiced by criminologists and intellectual leaders in criminal justice as well. Rarely do we hear any of those appeals that were common in the 1950s and 1960s calling for treatment and rehabilitation measures that might help offenders untangle themselves from lawbreaking. Indeed, those who describe criminals in this way have fallen silent and have been replaced by observers who tell us alarming things about "the criminal mind," "career criminals," and the lawless classes in American society. Some also advocate that certain lawbreakers, including violent juveniles, be disposed of entirely through capital punishment. Long prison sentences have been put forth as the cure for the errant ways of hardened "career criminals."

A Meaningless Threat

The threat of incarceration is meaningless. Study after study reveals that neither the threat of punishment nor increased incarceration has any real impact on the crime rate. This should not surprise anyone who considers the fact that those most prone to violent street crime, marginalized males, often find life on the street no better than life inside prison.

James W. Messerschmidt, *Capitalism, Patriarchy, and Crime,* 1986.

The past two decades have witnessed the spread of such dramatic and punitive responses to crime and criminals as we have moved to "get tough" with domestic enemies. The most visible impact of this hard line is found in the dramatic increase in the number of citizens, adults and juveniles alike, now packed into prisons, training schools and other custodial institutions. This trend is revealed in prisoner statistics for state and federal penal institutions which indicate that from 1958 to 1965, the year-end population count in those institutions hovered around 210,000 people, while from 1965 to 1973, the figure was below 200,000 inmates.

US Leads in Imprisonment

However, beginning in 1973, prison populations began an apparently inexorable growth, starting with 204,211 inmates in 1973, 285,456 prisoners in 1977, and 315,974 in 1980. In the years since 1980, this surge in prison populations has been even more marked. There are currently over 500,000 adults incarcerated in prisons and reformatories—not including those in jails or juvenile institutions which are also stuffed to overflowing with inmates. Virtually all of the nation's correctional facilities are experiencing severe pressures arising from this massive shift toward incarceration as the linchpin of correctional policy. The end result of warehousing miscreants and lawbreakers is that the United States now has the unenviable distinction of being the leader of the free world in the use of imprisonment as a social policy.

The facts are clear enough—criminal justice policies in American society have hardened markedly in the past decade or so. The increased use of incarceration is simply the most dramatic manifestation of the general shift toward punitive crime control measures. Less clear are the lessons citizens and policy makers ought to draw from such recent experiences. Are the policies validated by evidence indicating that they have reduced crime and protected law abiding citizens from lawbreaking? Or, have imprisonment and other hard-line solutions to the crime problem produced few if any tangible results? Clearly, it is time to ask whether current American crime control policies make sense. . . .

Formal vs. Informal Controls

There is one point that warrants particular emphasis. Much of the commentary on crime control that turns up in the public arena emphasizes the use of formal measures of social control in order to discourage further criminality on the part of offenders. Probation is one formal sanction on one end of a punitive scale, while imprisonment or execution are on the other pole. However, conformity, including law abiding conduct, is obtained principally through informal social controls—one's internalized standards or conscience, neighborhood influences, and social ties and traditions that bind the members of society together into a law abiding population.

Japan comes quickly to mind as a low-crime society in which law abiding conduct is maintained, not principally by the police or the courts, but by family solidarity and cultural traditions. The Japanese experience shows that where informal social controls are strong, the police and justice system agencies have relatively little work to perform, but where community controls are weak and citizens are atomized or alienated, even draconian measures of formal social control fail to stem the tide of criminality.

Sociological observers in the United States have frequently observed widely varying capabilities of local neighborhoods to deter crime, with high crime areas showing sundered social ties and defective neighborhood social controls. The implication of this finding is clear: the search for viable approaches to dealing with the crime problem in American society ought to emphasize measures that strengthen the informal social control mechanisms in our communities, rather than concentrating entirely upon ways to strengthen the hand of the state in crime control measures or zeroing in on tactics that will either attract apprehended offenders into more law abiding ways of behavior or which will frighten and intimidate them and drive them out of lawbreaking.

Why are the social influences that discourage criminality weak in some American neighborhoods and strong in others? The causes are the same ones that push some individuals into violent acts and crude and illegal forms of "income redistribution" such as robberies or burglaries. Those who have lost out in the struggle for meaningful work and educational opportunities, decent housing, and other less tangible but equally important rewards of American society end up with other disadvantaged citizens in neighborhoods where they are unable to sustain a sense of community and where they are vulnerable to attacks from lawbreakers in their midst.

Limits of Government

Will a no-nonsense approach to crime control, where violent and predatory criminals are made to pay for their offenses, reduce crime? Will increased financial support for crime control methods reduce crime? The answer is an emphatic *no*. . . .

It is fascinating that conservatives, who generally shun government intervention and argue that it is an ineffective and inappropriate source for handling social problems, look to government for crime control, just like liberals. Liberals want government to help, conservatives want government to punish, but both want *government* to solve the problem. The truth is that regardless of the financial investments in crime control made by federal, state, and local governments, the system will not reduce crime.

Kevin N. Wright, *The Great American Crime Myth*, 1985.

A look at the history of crime control measures in western societies shows that virtually every tactic the human mind could invent to be used in the "war on crime" has been employed somewhere, including such historically important measures as flogging, transporting, imprisoning or burning the cheeks of offenders. Also, some advocates of "new" approaches to crime control periodically attempt to revive some of the more barbarous of these tactics, i.e., those who have recently advocated a return to corporal punishment.

The Cost of Sanctions

Among criminologists, it was once fashionable to announce that punishment is a futile and immoral policy, but such pronouncement is too facile. Experiences in South Africa, for example, indicate that an unpopular minority government is quite capable of ruling with an iron fist, at least in the short run. Similarly, who is to say that the Malaysian policy of executing all drug dealers is a failure? Perhaps if we allowed no reduction of murder charges to manslaughter, made no exceptions for second degree murder, and put all convicted murderers to death, homicide rates might drop. There might be a noticeable reduction in crime if we were to maintain a level of two or three million citizens in prison. But is this the kind of nation in which most Americans want to live—

a fortress society? While criminal justice policies that emphasize draconian punishments may be effective, at least for short periods, severe sanctions raise profound moral and ethical concerns.

Two Approaches

Formal social control measures are extremely varied, but can be sorted into two types. The first, and currently most popular approach, is predicated on modern-day versions of imagery about the dangerous classes that were popular in 19th century England. It centers on instilling fear in lawbreakers and potential lawbreakers through tactics of terror and repression, along with sanitizing society, at least temporarily, by preventive detention of so-called "career criminals."

Some will protest such labels as tactics of fear and repression or terror as exaggerations at best. After all, Americans are not like Russians. We don't throw political dissenters in gulags nor do we employ the repressive measures that are now altogether too common in South Africa. Fear, repression, and terror are also apt terms for proposals that have been aired to extend capital punishment to juveniles and for policies of throwing a large and ever-increasing number of people in prisons and other custodial institutions.

It is important to note that a rehabilitative posture toward offenders need not excuse them from responsibility for their lawbreaking. Society can and should condemn lawbreaking while at the same time refraining from terror tactics.

The second approach, the "society as patient" perspective, assumes that crime is a reflection of societal conditions. This rehabilitation-social integration-preventive position shifts attention away from punishing offenders and toward efforts to alter "criminogenic" features of society, as well as to assist lawbreakers in disengaging themselves from criminal activity. . . .

Three Periods of Crime

There are three broad periods in the crime experiences of American society since the turn of the century. The first, roughly from about 1900 to the 1940s, was characterized by relatively low crime rates and by punitive approaches to offenders, relieved somewhat by humanitarian gestures. A substantial number of lawbreakers were imprisoned in penal institutions, but the rate of incarceration was relatively low. Most of the prisons of this period made little or no pretense of being in the rehabilitation business; instead, they were convict-run, harsh and punitive in their programs.

The late 1950s and 1960s witnessed the rise of "the rehabilitative ideal." Criminologists rushed to announce that punishment was an archaic response to crime and that it would soon disappear. Correctional administrators around the nation gave a good deal of lip service to treatment and intervention as the primary goals of their systems. In a number of states, the authorities moved to wrestle control of penal institutions away from convict leaders. Finally, in a few states such as California, concerted efforts were actually mounted to implement the rehabilitative ideal. In the 1950s and 1960s, a variety of experimental ventures were launched to test out new and hopefully more effective programs of correctional intervention.

In the third and most recent period, the exceedingly pessimistic "nothing works" view captured the attention of many correctional policy makers and lay people alike. Public support for treatment and intervention has withered away, at least in part because many criminological observers have rushed to embrace the contention that rehabilitation is an idea whose time has gone. We now find ourselves thrown back upon punishment and repression as devices to be employed in a desperate struggle to turn back the tide of lawbreaking. . . .

The Limits of Punishment

The American crime rate began a dramatic move upward in the early 1970s, reached a peak in 1980, and apparently began a slight descent in the years since 1980. On the other hand, the daily count of prisoners in adult correctional institutions rose from about 200,000 in 1970 to more than .5 million in 1987. Indeed, the prison population grew 10 times faster than did the general population between 1975 and 1985.

In addition, the number of felons doing time in jails increased markedly during the same period. Jails have received the overflow that cannot be accommodated in American prisons, most of which contain greater numbers of prisoners than they were designed to hold and many of which are under court order to reduce crowding or alleviate other conditions of inhumane treatment.

No Simple Solutions

Can we bring down the crime rate by putting more people in prison?

Perhaps; but not by much.

It is still widely believed that lowering crime by increasing its "costs" ought to be a simple matter, like cutting taxes or voting more money for defense. But research increasingly shows that things aren't so simple. Indeed, . . . most criminologists today—whether Left, Right, or Center—generally acknowledge that only a fraction of serious crime can be prevented by increased incarceration.

Elliott Currie, *Confronting Crime*, 1985.

The explosion of prison populations was the result of two related processes: more convicted felons were being sent to prison by judges than in earlier periods, and for longer sentences. Crime control through incapacitation of greater numbers of criminals has been the guiding principle of social policies in the 1970s and 1980s. Increased use of incarceration has been joined with efforts to raise the punitive force of lesser penalties handed out to less dangerous offenders. In short, punishment has been the order of the day.

What have we reaped from these policies? In particular, has increased incarceration had an appreciable effect upon crime rates? Is imprisonment a viable social policy?

Although incarceration is widely used in the United States, the extent varies from state to state. In 1983, the District of Columbia had an imprisonment rate of 558 people per 100,000 population, followed by Nevada with a rate of 354 inmates, while at the other extreme, New Hampshire and North Dakota had rates of about 50 prisoners per 100,000 population. Statewide index crime rates for the 50 states in 1984 show relatively little correlation with imprisonment rates. Should we conclude from this that imprisonment causes crime? Obviously not, but neither should we assume that increased imprisonment leads to significant reductions in lawbreaking. . . .

New Directions

Elliott Currie's assessment of the contemporary crime problem and proposals about how to curb it is correct in observing that garden-variety lawbreaking is related more to variations in the *quality* of work available to people than it is to simply being employed or not employed. He is also correct in his diagnoses of deficiencies in the social life of local neighborhoods and communities, negative learning experiences in schools that push people in the direction of criminal misconduct, and other pressures that contribute to criminality. Most of his recommendations for attacking the crime problem center on the same rents and tears in the social fabric:

> If we are serious about attacking the roots of this American affliction, we must build a society that is less unequal, less depriving, less insecure, less disruptive of family and community ties, less corrosive of cooperative values. In short, we must begin to take on the enormous task of creating the conditions of community life in which individuals can live together in compassionate and cooperative ways.

Proposals to reorder the social priorities in American life are considerably easier to enunciate than they are to bring about, but it is noteworthy that a number of European countries have already moved a considerable distance in the right directions. The obstacles to bringing about a world less ridden with crime are more political and ideological than anything else. Finally, major reforms in social and economic life in contemporary America represent our best hope for the future.

"[The] connections between drugs and crime . . . would be much diminished if drugs were legalized."

Legalizing Drugs Can Reduce Crime

Ethan A. Nadelmann

In the following viewpoint, Ethan A. Nadelmann argues that crime could be reduced by legalizing drugs. He writes that the illegal status of drugs automatically makes drug users criminals and makes drugs expensive. This causes addicts to commit crimes to support their habits, attracts organized crime, and contributes to police corruption. Nadelmann is an assistant professor of politics in the Woodrow Wilson School of Public and International Affairs at Princeton University in Rutgers, New Jersey.

As you read, consider the following questions:

1. What are the four links between drugs and crime, according to Nadelmann?
2. How are ghettos especially affected by drug laws, according to the author?
3. What does Nadelmann believe causes police corruption?

Ethan A. Nadelmann, "Shooting Up," *The New Republic*, June 13, 1988. Reprinted by permission of THE NEW REPUBLIC, © 1988, The New Republic, Inc.

Hamburgers and ketchup. Movies and popcorn. Drugs and crime.

Drugs and crime are so thoroughly intertwined in the public mind that to most people a large crime problem seems an inevitable consequence of widespread drug use. But the historical link between the two is more a product of drug laws than of drugs. There are four clear connections between drugs and crime, and three of them would be much diminished if drugs were legalized. This fact doesn't by itself make the case for legalization persuasive, of course, but it deserves careful attention in the emerging debate over whether the prohibition of drugs is worth the trouble.

Under the Influence

The first connection between drugs and crime—and the only one that would remain strong after legalization—is the commission of violent and other crimes by people under the influence of illicit drugs. It is this connection that most infects the popular imagination. Obviously some drugs do "cause" people to commit crimes by reducing normal inhibitions, lessening the sense of responsibility, and unleashing aggressive and other anti-social tendencies. Cocaine, particularly in the form of "crack," has earned such a reputation in recent years, just as heroin did in the 1960s and 1970s and marijuana did in the years before that.

Crack's reputation may or may not be more deserved than those of marijuana and heroin. Reliable evidence isn't yet available. But no illicit drug is as widely associated with violent behavior as alcohol. According to Justice Department statistics, 54 percent of all jail inmates convicted of violent crimes in 1983 reported having used alcohol just prior to committing the offense. The impact of drug legalization on this drug-crime connection is hard to predict. Much would depend on overall rates of drug abuse and changes in the nature of consumption, both imponderables. It's worth noting, though, that any shift in consumption from alcohol to marijuana would almost certainly reduce violent behavior.

Drug Buyers and Sellers

This connection between drugs and anti-social behavior—which is inherent and may or may not be substantial—is often confused with a second link between the two that is definitely substantial and not inherent: many illicit drug users commit crimes such as robbery, burglary, prostitution, and numbers-running to earn enough money to buy drugs. Unlike the millions of alcoholics who support their habits for modest amounts, many cocaine and heroin addicts spend hundreds, maybe even thousands, of dollars a week. If these drugs were significantly cheaper—if either they were legalized or drug laws were not enforced—the number of crimes committed by drug addicts to pay for their habits would drop dramatically. Even if the drugs were taxed heavily to discourage consumption, prices probably would be much lower than they are today.

The third drug-crime link—also a byproduct of drug laws—is the violent, intimidating, and corrupting behavior of the drug traffickers. Illegal markets tend to breed violence, not just because they attract criminally minded people but also because there are no legal institutions for resolving disputes. During Prohibition violent struggles between bootlegging gangs and hijackings of booze-laden trucks were frequent and notorious. Today's equivalents are the booby traps that surround marijuana fields; the pirates of the Caribbean, who rip off drug-laden vessels en route to the United States; and the machine-gun battles and executions of the more sordid drug mafias—all of which occasionally kill innocent people. Most authorities agree that the dramatic increase in urban murder rates over the past few years is almost entirely due to the rise in drug-dealer killings, mostly of one another.

What Legalization Can Do

Legalizing drugs would reduce enormously the number of victims of drug use who are not addicts: people who are mugged, people who are corrupted, the reduction of law and order because of the corruption of law enforcement, and the allocation of a very large fraction of law enforcement resources to this one particular activity. There are millions of people who are not addicts who are being harmed by the present system.

Milton Friedman, *Reason*, October 1988.

Perhaps the most unfortunate victims of drug prohibition laws have been the residents of America's ghettos. These laws have proved largely futile in deterring ghetto-dwellers from becoming drug abusers, but they do account for much of what ghetto residents identify as the drug problem. Aggressive, gun-toting drug dealers often upset law-abiding residents far more than do addicts nodding out in doorways. Meanwhile other residents perceive the drug dealers as heroes and successful role models. They're symbols of success to children who see no other options. At the same time the increasingly harsh criminal penalties imposed on adult drug dealers has led drug traffickers to recruit juveniles. Where once children started dealing drugs only after they had been using them for a few years, today the sequence is often reversed. Many children start using drugs only after working for older drug dealers for a while.

The conspicuous failure of law enforcement agencies to deal with the disruptive effect of drug traffickers has demoralized inner-city neighborhoods and police departments alike. Intensive crackdowns in urban neighborhoods, like intensive anti-cockroach efforts in urban dwellings, do little more than chase the menace a short distance away to infect new areas. By contrast, legalization of drugs, like legalization of alcohol in the early 1930s, would drive the drug dealing business off the streets and out of apartment buildings and into government-regulated, tax-paying stores. It also would force many of the gun-toting dealers out of business and convert others into legitimate businessmen. Some, of course, would turn to other types of criminal activities, just as some of the bootleggers did after Prohibition's repeal. Gone, though, would be the unparalleled financial gains that tempt people from all sectors of society into the drug-dealing business.

Corruption

Gone, too, would be the money that draws police into the world of crime. Today police corruption appears to be more pervasive than at any time since Prohibition. In Miami dozens of law enforcement officials have been charged with accepting bribes, ripping off drug dealers, and even dealing drugs themselves. In small towns and rural communities in Georgia, where drug smugglers from the Caribbean and Latin America pass through, dozens of sheriffs have been implicated in corruption. In one New York police precinct, drug-related corruption has generated the city's most far-reaching police scandal since the late 1960s. Nationwide, over 100 cases of drug-related corruption are now prosecuted each year. Every one of the federal law enforcement agencies with significant drug enforcement responsibilities has seen an agent implicated.

It isn't hard to explain the growth of this corruption. The financial temptations are enormous relative to other opportunities, legitimate or illegitimate. Little effort is required. Many police officers are demoralized by the scope of drug traffic, the indifference of many citizens, a frequent lack of appreciation for their efforts, and the seeming futility of it all; even with the regular jailing of drug dealers, there always seem to be more to fill their shoes. Some police also recognize that their real function is not so much to protect victims from predators as to regulate an illicit market that can't be suppressed but that much of society prefers to keep underground. In every respect, the analogy to Prohibition is apt. Repealing drug prohibition laws would dramatically reduce police corruption. By contrast, the measures currently being proposed to deal with the growing problem, including more frequent and aggressive internal inspection, offer little promise and cost money.

The final link between drugs and crime is the tautological connection: producing, selling, buying, and consuming drugs is a crime in and of itself that occurs billions of times each year nationwide. [In 1987] alone, about 30 million Americans violated a

Ed Gamble, *The Florida Times-Union*. Reprinted with permission.

drug law, and about 750,000 were arrested, mostly for mere possession, not dealing. In New York City almost half of the felony indictments were on drug charges, and in Washington, D.C., the figure was more than half. Close to 40 percent of inmates in federal prisons are there on drug-dealing charges, and that population is expected to more than double within 15 years.

Clearly, if drugs were legalized, this drug-crime connection—which annually accounts for around $10 billion in criminal justice costs—would be severed. (Selling drugs to children would, of course, continue to be prosecuted.) And the benefits would run deeper than that. We would no longer be labeling as criminals the tens of millions of people who use drugs illicitly, subjecting them to the risk of arrest, and inviting them to associate with drug dealers (who may be criminals in many more senses of the word). The attendant cynicism toward the law in general would diminish, along with the sense of hostility and suspicion that otherwise law-abiding citizens feel toward police. It was costs such as these that strongly influenced many of Prohibition's more conservative opponents. As John D. Rockefeller wrote in explaining why he was withdrawing his support of Prohibition:

> That a vast array of lawbreakers has been recruited and financed on a colossal scale; that many of our best citizens, piqued at what they regarded as an infringement of their private rights, have openly and unabashedly disregarded the 18th Amendment; that as an inevitable result respect for all law has been greatly lessened; that crime has increased to an unprecedented degree—I have slowly and reluctantly come to believe.

"Removing legal sanctions and lowering drug cost. . . . will result in a surge in incidences of random violence and higher crime rates."

Legalizing Drugs Cannot Reduce Crime

Robert E. Peterson

In the following viewpoint, Robert E. Peterson argues that crime would not be reduced by legalizing drugs. He argues that the black market for drugs could never be fully stopped, and that legalization would greatly increase drug addiction and drug-influenced crimes. Peterson is the deputy attorney general in Pennsylvania.

As you read, consider the following questions:

1. What does Peterson believe motivates the current calls for drug legalization?
2. According to the author, why would the black market for drugs be difficult to eliminate?
3. How would cheaper legal drugs increase crime, according to Peterson?

Robert E. Peterson, "Stop Legalization of Illegal Drugs," *Drug Awareness Information Newsletter*, July 1988. Reprinted with permission.

The argument that the only solution to the drug problem is to legalize illicit drugs has resurfaced with a fiery vengeance. . . .

Many of those advocating drug legalization do not realize the damage they are doing. They have never talked with the kids who bravely refuse to use or to the young addicts struggling to recover a shattered life. As Congressman Charles Rangel angrily states, to many people the legalization issue is "idle chitchat as cocktail glasses knock together at social events." It is our duty and responsibility to speak out for those who often cannot speak for themselves. We must publicly challenge every assertion that drugs should be legalized. . . .

Why Legalize?

There is both an old school and a new school of thought on why drugs should be legalized. The old school dates back to the hippy era and argues that drug use should be allowed as a matter of individual liberty and that people should have the right to use whatever drugs they want, regardless of the consequences to society. The old liberal school will support almost any argument to legalize drugs, such as: claiming drugs are not that dangerous; or that there is a compelling medicinal need for illicit drugs; or that drug laws are an evil plot by big brother government; or that people only use drugs because they are illegal. This group has generally lost ground over the past ten years as the marijuana decriminalization push stagnated and public concern about the drug issue mounted.

America has grown increasingly intolerant of illicit drugs as the destructive impact of these substances has expanded. Ironically, in the midst of increasing drug intolerance, a renewed cry for drug legalization is being heard. This call for drug legalization is primarily based on fear and frustration. The inability of law enforcement to single-handedly solve America's drug problem is cited as evidence of the futility of imposing legal prohibitions on drugs. The costs of enforcement, it is argued, outweigh the benefit society derives from such enforcement. Faulty economic theory is simplistically applied to bolster the legalization position.

I call such economic theory "blind-side economics" because it overlooks historical experience, neglects social and economic realities, ignores the biological and psychological effects of illicit drugs, and misinterprets lessons from our recent experience with these deadly substances. The frustration of those concerned about the drug issue is understandable. The call for drug legalization is not.

The legalization argument sounds deceptively logical when viewed as an abstract theory or when coupled with distorted analogies or facts out of context. However, the argument completely self-destructs when it is placed in the context of human experience and history, and when examined in conjunction with the scientific biological nature of illicit drugs. . . .

Law Enforcement Can Work

The advocates of drug legalization claim that the war on drugs cannot be won and we must withdraw now and cut our losses. In support of this claim they cite the fact that drug availability, drug consumption, and drug-related violence has increased in spite of stronger law enforcement efforts and tougher drug laws.

History and the experience of other nations reveals that the most effective means of solving a drug epidemic is to apply strong enforcement in conjunction with a public education and user rehabilitation campaign. . . .

The experience of other nations indicates that applying tough law enforcement measures in conjunction with public education and rehabilitation efforts is the only way to successfully solve a drug crisis. Liberalizing drug laws only brings about an increase in drug use, drug addiction, and drug-related criminal activity. It is true that law enforcement cannot win this war alone and prevention, education and treatment efforts have only just started to work in conjunction with enforcement. . . .

Bob Dix, *The Union Leader*. Reprinted with permission.

Legalization proponents say that if drugs were legal and made less expensive then illegal drug trafficking would cease and crimes committed by drug users would dramatically decline. They also claim that various schemes of governmental regulation of drugs could be tried. In defense of this claim they analogize the current drug laws with alcohol prohibition and assume that drug users only commit crimes to pay for high priced drugs.

Legalization proponents use the alcohol system analogy to demonstrate the problems of prohibition, but they often call for a system of drug legalization that does not resemble the alcohol model. Some have argued that a restrictive government regulatory system could be implemented to control drug purity and price. This notion does not conform with logic, reason, or experience.

A strong black market in illicit drugs will persist unless all drugs of all potencies are competitively manufactured and marketed. The reason that we do not have a strong black market in alcohol products is that consumers can easily obtain a beverage with the taste, potency and cost of their choice. In the Soviet Union, where alcohol product quality and quantity is controlled by the government, illegal alcohol production and the consumption of dangerous substitutes is rampant. Drugs are easier to smuggle and manufacture than alcohol and government approved cocaine could quickly be converted into deadly pellets of crack. Great Britain found that allowing limited distribution of heroin to addicts resulted in a stronger black market.

To eliminate the illicit drug market, pure cocaine, crack, PCP and heroin would have to be readily available at low cost. The black market in drugs would disappear, but a black plague of drug addiction, overdose deaths and crime would sweep the nation.

Legalization and Street Crime

A popular misconception among legalization proponents is that drug users commit crimes solely to support expensive drug habits. This misperception leads to the false conclusion that lowering the cost of drugs would reduce the level of drug-related crime. In reality, cheaper legal drugs would increase the level of violent and property crime.

Drug users will commit crime to obtain drugs regardless of drug price. Crime levels have dramatically risen in areas where drug prices have dropped. In areas where crack now sells for only $3 per dose (a price that a legal, taxed market would find hard to beat), violent crime has skyrocketed. Amsterdam has found that de facto legalization and readily available low cost drugs has led to a wave of theft and vandalism. Drug abusers who formerly sold drugs to support their habit would now steal to buy legal drugs. The amount of drugs consumed by addicts also would rise with falling drug price.

Dr. Robert Gilkeson, M.D., a pediatrician, neuropsychiatrist, and director of the Center for Drug Education and Brain Research, states that "drug use [is] actually the cause of sociopathic and 'criminal' behavior." Drug users commit crimes that are totally unrelated to the cost of the drug. In Philadelphia, 50% of the child abuse fatalities involve parents who heavily use cocaine. Cheaper legal cocaine would result in more children murdered and more babies born addicted. Bizarre sexual behavior, youth suicides and murder are committed because drugs impair normal thought processes. Over 80% of criminals arrested for violent felonies were on drugs when they committed their crime, according to the Department of Justice. Rapes, assaults, and murders that are unrelated to a need for drug funds are included in these statistics.

The Fantasy of Legalization

The idea that legalization would take the profit out of drug crime by driving down prices, thus persuading pushers of the virtues of honest labor, is a socially deluding fantasy. Right now, you can get all the crack you want in New York for $3 to $5 a vial, a good enough price so that the hard-working mass-marketers of the poison can earn millions a week.

A.M. Rosenthal, *The New York Times*, April 22, 1988.

By removing legal sanctions and lowering drug cost a broader and more frequent demand for drugs will be created. Increased drug use will result in a surge in incidences of random violence and higher crime rates. . . .

Alcohol prohibition failed because a popular legal substance, with a long cultural and social history, was banned without the moral consensus of the people. Today, less than 18% of the public favors a return to alcohol prohibition and over 85% favor a 21-year-old drinking age. On the other hand, public support for our drug laws and strong drug law enforcement has never been stronger. Over 73% of the public oppose legalizing marijuana and tough drug laws are overwhelmingly favored. The few vocal proponents of legalization inaccurately conclude that the nation does not have a moral consensus on this issue. Few other laws receive such strong support from the American people as those that prohibit illegal drug use. . . .

All laws are expressions of the moral will of the people. However, laws cannot make a wrong into a right. Laws that allowed slavery did not make slavery right or just. Illicit drug use is wrong. It enslaves the user and victimizes all of society. The current law reflects our overwhelming recognition of that fact. In a democratic society, the will of the people, expressed through a system of laws, is the rule of the land.

"Programs that fight unemployment fight crime as well."

Youth Employment Programs Can Reduce Crime

William H. Kohlberg

William H. Kohlberg is president of the National Alliance of Business, an organization that works to involve businesses in education and job training programs. In the following viewpoint, he argues that a major cause of crime is unemployment, especially among minority youth. Kohlberg advocates programs in which businesses, schools, and communities work together to provide training and jobs for young people who might otherwise become involved in crime.

As you read, consider the following questions:

1. How does Kohlberg define "at-risk youth"?
2. What is the relationship between education, drugs, and crime, according to the author?

William H. Kohlberg, "Employment, the Private Sector, and At-Risk Youth," *The Annals of the American Academy of Political and Social Science*, November 1987, Vol. 494, November 1987, copyright 1987 by The American Academy of Political and Social Science. Reprinted by permission of Sage Publications, Inc.

The United States has many features that make it unique among nations. Sadly, one of these is a uniquely high crime rate. We all recognize that however significant the police and the criminal justice system are in addressing crime as it occurs, real reduction in our crime rate requires policies that address the social pathology that gives birth to excessively high levels of crime and violent behavior. Many factors contribute to this pathology, and its cure requires a coordinated attack from a variety of angles.

The special concern of the organization I represent, the National Alliance of Business, is unemployment. No one doubts that an increase in unemployment leads to an increase in crime. The sense of frustration and despair that joblessness can provoke finds expression in a variety of ways: theft, substance and alcohol abuse, and spouse and child abuse. Programs that fight unemployment fight crime as well.

Yet we know that crime rates remain high in the United States whether unemployment rises or falls. We recognize, moreover, that a disproportionate amount of crime is committed by youth whom we refer to as at risk. Any substantial reduction in our nation's crime rate requires that we address effectively the problems of at-risk youth. . . .

Youth at Risk

We use the term "at-risk youth" to describe young people who are in danger of dropping out of school and out of the labor market due to a variety of social, economic, and educational problems. Obviously, these are youth who are also very much at risk of leading lives marred by crime and violence. It is also as accurate to say that we as a nation are at risk if we do not address the problem.

Current data on American youth, and predictions based on that data, tell a story of impending crisis and profound economic and social costs.

Each year, about 700,000 high school students drop out. Another 300,000 are constant truants. In some of our cities, the dropout rate is 50 percent. One out of every four ninth-graders will not graduate from high school. One out of every eight 17-year-olds in this country is functionally illiterate. For minorities and the poor, the rates are significantly higher. In Japan, in contrast, virtually every high school student graduates, and illiteracy has been reduced to the vanishing point.

The lives of millions of our young people are marked by crime and despair. Young people under 21 account for more than half of all arrests for serious crimes, and young people are the victims of crime as well. Moreover, the involvement of the young in crime has been increasing over the last several decades. The homicide rate for nonwhite teens rose by 16 percent between 1950 and 1978, while for white teenagers the rate jumped by 232 percent.

The skyrocketing of drug and alcohol abuse among teenagers over the past 20 years hardly needs mention. During the period 1960-80, arrests of people under 18 for drug abuse increased by an incredible 6000 percent. Arrests for drunkenness among high school seniors rose by 300 percent. . . .

One of the most dramatic effects of poverty is its impact on educational attainment. Only 43 percent of black young people who come from poor homes ever graduate from high school. For whites, the figure is not much better—a graduation rate of only 53 percent.

The Need for Employment Policies

It is hardly accidental that every advanced industrial society with a far lower level of violent crime than ours has also developed much more humane and effective employment policies. Usually they include both substantial public expenditure for job training and retraining of the work force and active policies to ensure high levels of employment—including, where necessary, creation of public jobs. In the United States, such measures have always been comparatively underdeveloped; this left us thoroughly unprepared to cope with the wrenching technological and economic changes of the postwar era.

Elliott Currie, *Confronting Crime*, 1985.

Uneducated young people cannot find jobs. Young people who enter their twenties with neither a high school diploma nor work experience are in great danger of spending a lifetime in idleness and frustration. Yet large numbers of our youth, particularly minority youth, find themselves in this situation. For example, scarcely more than half of young black males aged 16-19 are in the labor force; less than one-third are employed; and one-fourth have never been employed.

Addressing the Problems

The picture of the phenomenon we call at-risk youth that I have just drawn is a complex one. When trying to address the problems of at-risk youth, we find that although they can be analyzed separately they are interrelated and cannot be approached piecemeal. There is a ripple effect involved. Young people who regularly use drugs are less likely to do well in school, are more likely to engage in casual criminal behavior, and are less likely to develop stable employment patterns. Young people who drop out of school are less likely to find employment and more likely to become involved with drugs and crime. In effect, these factors tend to assume the form of a circle of antisocial and self-destructive behavior. Young persons may enter the circle at any point, by using drugs, for example, or by committing petty crimes or dropping out of school. If they persist in such activity, however—if they remain on the circle—some or all of the other types of antisocial behavior will begin to appear in their lives. Moreover, these forms of behavior reinforce one another. The longer one is on the circle, the more difficult it is to leave.

In addressing the problems of at-risk youth, the National Alliance of Business seeks to break the circle by striking at the point of unemployment. This is our particular area of concern and expertise. High levels of youth unemployment have critical implications for our nation's present and future productivity, security, economic competitiveness, and social stability.

The combined efforts of public and private leaders, government, community organizations, and families will be crucial to addressing the issues facing our nation's young people. Unemployment problems among young people cannot be solved in isolation, and success in moving at-risk youth into the economic mainstream can have a ripple effect of its own in reducing crime, drug use, and other undesirable forms of behavior. . . .

Past Efforts

Past efforts have established a wide range of individual programs to address the problems of at-risk youth, but they have not achieved the overall results that had been hoped for. They have not focused on the extent to which these problems are interconnected—a teenager misusing drugs or alcohol is likely to have problems in school and in looking for a job; a high school dropout is more likely to become involved in drugs or crime.

We must adopt a holistic approach to the problems of youth, one that is aware of the ways in which these problems affect one another and one that can address these interrelationships. Such a grand strategy cannot be conceived, much less implemented, from Washington. Both the federal and state governments can do much to make a coordinated youth effort possible, but the actual coalition building must take place at the local level.

It is critical to business and society at large that we meet this historic opportunity successfully, but no single sector of our economy or society is equipped to deal with these issues alone. The effort must be a partnership between key elements of the public and private sectors.

For years now, we at the National Alliance of Business have been particular advocates of public-private partnership in the field of job training. This partnership approach is the basis of the Job Training Partnership Act (JTPA), which provides the framework for job training for the structurally unemployed in the United States.

JTPA embodies a landmark concept in federal policy that is systemized nationwide. At the local level, over 600 private industry councils (PICs) set job-training policy and oversee the operation of training programs, in partnership with local elected officials. The PICs draw their membership from business, education, trade unions, community-based organizations, and other groups. . . .

PICs are excellent vehicles for convening and galvanizing community action. They are one of the few community institutions that have at the same table education, labor, business, and community-based organizations.

We see potential for increasing the role of PICs in a number of human resource development areas, most particularly that of at-risk youth. The private sector needs to be involved in a broader range of human resource issues because the private sector is where the jobs are, and private employers have a growing interest and stake in the success of human resource development efforts. . . .

The Boston Compact

An outstanding example of what a PIC can do, and one we are trying to re-create in other sites around the country, is the Boston Compact. Working through a PIC, the Boston business community agreed to give high priority to high school graduates from the city if the school system agreed to institute a program to improve daily attendance, dropout rates, academic preparation, and job placement.

Career-experience teachers were assigned to participating schools by the Boston PIC to help achieve these goals. Area colleges, universities, and trade union apprenticeship programs have also joined the Compact, promoting the school-to-work transition for graduating seniors. In 1985, one Boston official said, eighty-seven percent of the high school graduates in Boston who got full-time jobs were placed by [the Boston Compact]. Right now in Boston, every young person who makes it through high school can be assured of going on to a job. No other high school system in the country can make that claim.

Over the next two years, we will be working with seven cities to help them develop and implement their own versions of the Boston Compact. Boston has the advantage of a booming local economy, which few other communities can match. Yet the Compact has had difficulty in reducing dropouts. We would like to improve on the Compact while learning from it.

Impressive as its results are, the Compact is only part of the solution, operating in only one city—but that is how partnerships begin. Every city needs to look at what its needs are, what its problems are, and what its resources are.

"When others are allowed to do their own thing without fear of censure . . . we are creating an environment conducive to crime."

Citizen Action
Can Reduce Crime

William Wilbanks

William Wilbanks is a criminal-justice professor at Florida International University in Miami. In the following viewpoint, he blames the rise of crime on the failure of families, schools, and communities to instill traditional values and to control behavior. Wilbanks argues that crime can only be reduced by restoring a sense of community in American cities and counteracting prevailing self-centered attitudes.

As you read, consider the following questions:

1. Why do people refrain from breaking laws, according to Wilbanks?
2. According to the author, why has crime risen in the past 25 years?
3. What three problems prevent people from becoming involved in fighting crime, according to Wilbanks?

William Wilbanks, "You Can Do Something About Crime . . . You Can T.H.I.N.K." Revised and expanded for Greenhaven Press, January 1989.

I have been a criminologist for 20 years. I spent four years studying crime and the criminal justice system in graduate school (receiving a Ph.D. in criminal justice) and have taught in this field for 16 years. I am well-read in the criminological literature and have contributed to that literature via my own research and writing (publishing five books and over 30 articles in professional journals). I am quite comfortable discussing crime and criminal justice with my colleagues and students. . . .

I am most uncomfortable discussing crime and criminal justice issues with laypersons and the media (e.g., radio talk show hosts) since they tend to be "bottom-line" people in that they want to skip over all the talk of facts about crime and theories about crime to the bottom-line—"What can we do to reduce crime?" But that is precisely the question that embarrasses criminologists. We are strong on theory, research, and evaluation but short on solutions. We know what doesn't work but we are not sure what does (or would) work.

Nothing Works

Criminologists are even less prone than laypersons to offer solutions to the crime problem because we are aware of the literature suggesting that the panaceas usually suggested by the layperson (e.g., increase the use of the death penalty, give tougher and/or mandatory sentences, eliminate plea bargaining, abolish the insanity defense) have not and likely would not significantly reduce crime. A good summary of the evidence against the commonly accepted panaceas is given in Samuel Walker's *Sense and Nonsense about Crime*. In the mid-1970's Robert Martinson, a criminologist, became famous when his evaluation of all types of rehabilitative programs indicated that "nothing works". Students and the public often get the impression from criminologists that the motto of the field is "nothing works".

Criminologists do suggest some solutions to the crime problem but their solutions generally concern broad changes in culture (i.e., changes in "informal social controls") or the socio-economic system which are not seen as practical since it is difficult to make such basic changes in our society. For example, Wilson and Herrnstein in *Crime and Human Nature* suggest that the increase in crime in the past 20 years is largely due to the shift from a culture that emphasized self-control to one that now emphasizes self-expression. Unfortunately, this diagnosis of the problem does not suggest a solution as culture is difficult to change.

I share the bias of most criminologists in believing that increasing informal social controls is likely to be more effective than increasing the formal controls of the criminal justice system. I know that I (and most other law-abiding persons) refrain from law-breaking more because of the fear of disapproval from "significant others'' than because of fear of being arrested and going to jail. In my view, crime has increased not because of the breakdown of the criminal justice system but because of the breakdown of informal social controls. . . .

Comparisons

Many laypersons look back with nostalgia to the ''good ol' days'' when crime rates were lower and incorrectly attribute the lower crime rates to the ''old'' and more efficient (perhaps less ''handcuffed'') criminal justice system. But the lower crime rates of the past were not due to a better criminal justice system—they were due to more effective informal social controls. Families, churches, schools, etc., were more effective in the ''good ol' days'' in socializing, monitoring and controlling youth than they are today. There was not as much need for the back-up controls of the criminal justice system and thus the number of law violators being caught up in the criminal justice system was much smaller than today.

ROTHCO
ORIGINAL.

"IT'S A BURGLAR, ALL RIGHT, BUT HE'S BREAKING IN NEXT DOOR, NOT HERE!"

China and Japan do not have less crime than the U.S. because they have a better criminal justice system than we do. They have less need for the formal controls of the criminal justice system because their community (informal social) controls are so much better than ours. They do a much better job of socializing their population and of monitoring the behavior of deviants. Likewise, Vermont does not have less crime than Florida because the Vermont criminal justice system is so much better than the criminal justice system in Florida. There is less need for the criminal justice system in Vermont because informal social controls are so much more effective there.

Most people recognize that these inter-country and intra-country comparisons at one point in time do not support the view that the criminal justice system is the major factor to blame when explaining sharply different crime rates. But for some reason the comparison of U.S. crime rates over time seems to elicit the view that the changing (for the worse) criminal justice system is the major reason why crime in the U.S. has increased in the last 25 years. Few who hold this view seem to have considered the possibility that the criminal justice system may be even better than in the "good ol' days" but is simply overwhelmed by the "hordes" of offenders who have been created by the breakdown in informal social controls. . . .

A Sense of Community

Perhaps the best way to illustrate the strength of informal controls is to think of the small towns that many of us grew up in. I grew up in Belton, Texas, a town in Central Texas with a population around 8,000. My brothers and I were well known in that small community and we were under surveillance by someone who knew us (and who would report to our mother) no matter where we went. There were a lot of "nosy neighbors" and people who cared enough to let us know when we stepped out of line. There was no attitude of "let them do their own thing" as there was a sense of community and people had to conform to the norms of that community.

This sense of community can be achieved in a modern urban environment as one has only to look at the ethnic neighborhoods in some of our older cities. Those who step out of line in a closely-knit Polish or Italian or Jewish neighborhood are reminded of what is right and wrong and what hurts the community. Certainly Japan and China have proven that modern cities can achieve a sense of community and informal social control in the 1980's.

Unfortunately, most of the urban areas in the U.S. have little sense of community and few informal social controls. Our urban communities are "atomized" in that they are an aggregation of individuals who have no "connection" with their neighbors.

Anonymity (i.e., "privacy") and individualism seem to be encouraged in our modern culture and we want our neighbors to "mind their own business" and thus we actually discourage the type of close-knit community that monitors and checks the behavior of its residents. We have achieved our privacy and individualism at the expense of a much higher crime rate where "doing one's own thing" to many has involved criminal behavior.

Two Neighborhoods

The importance of informal social controls in determining the extent of criminal behavior is well illustrated by a study of two neighborhoods in Cambridge, Massachusetts, one with a high rate of juvenile delinquency and one with a low rate. Social characteristics in the two neighborhoods were much alike. But in the high delinquency area, there was higher variation in religion and ethnic background. Neighbors knew fewer neighbors by name, had fewer interests in common, and disliked their community more. Persons in the high-delinquency neighborhood were no more accepting of delinquency, but were less likely to take action if they were not the direct victims. The residents of the low-rate area were more likely to take action if they saw a delinquent act in progress. When people ignore such acts, there develops an atmosphere where delinquency can grow more easily.

National Crime Prevention Institute, *Understanding Crime Prevention*, 1986.

Criminals and those contemplating theft or aggression are calculating individuals. They sense that they will not face any social censure if they steal or assault. Such acts have an immediate reward and there is little indication that anyone in the community knows or really cares. We put up signs in our neighborhoods warning criminals that the community is protected by Neighborhood Watch but most criminals know that these signs are an empty warning in that most neighborhoods are not "organized" to monitor and check the behavior of stranger intruders. . . .

Three Problems

The problem of a breakdown of informal social controls in the U.S. is due to three problems: (1) We don't know and don't want to know what illegal activities are going on around us. (2) We don't care if we do know—let them do their own thing. (3) We don't know what to do if we do know and do care. Let me illustrate the first problem. Most of us live in our little private worlds and don't want to be bothered with the activities and problems of others. Therefore we don't try to get to know our neighbors as they might then make demands upon us or interfere with our privacy. Our attitude is "leave me alone and I will leave you alone".

But it is that attitude that has created the atomized community that we live in. Neighborhood Crime Watch is an effort to organize so that we know what is going on in our neighborhoods—it is an effort to create a small-town environment in the midst of a big city.

The second problem (we don't care if we do know) is more difficult to solve. We have to become convinced that "no man is an island" and that when others are allowed to do their own thing without fear of censure that we are creating an environment conducive to crime. Why are we surprised when we ignore the criminal behavior of others because "it doesn't hurt me" that others are not concerned when someone else does hurt us? We have to care enough to want to do something.

The third problem (we don't know what to do if we do know and care) is perhaps the most difficult. What do I do if I know of illegal activity. I can't tell the criminal as he may intimidate or harm me. If I tell the police they will say they cannot act without more evidence or they may suggest that they do not have the manpower to deal with minor criminal activity (e.g., a student selling a "joint" to another). . . .

A Partial Solution

I want to propose a partial solution to the crime problem—one that will help strengthen informal social controls and perhaps change the thinking of some who may be only beginning to commit criminal acts. I propose that we T.H.I.N.K. (Tell Him/Her It's Not Kool). In many cases we do know of criminal activity in our midst but we ignore it. Why don't we get involved in the crime problem by anonymously informing the offender that we do not think his/her behavior is "Kool" (appropriate)? We can send that person a T.H.I.N.K. card that suggests that there are persons who do not approve of his behavior and that the self that he thinks he is projecting is not consistent with how others perceive him.

Let's take an example that probably applies to 90% of Americans. Most of us know persons who use (or perhaps even sell) illegal drugs such as marijuana or cocaine. But we ignore that as "it's none of our business" and after all they may even be friends and we wouldn't want to see them get in trouble. But the "drug problem" is tearing our nation apart and drug addiction is closely intertwined with our crime problem. If there were no demand for drugs there would be far fewer homicides (up to one-third of homicides in some cities are "drug-related") and fewer robberies and burglaries (since many are attempts to get money to buy drugs). The demand for drugs creates much of our crime. So why are we so tolerant of those who help create that demand? They are indirectly hurting us and our community.

Let's try to change their behavior by T.H.I.N.K. Let's send them an anonymous note that looks something like the following:

T.H.I.N.K.

I am an acquaintance of yours. I know you think of yourself as a law-abiding person and that you are concerned about the crime problem in our community. But did you ever stop to THINK that much of the crime problem is due to the illegal drug trade? And there would not be an illegal drug trade without persons like yourself who buy and use those drugs. I know you believe you are not hurting anyone and that your drug use is nobody's business. But your drug use along with that by countless thousands is part of the crime problem. Won't you reconsider your contribution to the crime problem? Perhaps you think no one really cares that you use drugs—but I do and countless thousands also care. Won't you consider the possibility that you are part of the problem and not part of the solution?

This note is anonymous as I am concerned about you and don't want to see you get in trouble. I am not a fink—I am a concerned citizen. I want you to know that I do not see you as chic, sophisticated or cool. I see you as someone who, perhaps unwittingly, is contributing to the crime problem. I am sending you this card so that you might re-evaluate your behavior in light of how you are perceived by others. I am hoping to change behavior by T.H.I.N.K.—Telling Him/Her It's Not Kool.

Obviously, the T.H.I.N.K. cards can be created for those engaged in drunk driving, spouse abuse, child abuse, vandalism, assaults (e.g., bullies whose self-image is cool) or even burglaries and robberies. Maybe we don't have the courage to directly approach persons whom we know are engaged in illegal activity but how can we refuse to T.H.I.N.K. via an anonymous message? Do we care enough to take ten minutes to write a T.H.I.N.K. card and to spend 25 cents on a stamp? . . .

I would suggest that those organizations in the community, like Crime Watch, Mothers Against Drunk Driving, etc. might want to consider the use of T.H.I.N.K. cards to help restore a sense of community to their city. I also believe such organizations are an excellent source for volunteers to write T.H.I.N.K. cards for those who need help in composition. What do you think?

"Building prisons is not the answer; building people is."

Community-Based Organizations Can Reduce Crime

Elizabeth Lyttleton Sturz and Mary Taylor

The following viewpoint is written by two workers at Argus Community, Inc., a New York City organization that works with juvenile delinquents and drug abusers. Elizabeth Lyttleton Sturz, president of Argus, has worked as a journalist, public relations director, and writer. Associate director Mary Taylor experienced drugs and streetlife firsthand before earning a master's degree in social work. They argue that community-based organizations which provide quality treatment and care for at-risk youth and drug abusers can help many people turn away from crime.

As you read, consider the following questions:

1. Which values do the authors believe are important to teach to youth?
2. According to Sturz and Taylor, what are the essential elements of a successful community organization?

Elizabeth Lyttleton Sturz and Mary Taylor, "Inventing and Reinventing Argus," *The Annals of the American Academy of Political and Social Science*, November 1987, Vol. 494, November 1987, copyright 1987 by The American Academy of Political and Social Science. Reprinted by permission of Sage Publications, Inc.

Argus has existed as a community-based organization (CBO) in the South Bronx since 1968. It provides an alternative life program for adolescents and adults who have been on the treadmill of unemployment, underemployment, street hustling, welfare, substance abuse, crime, and prison and who saw no way out for themselves.

Of the adolescents who have attended Argus over the years, about a third were caught up in the juvenile and criminal justice systems, accused or convicted of theft, assault, mugging, robbery, possession or sale of drugs, and so forth. Many came through family court as persons in need of supervision or as neglected, abused, or abandoned. Nearly all used drugs. All were dropouts. Many had serious educational deficits. About a third were adolescents brought to Argus by relatives who could not cope with their troublesome behavior and who clung to the hope that their children would somehow find their way out of the South Bronx. They had been told that Argus could help. And we have been able to succeed with substantial numbers, first folding them into the bosom of our community, where they could heal, learn new ways, and grow in competence and self-esteem; then transplanting them firmly into the broader community, where they could continue to thrive—or if they did not, bringing them back for another try. . . .

Why We Need CBOs

CBOs are needed for economic and societal as well as humane reasons, and we believe that, given the resources, carefully constructed, well-run community organizations could achieve desirable outcomes on a broad scale.

Indeed, the plight of families, children, and communities is so drastic and the consequences for the future so catastrophic that sooner or later our country must be moved by enlightened self-interest, if not by compassion, to provide responsible elements in communities with the resources and the support to wrestle with these problems. . . .

It is not just ghetto dwellers and the poor who could benefit, but middle-class families and children as well. They, too, are experiencing social upheaval leading to an erosion of values, broken homes, alienation, underachievement, child abuse, teen pregnancies, teen suicide, substance abuse, violence, and crime. . . .

Can CBOs Have an Impact?

Can CBOs reduce crime among youths, where it is most prevalent? Can they foster positive values? By values we mean respect for law and order, respect for self and others, realizing one's potential, reaching out to help others. Can CBOs act as extended families; make up for past deprivations; fill in educational gaps; motivate young people to develop the behavior, attitudes, and competencies that open doors in the labor market? Can CBOs be of help to the business community in its search for responsible, committed, drug-free and alcohol-free employees—a search that in light of foreign competition has become a matter of survival for American businesses?

We believe that the answer is yes on two conditions: (1) that CBOs are well managed, properly staffed, and effectively run; and (2) that society commits sufficient resources to the initiative, that is, that there be an effort commensurate with the need.

A Sense of Family

A good number of inner-city neighborhood nonprofit organizations have become sufficiently empowered to use crime prevention successfully as a means to the ultimate end of securing community regeneration, economic development, housing rehabilitation, and youth employment. In part, the development process has been made secure by reducing opportunities for crime, for example, through neighborhood patrols, block watches, and escort services. But to avoid merely displacing violence to other locations, the causes of crime also have been addressed. One way has been through replacing or supplementing weakened families with alternative, community-based extended families that, along with ethnic and cultural identification, help restore to children and teenagers the consistent discipline and self-respect created by strong natural families. In other words, a broad sense of family can be suggested that includes any emotional connecting and bonding among individuals, such attachment supplying social support and discipline.

Lynn A. Curtis, *The Annals of the American Academy of Political and Social Science,* November 1987.

Building prisons is not the answer; building people is. Prisons do not work because we cannot build enough of them and we cannot keep misdoers inside forever. Moreover, the numbers of misdoers are swelling. Repeat felons are turned back into foster care programs because the courts are swamped. Prisons are bursting at the seams. On the other hand, there is national concern about youths detained in adult jails for want of community resources.

Basic Recipes for a CBO

Granted that we can build and rebuild people and families— every successful society on the face of the earth has done it— what are the essential ingredients of a CBO devoted to such a purpose? In trying to answer this question, we will rely on the Argus model because that is what we know best. We have invented and reinvented Argus over 18 years and have harvested some grains of knowledge that may be useful.

First, there are certain elements that should be present because, in our experience, it is precisely the lack of these elements in the family, in the schools, in the justice system, and in the workplace that encourages antisocial behavior and chaos. These elements include modeling and teaching values as defined earlier; setting up and maintaining a safe environment—cooperation here from the police is helpful; responsible authority figures and peer groups who act as an extended family, providing warmth, nurturance, communication, and structure; rules that allow enrollees and staff to experience the consequences of positive and negative behavior; marshaling well-designed, realistic academic, prevocational, and vocational training resources; setting positive short-range and long-range goals; the development of new identities and aspirations; and the cooperation of the private sector, including, especially, employers.

How do we set up the chain of events that ends with young people in jobs and employers being supplied with the human material they need? Essentially, it is a process that responds to the whole person, attempting to fill in gaps, restoring trust in family, law, and societal values, changing feelings and attitudes—in short, developing the self-esteem and new identities and responsible behavior that can open doors. . . .

The Treatment Model

We are healers in a spiritual and moral, not a medical, sense. We do not subscribe to the model that says that people who commit antisocial acts are sick. Sometimes the problems are biochemical or medical, as research findings over the past 20 years have clearly shown. These problems require medical treatment or whatever steps are necessary to protect society. Apart from that subset, social scientists refer to a complex of factors, economic and psychological, leading to antisocial behavior: the one-parent, female-dominated family, the culture of poverty, the culture of crime, and recently a permanent underclass are frequently blamed for the disruptive behavior of inner-city youths. A failed welfare system, unresponsive schools, and the lack of jobs and opportunities are cited also, although not as often, perhaps because we are not ready to put our words, much less our money and our best efforts, into a solution. It appears more prudent and less costly—over the short run—to probe the past histories and inner lives of troubled and troublesome people, seeking the origins in early traumas and family conflicts.

This model provides a cop-out for kids—and people of all ages—who do not want to grow up. Who does? It is tough to deal with the here and now, assume responsibility for one's own life, shape oneself and one's future, and learn to communicate and to care about people. But that is our task if we are to be successful as human beings or as a society. For the test of a successful society is its ability to incorporate the young. That is precisely what this country is not doing at present and what it must learn to do on a large scale if we are to thrive or even remain alive on this planet. It is a task that never ends and that cannot be undertaken solely by teen mothers or grandmothers or fathers or even two parents together raising children on their own in a small walled-off space without guidance or a supportive network and without strong social underpinnings.

A history of deprivation or abuse in the family or in society deserves sympathy and understanding. But at Argus we do not encourage our kids to wallow in their sorrows, nor do we believe that a solution can be found by raking over the past. People serve themselves best by focusing on what they can learn from their unique experience, however painful it has been, by realizing how strong they are to have survived, and by putting that strength to work to build a here and now and a future.

A Message for Policymakers

SOS. Formulate a national policy. Address the problem. Arrange to bring help into communities so that they can begin to build supports for beleaguered families, schools, drug-free treatment, and justice systems. Argus and other agencies have demonstrated that CBOs can effectively fill in emotional, parental, educational, and vocational gaps. We can create and maintain drug-free and crime-free environments where growth, motivation, and learning can take place. We can act as launching pads for a broader, brighter future for numbers of people.

The problem is huge and complicated, of course. But our experience has shown that angry, alienated teenagers can be pulled in, can be brought to the point where they not only do not steal and assault but have something of value to give to society. The message to these teenagers has to be: "You are valuable, society cares about you. You have the obligation and the resources to reach your potential."

The effort and the message have to be underwritten by the government and carried out by the community. . . . They have to "trickle up," not down. In our experience, the CBO can be a proper vehicle for the process.

"Environmental design . . . can make people feel more secure even when they live in dangerous circumstances."

Environmental Design Can Reduce Crime

Edward Krupat and Philip E. Kubzansky

Edward Krupat and Philip E. Kubzansky argue in the following viewpoint that city residences and stores could be designed to make crime more difficult to commit. Krupat is a professor of psychology at the Massachusetts College of Pharmacy and Allied Health Sciences in Boston, and Kubzansky is a professor of psychology at Boston University.

As you read, consider the following questions:

1. According to the authors, how have attempts to improve slums worsened the crime problem?
2. How do burglars determine which houses to break into, according to Krupat and Kubzansky?
3. Do the authors believe environmental design alone can reduce crime?

Edward Krupat and Philip E. Kubzansky, "Designing To Deter Crime," *Psychology Today,* October 1987. REPRINTED WITH PERMISSION FROM PSYCHOLOGY TODAY MAGAZINE copyright © 1987 (PT Partners, L.P.)

No matter what city you live in, it is impossible to open the local paper without being bombarded by stories of fear and crime. Evidence of public vandalism and concerns about being mugged or robbed are part of daily life in the city. The causes of urban crime and its possible remedies have been debated endlessly by social reformers, from politicians to philosophers, but few have been able to do anything significant to reduce this critical social problem.

Based on the premise that slums were the breeding ground of crime, planners in the 1950s and '60s tore down entire neighborhoods of old, decaying buildings and replaced them with new high-rise housing developments. They also improved street lighting and hired extra police to patrol problem areas. Yet, to their surprise and disappointment, crime still flourished. Police presence and better lighting did little to reduce either crime or fear. In fact, people seemed more afraid to use the newly created open spaces of their housing projects at night than they had been to walk the streets of their old slum neighborhoods.

Defensible Space

Architect Oscar Newman looked at these efforts in his controversial book, *Defensible Space*, and labeled them misguided. He claimed that crime occurred because of this new design, not in spite of it, and concluded, "the new physical form of the urban environment is possibly the most cogent ally the criminal has in his victimization of society." Better lighting, more police and stronger locks could not deter crime, Newman said, unless residents became the critical agents in their own security.

Newman believed that the proper design, one that fostered "defensible space," could arouse the strong, but latent, territorial feelings of city dwellers and stir them to action. First, it should generate opportunities for people to see and be seen continuously. Knowing that they are, or could be, watched makes residents feel less anxious, leads them to use an area more and deters criminals by making them fear being identified and caught.

Second, people must not only watch but also be willing to intervene or report crime when it occurs. Newman proposed reducing anonymity and increasing territorial feelings by dividing larger spaces into zones of influence. This can be accomplished on a small scale by clustering a few apartments around a common entrance or a common elevator. On a larger scale individual yards or areas can be demarcated by having paths and recreational areas focus around a small set of apartment units or by having each building entry serve only a limited number of apartments.

Newman and his followers tested these ideas by studying housing developments in cities across the country, from New York to San Francisco, and concluded that rates of crime, vandalism and turnover were lower in places that conformed to the principles of defensible space. In a variety of large and small cities, housing projects and urban neighborhoods have been redesigned in accord with defensible space principles. While the results have not been consistent, reductions in crime and fear and increases in a sense of community have been found in several places.

The Goals of Design

Physical design can be used to stimulate social attitudes and behavior which can help reduce both the opportunities for crimes and the fear of crime through:

Intensified use of streets, parks and land around structures;

Increased visibility of intruders to legitimate occupants and users;

Increased tendency for people to look out for each other and to act if a crime is observed;

Increased ability to discriminate between people who belong in an area and those who are intruders; and

Increased sense of shared interest in improving and maintaining the quality of the physical and social environment.

National Crime Prevention Institute, *Understanding Crime Prevention*, 1986.

Still, many disagreed. Some have argued that the principles are too mechanistic and narrow to account for the complex issues of fear and crime. Other critics object to the concept of territoriality that forms the basis of the theory, while still others believe that Newman and his colleagues did a poor job of picking matched sites for comparison and analyzing their data.

The Criminal Perspective

More recent studies have looked at crime from the opposite perspective, that of the criminal. Social psychologists Ralph Taylor and Stephen Gottfredson of Temple University and other researchers believe that criminals form mental images of potential target sites in deciding where to commit a crime. They read the nonverbal cues given off by the target to pick up messages about the opportunities, risk and convenience involved.

Social psychologists Irwin Altman and Barbara Brown of the University of Utah have expanded on this idea. They suggest that burglars ask themselves five kinds of questions:

• *How detectable am I? For instance, where are windows and doors positioned, and how far is it from the street to the house?*

• *Are there any real barriers present? Does the place have strong locks, a gate or an alarm system?*

• *Are there any symbolic barriers present? Are there any nameplates, "Neighborhood Watch" signs or similar indicators of territoriality and vigilance?*

• *Are there traces of presence or activity on the part of the residents? Is the newspaper still in the driveway, and are the lights on?*

• *What is the social climate of the area? Are people staring at and questioning me, or can I go about my business ignored by others?*

In 1984 sociologist Stephanie Greenberg, then of the University of Denver, and urban planner William Rohe of the University of North Carolina at Chapel Hill tested this "criminal opportunity" theory in three pairs of Atlanta neighborhoods. They were matched on racial and socioeconomic makeup but differed greatly in their levels of crime. The researchers found that the low-crime neighborhoods were more residential, had less public parking and had fewer through-streets.

To get a closer look into the mind of a burglar, Altman and Brown went right to the scene of the crime. The Salt Lake City Sheriff's Office gave them the locations of 102 suburban middle-class homes that had been broken into over the previous 15 months. The researchers compared these homes to similar homes that hadn't been burglarized. Their research team walked along the block coding each home—or should we say, casing it—for the presence or absence of 200 specific environmental cues that might give off a special scent of criminal attractiveness.

Several differences were clear. Burglarized homes were more likely to be on a street with signs revealing it was a public thoroughfare, where strangers might commonly be found. Non-burglarized blocks had a more private sense about them: They looked hard to enter, were clearly set off from public areas and often had large names or numbers on them. These cues, all suggesting the owners' presence, activity and territorial commitment, apparently signaled criminals to keep away.

The 7-Eleven Solution

The Southland Corporation, owner of the 7-Eleven convenience chain, has redesigned its stores with a special eye toward the criminal's aversion to surveillance. The chief architect of this plan, Ray D. Johnson, has excellent credentials. Before working for 7-Eleven, Johnson served 25 years for robbery and burglary in the California state penitentiary system. Now working on the other side of the law as a consultant on crime prevention, Johnson and his colleagues rearranged the physical design of 60 7-Elevens in southern California.

Knowing that robbers like concealment, they provided just the opposite. To allow clear sightlines from the street into the store, they moved cash registers up front and removed all advertising from the front windows. They also put bright floodlights outside the entrance, forcing potential robbers to perform where any passerby could look in and see.

They also installed special cash drawers that make it impossible to get at more than $10 every two minutes. This gives the would-be robber the choice of getting away with very little cash, waiting "onstage" to make the payoff worthwhile or simply going elsewhere. As Johnson says, "It takes too much time. With the register so visible from the street, no robber would hold a gun on anyone that long. When you're worried about getting caught—and every robber is very worried every time—two minutes is an eternity. It's just not worth it to wait that long for another $10."

Crime and Privacy

Think about some common crimes. . . .

- Burglary occurs most frequently in empty apartments, offices, or buildings.
- Robberies are crimes of anonymous streets, empty elevators, hidden stairwells, and poorly designed stores.
- Rapes happen mostly indoors under cover of night.
- Vandalism—also a nighttime crime—sullies unwatched, unlit spaces.

These crimes are the product of desire, opportunity, and perceived risk. All three elements have a spatial dimension—privacy. Amos Rapoport, an environmental behaviorist, defines privacy as the "control of unwanted interaction." In the case of crime, unwanted interaction cuts two ways. The victim wants to be protected from the intrusion of a criminal and the criminal wants to be protected from observation by witnesses and police. The way spaces are defined determines whose purpose gets served. Spaces designed to limit access and open activities to public view suffer less crime. Spaces that are freely accessible and closed off from view invite it.

Georgette Bennett, *Crimewarps*, 1987.

Johnson's insights proved to be right on the money. The Southland Corporation found that robberies were 30 percent lower in the 60 redesigned stores than in 60 similar stores that had not been redesigned. "Our experience has been that robbers frustrated by small takes don't shoot; they leave," says Richard Nelson, security manager for Southland.

The new design has proven itself over time against other convenience stores, as well. While the average loss at convenience store holdups was $607 and the number of robberies rose 47 percent in the late 1970s and early 1980s, 7-Eleven's losses averaged $45 and its number of robberies went down 56 percent.

Anthropologist Sally Merry of Wellesley College combined the resident and criminal perspective during 18 months as a participant-observer in a low-to-moderate-income housing project in Boston, which Merry refers to as "Dover Square." Merry got to know many of her fellow residents and interviewed several young men who were responsible for much of the street crime in the neighborhood. The section Merry studied consisted of four-story buildings, built in 1965, that reflected several of the design factors later recommended by Newman. Yet it had the highest per capita robbery and assault rates in the city.

More than half Chinese and one quarter black, with a sprinkling of whites and Hispanics, Dover Square is, in Merry's words, "a neighborhood of strangers." It is a pot that simmers and boils but rarely melts or blends. Few friendships stretch across racial or cultural lines, and each of the groups harbors strong and often negative stereotypes of the others.

Different Perspectives

In Merry's interviews and surveys, she found several differences between the residents' perspective and that of the criminals. The places the residents considered most dangerous were not necessarily those where the most crime took place. They felt safest when they were familiar with an area and the people who used it and felt unsafe if the turf was unfamiliar. And although they did identify a number of architectural features that they associated with danger, these were not major concerns.

The criminals, on the other hand, equated the safety of a place with the number of crimes that took place there, and they were particularly conscious of an area's architectural features. Several of them spontaneously mentioned that they looked for places with poor surveillance, such as narrow, enclosed pathways or where windows were obstructed by fences.

One of the young criminals had a favorite spot where no one could hear or see his victims. Describing it, he explained, "Someone can back you in there, and if you scream, all you can hear is the echo." Another young robber mentioned that he carefully avoided one spot because there are "so many eyes there."

Merry's research on criminals and residents helped make a critical distinction between space that is defensible and space that is defended. She notes that a neighborhood may be architecturally designed to encourage defense against crime but still not be defended because there is little or no social cohesion. Even when buildings are low and the entrances and public spaces focus around a small set of families, people will not react to crime when they believe that they are on someone else's turf, when they do not consider the police effective or when they fear retribution.

Designing defensible space is neither the panacea that some proponents have hoped, nor is it as irrelevant to crime and fear as some detractors have contended. Environmental design does address the when and where of crime and can make people feel more secure even when they live in dangerous circumstances. But it can never eliminate crime because it does not attack its root causes; design, as some critics have suggested, may only move crime from one place to other, more vulnerable areas. It remains easier to remodel buildings than to create opportunities for teenagers who live in poverty, and until that is done the motivation for crime will not disappear.

Design also cannot generate a social environment in which people of different races and cultures understand, care for or share responsibility for one another. As Merry says, "Design can provide preconditions for effective control, but it cannot create such control if the social fabric of the community is fragmented." Environmental design is hardly the ultimate solution to the puzzle that we call urban crime, yet it does add some new and important pieces that make the picture a good deal clearer.

Recognizing Statements
That Are Provable

From various sources of information we are constantly confronted with statements and generalizations about social and moral problems. In order to think clearly about these problems, it is useful if one can make a basic distinction between statements for which evidence can be found and other statements which cannot be verified or proved because evidence is not available, or the issue is so controversial that it cannot be definitely proved.

Readers should constantly be aware that magazines, newspapers, and other sources often contain statements of a controversial nature. The following activity is designed to allow experimentation with statements that are provable and those that are not.

The following statements are taken from the viewpoints in this chapter. Consider each statement carefully. *Mark P for any statement you believe is provable. Mark U for any statement you feel is unprovable because of the lack of evidence. Mark C for any statements you think are too controversial to be proved to everyone's satisfaction.*

If you are doing this activity as a member of a class or group, compare your answers with those of other class or group members. Be able to defend your answers. You may discover that others will come to different conclusions than you. Listening to the reasons others present for their answers may give you valuable insights in recognizing statements that are provable.

P = *provable*
U = *unprovable*
C = *too controversial*

1. Crime rates have long been much higher in America than in Europe.

2. Criminals are calculating individuals.

3. Opinion polls have shown that Americans believe a crime wave has engulfed the United States.

4. The United States has one of the highest incarceration rates in the world.

5. The policy of imprisoning criminals has failed to control crime.

6. Far more people are capable of committing crimes than actually do.

7. Legalizing drugs would cause a plague of drug addiction to sweep across the nation.

8. Legalizing drugs would eliminate the black market and reduce crime.

9. Every federal law enforcement agency involved with drug laws has been touched by corruption.

10. Crime rates remain high in the US whether employment rises or falls.

11. The example of other countries shows that the most effective means of solving a drug epidemic is to combine strong enforcement with public education and rehabilitation programs.

12. Criminals prefer working in places where they cannot be seen by anyone passing by.

13. Building people, not prisons, is the answer to reducing crime.

14. The consultant who helped redesign 7-Eleven stores to make robbery more difficult was himself a former criminal.

15. Juvenile delinquents transplanted into supportive communities have succeeded in transforming their lives.

16. Young people who regularly use drugs are more likely to engage in criminal behavior.

17. Most people abstain from crime because they want to avoid disapproval from their friends and relatives.

18. Major social and economic reforms are America's best hope for ending crime.

Periodical Bibliography

The following articles have been selected to supplement the diverse views presented in this chapter.

Gary S. Becker	"Should Drug Use Be Legalized?" *Business Week*, August 17, 1987.
Robert M. Bohm	"Crime, Criminal, and Crime Control Policy Myths," *Justice Quarterly*, June 1986.
Warren T. Brookes	"Are Courts Soft on Crime?" *Conservative Digest*, May 1985.
Dan Feldman	"Longer Sentences Do Not Deter Crime," *The New York Times*, October 3, 1987.
Ted Gest	"What Should Be Done," *U.S. News & World Report*, August 22, 1988.
George Kannar	"Liberals and Crime," *The New Republic*, December 19, 1988.
Peggy Mann	"Reasons To Oppose Legalizing Illegal Drugs," *Drug Awareness Information Newsletter*, September 1988. Available from 57 Conant St., Room 113, Danvers, MA 01923.
Tom Morganthau	"Should Drugs Be Legal?" *Newsweek*, May 30, 1988.
Charles Murray	"Crime in America," *National Review*, June 10, 1988.
Howard A. Palley and Dana A. Robinson	"Black on Black Crime," *Society*, July/August 1988.
Reason	"America After Prohibition," October 1988.
Raymond Shonholtz	"The Citizen's Role in Justice: Building a Primary Justice and Prevention System at the Neighborhood Level," *The Annals of The American Academy of Political and Social Science*, November 1987.
Jerome H. Skolnick	"Drugs: More or Fewer Controls?" *Los Angeles Times*, June 22, 1988.
Sherry Sylvester	"Crime Prevention and Criminal Justice in Search of a Silver Bullet," *The Annals of The American Academy of Political and Social Science*, November 1987.

How Should White-Collar Crime Be Controlled?

Chapter Preface

The term *white-collar crime* was created by noted criminologist Edwin H. Sutherland in a speech given in 1939. He defined it as "a crime committed by a person of respectability and high social status in the course of his occupation," and gave such examples as antitrust violations, false advertising, theft of trade secrets, and bribery. Many of the crimes Sutherland described are committed by corporations as well as individuals. Sutherland's term *white-collar crime* quickly passed into common use among both social scientists and the general public.

Examples of white-collar criminals in the news today include the broker who uses inside information to reap a profit on the stock market, the bank president who lends depositors' money to himself, the weapons manufacturer who overcharges the Pentagon for weapons, and the company that illegally dumps toxic waste underground. White-collar crime shows no signs of abating. The viewpoints in this chapter debate how society should respond to the problem.

"Corporate crime and violence . . . is more pervasive and more damaging than all street crime."

White-Collar Crime Is Serious

Russell Mokhiber

Russell Mokhiber is a lawyer and editor of the *Corporate Crime Reporter*, a Washington-based newsletter. In the following viewpoint, he argues that the most damaging crimes in the US are committed by businesspeople and corporations. He defines crime to include such acts as marketing unsafe products, forcing people to work in dangerous conditions, and polluting the environment. Mokhiber concludes the social costs of these acts greatly exceed that of all street crimes.

As you read, consider the following questions:

1. What examples of corporate crimes does Mokhiber provide? Do you agree or disagree that they should be labeled as crimes?
2. Why does the author believe the definition of crime is important?
3. How much does corporate crime cost the US, according to Mokhiber?

Name a crime.

Many would respond "burglary" or "robbery" or "murder." Few would respond "monopoly" or "knowingly marketing unsafe pharmaceuticals" or "dumping of toxic wastes."

Name an act of violence.

Similarly, many would respond with examples of violent street crimes, such as assault. Few would respond with examples of violent corporate crime, such as the marketing of a dangerous automobile or the pollution of a community's water supply.

The Damage of Corporate Crime

People respond this way despite a near universal consensus that all corporate crime and violence combined, both detected and undetected, prosecuted and not prosecuted, is more pervasive and more damaging than all street crime. The electrical price fixing conspiracy of the early 1960s alone cost American consumers $2 billion, more than all the burglaries in America in one year. According to the Federal Bureau of Investigation, there were 19,000 victims of street murder and manslaughter in 1985. Compare that one-year total with the numbers of victims of corporate crime and violence in the United States today:

- One hundred and thirty Americans die every day in automobile crashes. Many of those deaths are either caused by vehicle defects or preventable by available vehicle crashworthiness designs.
- Almost 800 Americans die every day from cigarette-induced disease.
- Over the next 30 years, 240,000 people—8,000 per year, one every hour—will die from asbestos-related cancer.
- The Dalkon Shield intrauterine device seriously injured tens of thousands of women who used it.
- An estimated 85,000 American cotton textile workers suffer breathing impairments due to cotton dust (brown lung) disease.
- 100,000 miners have been killed and 265,000 disabled due to coal dust (black lung) disease.
- One million infants worldwide died in 1986 because they were bottle-fed instead of breast-fed.
- In 1984, 2,000 to 5,000 persons were killed and 200,000 injured, 30,000 to 40,000 of them seriously, after a Union Carbide affiliate's factory in Bhopal, India, released a deadly gas over the town. . . .

Why is it that despite the high numbers of victims, when people think of crime, they think of burglary before they think of monopoly (if they think of monopoly at all), of assault before they think of the marketing of harmful pharmaceuticals, of street crime before they think of corporate crime? And what can be done to curb corporate crime and violence? . . .

When a chemical company dumps deadly mercury into a lake and no law prohibits such dumping, has a crime been committed? Or when the company dumps toxic wastes into the lake, in apparent violation of federal law, but the police look the other way, has a crime been committed? Or if instead, the cops cite the toxic dumper, run to civil court and obtain an injunction against further dumping, has a crime been committed?

Profit and Loss

Corporate murderers are not like your typical killer on death row. Corporate murderers do not set out to kill. There's no profit in that. They are simply willing to accept a certain amount of death and physical torment among their workers and customers as a sometimes necessary byproduct of the free enterprise system. . . . When it was suggested to Alfred P. Sloan, Jr., president of General Motors circa 1930, that he should have safety glass installed in Chevrolets, he refused with the explanation, "Accidents or no accidents, my concern in this matter is a matter of profit and loss."

Robert Sherrill, *Utne Reader*, March/April 1987.

The answers to these questions vary with the definition of crime, and the definition of crime varies with the person putting forth the definition. Some argue that an act is criminal only if a criminal court has officially determined that the person or entity accused of violating the law has committed a crime. Few harmful corporate illegalities or other wrongdoings fit this narrow legal definition of crime.

Were the stakes in human terms not so high, this debate over the definition of crime could be relegated to the stacks of law libraries and written off as another less than meaningful academic squabble. The word *crime*, however, carries with it explosive connotations. The corporate justice system has developed so as to shield the corporation from those connotations and the stigma of the criminal process. This shapes the public perception of the nature of the harm inflicted by corporate misconduct. The result is that in referring to corporate transgressions we speak of civil wrong, not criminal wrong; of consents, not convictions; of suits, not indictments; of "neither admit nor deny," not guilt or innocence.

Many corporate misdeeds that fall outside the narrow definition of crime as "conviction" qualify as crimes in a more fundamental sense of the word in that they contain the essential characteristic of crime as defined by [Edwin] Sutherland: that is,

161

"behavior which is prohibited by the State as an injury to the State and against which the State may react, at least as a last resort, with punishment.". . .

The Costs of Corporate Crime

The total cost of corporate crime has never been estimated, despite the need for accurate figures. The problem involved in quantifying the costs of corporate crime turns on the philosophical and political question discussed above: what is corporate crime? Any definition, however imperfect, raises another question: who are the victims of the crime? Once the victims are identified, the costs of the injuries must be measured.

The costs of corporate crime will fluctuate wildly with only the slightest modification of any number of variables. Take, for example, the definition of crime. As of this writing, it is legal for automobile companies to market their products without passive restraints, restraints that would save thousands of lives and injuries every year. Legislation that would make it a crime to market autos without passive restraints has been thwarted by the auto industry for over a decade. If not for the industry's considerable efforts to defeat this legislation, it would be a crime today to market such automobiles. Under all the definitions of crime discussed above, thousands of persons who are killed or injured after crashing through the metal and glass of their automobiles are not victims of auto industry crime. Why? Because there is no law to prohibit the manufacture of autos without passive restraints. Why? Because the auto industry pressured the federal government to defeat this legislation.

Sometimes, even with well-defined crimes, the extent of the victimization and the costs thereof will be literally impossible to measure. A chemical company dumps toxic wastes illegally into a river that provides drinking water for local residents. How are the effects of this crime to be measured? How many cancers will these toxics cause twenty years from now? Were the cancers caused from drinking the water, or from smoking cigarettes, or breathing polluted air?

Billions of Dollars

Despite these analytical problems, efforts are underway to map out the academic terrain in search of a workable formula to determine the costs of corporate crime. [Marshall] Clinard estimates that the total cost of corporate crime runs into the billions of dollars, and supplies the following as indices of that cost:

- The Judiciary Subcommittee on Antitrust and Monopoly estimates that faulty goods, monopolistic practices, and similar law violations annually cost consumers between $174 billion and $231 billion.

162

- A Department of Justice estimate put the loss to the taxpayers from reported and unreported violations of federal regulations of corporations at $10 billion to $20 billion each year.
- The losses resulting from the conspiracy of the largest plumbing manufacturing corporations totaled about $100 million.
- During the 1970s Lockheed Corporation admitted to illegal payments of more than $220 million, primarily in concealed foreign payments. . . .

Corporate Crime Kills

Corporations perpetrate violence not only on workers, but also consumers and citizens. Corporate injuries of childbearers as consumers is a good example. Approximately 8,000 pregnant women who had taken the prescription drug thalidomide ended up giving birth to terribly deformed babies. The corporation that developed and distributed the drug deliberately falsified the test data and concealed the truth about the drug's serious side effects.

James W. Messerschmidt, *Capitalism, Patriarchy, and Crime*, 1986.

It may prove difficult to measure the direct costs of chemical crime, auto crime, oil crime, and other corporate crimes to consumers, employees, neighbors, citizens, and society as a whole, but the evidence points to a problem of a magnitude that dwarfs the costs associated with much more highly publicized street crime. . . .

White-Collar Violence

Finally, indications are that violent corporate crime is taking staggering tolls. Approximately 28,000 deaths and 130,000 serious injuries each year are caused by dangerous products. And in the workplace, the toll is even greater: 5.5 million on-the-job injuries, with hospital treatment for 3.3 million; at least 100,000 worker deaths each year from exposure to deadly chemicals and other safety hazards; and 390,000 new cases of occupational disease. Of the 38 million workers in manufacturing industries, 1.7 million are exposed to a potential carcinogen each year. Workplace carcinogens are believed to cause an estimated 23 to 38 percent of all deaths resulting from cancer each year.

But these are only vague indications of the enormity of the problem. The absence of research in this area leaves us guessing as to the true cost of corporate crime.

"White-collar crime is largely a diversion from the real crime problem."

White-Collar Crime Is Not Serious

Morgan O. Reynolds

Morgan O. Reynolds is a professor of economics at Texas A&M University in College Station, and has written extensively on economics and labor. In the following viewpoint, he questions the assertion that white-collar crime is more serious than street crime. He argues that corporations adequately police themselves and that much white-collar crime results from unnecessary government regulation.

As you read, consider the following questions:

1. What distinctions does Reynolds make between different kinds of white-collar crime?
2. Why does Reynolds believe that the cost of white-collar crime is hard to determine?
3. How does the federal government contribute to the crime problem, according to the author?

Morgan O. Reynolds, *Crime by Choice: An Economic Analysis.* Dallas, TX: The Fisher Institute, 1985. Reprinted with permission.

When the topic turns to crime, most people mean the crime in the streets which threatens them, not the financial manipulations known as white-collar crime. Some in the intellectual community, however, have tried to change the middle class assumption that crime occurs mainly in lower class places. After the Watergate scandals and the concern over overseas corporate bribes, some intellectuals and consumer advocates tried to convert the revulsion against crime into a revulsion against people in high places, especially in business. Subtly, if not by explicit statement, writers conveyed the idea that crime in high places makes crime in low places legitimate—the peculiar notion that two wrongs make a right.

White-collar crime is a term which seems to cover everything from embezzlement, tax fraud, computer crimes, land schemes, investment swindles, price-fixing, hazardous products, pollution, false advertising, shoplifting, credit-card frauds, and so on. With such a broad definition, the economic toll can be nearly as high as the analyst likes. Consumer advocates, for example, claim that corporate crime costs the nation $200 billion a year in price fixing, poisoned air, land, and water, corruption of government officials, and tax evasion.

Types of Crimes

Given the sprawling nature of white-collar crime, we should distinguish between those crimes that are widely agreed to be criminal offenses—basically the use of deceit and fraud to take the property of another—and offenses that are more debatable, especially violations of government regulations of doubtful value. In terms of employee theft, the media has heavily publicized computer crime. A trio convicted in 1982 of bilking the Wells Fargo Bank's computer system of $21.3 million was a highlight. Data transmission lines electronically shuffle a staggering $400 billion among banks each day, a tempting target. While it is true that computer crimes increase the cost of doing business ($150 million was reportedly spent in 1982 on computer security), the problem is kept within bounds by the efficiency of private enterprise and the consensus that protecting business property is mostly a matter of private precautions rather than government crime control. True, many businesses fail to cooperate with the police after a loss because of embarrassment, preferring quiet dismissals and revised procedures for internal control instead. More prosecutions would reduce the problem, but individual enterprises have little incentive to consider the general problem. Controlling the various forms of employee pilferage, fraud, and theft is largely a task for the checks and balances of internal controls.

Other kinds of white-collar crime that are serious crimes include scams in land, tax shelters, and investment schemes run by con men and swindlers. To a large extent this problem is controlled by the prudent behavior of consumers and investors who follow the admonition "caveat emptor" and generally deal with reputable firms. These crimes blur the border between criminal and civil law. The Racketeer Influence and Corrupt Organizations Act of 1970 melded civil and criminal law into a potent package, but its use remains controversial because ordinary commercial disputes can come under RICO on the grounds that an otherwise legitimate enterprise has been acting "like a racketeer by engaging in a pattern of fraud."

Government Regulations

Much of the alleged crime in the suites occurs because of the growth of government. Each year more than 20,000 new bills are submitted to Congress and about 1,000 become law; state and local governments add thousands more. More than 10,000 administrative laws are produced each year by federal agencies. The Internal Revenue Code has 40,000 pages. The *Dictionary of 1040 Deduc-*

Michael Witte. Reprinted with permission.

tions for 1982 lists more than 1,800 credits, deductions, exclusions, deferrals, and other dimly understood avenues of tax escape for the personal income tax. Hundreds more are available to corporations, partnerships, estates, and trusts. The tax code is a thicket of provisions intended to promote or discourage certain kinds of behavior far removed from the function of raising revenue. Complexity and the fact that taxpayers can see less and less difference between cheating and permissible legal tricks erodes compliance.

Government officials cannot possibly enforce all the laws and regulations on the books. The laws are like wish lists submitted by politicians, lawyers, and bureaucrats. When laws abound, compliance *must* disintegrate. Even ignorance of the law must become an acceptable defense to some extent. An interventionist society must be dishonest and the erosion of honesty is creating a nation of cheaters. To call the whole nation criminal debases any sensible definition of crime.

Debatable Crimes

Though most businesses in the United States are law-abiding, some have been guilty of serious misbehavior. What kinds? Of the 25 largest corporations by sales, in 1981, 14 had paid some kind of civil penalty in excess of $50,000, experienced a criminal conviction, or had entered a no-contest plea since 1976. Eleven had no offenses. The most common offense, by far, was that nine oil companies had paid fines for alleged overcharges, incidents that occurred because government officials fixed complex price schedules below free market levels and declared some oil "new" and other oil "old," producing incentives to defy government. Ironically, the second most common offense (3) was private price-fixing (violations of antitrust law), but these are offenses that are based on arguable evidence and dubious economic theories. Private trade rings have been less effective than the industry-wide price fixing imposed by unions, which are supported by government, the agricultural marketing orders which government uses to fix prices in the interest of producer groups, and other government-created monopolies. This does not excuse business violations of law, but government officials should be held to the same standards as businessmen are. Instances of fraud, pollution, and defective products are not confined to the private sector. The public schools, public sewage treatment plants, the Social Security System, and the depreciating currency are examples of the defective and deceitful products produced by government.

Corruption

The age-old problem of corruption in the public sector—bribes to bureaucrats, judges, and politicians, vote frauds, and so on—require two essential conditions to occur on a sustained basis: 1) a bureaucratically-created scarcity, and 2) a separation between the bureaucrat's wealth and the negative consequences of corruption. The convictions of hundreds of county commissioners in Oklahoma and Texas provide ready examples. The traditional way of doing business was that firms selling road and bridge supplies to counties routinely paid bribes to commissioners. Back in the 1930s, so the story goes, county commissioners in Oklahoma asked for a raise in their $45 weekly salary. They didn't get the raise. If they weren't smart enough to figure out how to get more money, a colleague told them, they didn't deserve to be commissioners. County taxpayers, of course, picked up the tab for the higher priced building supplies, generally inflated by 20–30 percent to account for bribe costs. Corruption was accepted by the "good old boy" network and the custom that getting elected to county commissioner meant that you were going to live a little better. Speeches at county commissioners' conventions even advised on how much to take in certain situations. State and federal prosecution ultimately intervened because county commissioners in Oklahoma had set district attorney's salaries and staff size and so commissioners' corruption was not likely to be prosecuted locally. The whole scene resembles doing business overseas, where government officials control virtually all economic activity and demand pay-offs as a routine matter before they will allow businessmen to do business. These cases come closer to extortion than bribery. Public officials who have sworn to uphold the law for the benefit of the general public decide to personally profit from allocating bureaucratic favors. Owners of private enterprises have the same problem of internal controls against employee abuse, but owners have more incentive and are more efficient than the general public is in controlling malfeasance. . . .

Not Real Crime

White-collar crime is largely a diversion from the real crime problem. White-collar crime increases the cost of doing business, and thereby cuts down on production and trade, but it is kept within bounds by the efficiency of private enterprise. Much corporate crime is artificial because it occurs due to the expansion of the regulatory state, which seems to have lost any sense of limits to its competence. Disrespect and disregard for law have spread among the general public and among business managers. Tax "avoision" is a consequence of the web of tax rules that has undermined compliance.

"If corporate crimes are to be deterred, action must be taken against the human decision-makers actually responsible."

Executives Should Be Punished for White-Collar Crime

Ernest Conine

Many people have questioned instances in which corporations were found guilty of crimes but no individuals were prosecuted. In the following viewpoint, Ernest Conine argues that the only way to control white-collar crime is to punish individual criminals, including executives of corporations guilty of crime. Conine is an editorial writer for the *Los Angeles Times*.

As you read, consider the following questions:

1. Why does the author believe the punishment of individuals is necessary?
2. How does Conine respond to the issue of overcrowded prisons?
3. What is the purpose of prison, according to Conine?

A lot of corporate executives swallowed hard when an Illinois court sentenced three officials of a silver-recycling plant to 25 years in prison and $10,000 fines for murder.

The three executives didn't shoot anybody. Their crime was to knowingly expose workers to deadly cyanide fumes; one of the workers died. This is believed to be the first time that corporate officials have been found guilty of murder for a worker-safety infraction.

Legal scholars who argue that manslaughter charges would be more appropriate in such a case may be right, but they are missing the point: In most instances, when a corporation commits a crime, company executives, especially top executives, are not held personally responsible at all.

Dishonesty is probably no more rampant in business than in other callings, but the temptations are there, in terms of both personal gain and pressures to go along with an atmopshere that encourages bending of the rules to improve a company's "bottom-line" performance.

A Welcome Trend

The Illinois case is an extreme example of what appears to be a growing and welcome trend toward holding culpable executives responsible for criminal acts that are committed by their companies with their knowledge or participation.

There have always been notable departures from the prevailing leniency toward executives. For example, in 1960 three General Electric officials were sent to jail for price-fixing. More recently a small manufacturer was sentenced to prison for selling the government defective cord for use in parachutes.

Typically, though, executives of large corporations have claimed that they were unaware of the criminal conduct of their companies, and prosecutors have usually been disinclined to take the time and trouble to prove otherwise.

Crimes with No Criminals

Sperry Corp. pleaded guilty to making false statements in request for payments on defense contracts. The company was fined, but no individuals were charged.

National Semiconductor Corp. pleaded guilty to 40 counts of fraud involving incomplete testing of parts sold to the military. The company paid a fine of $1.75 million, but refused to identify the employees or officials responsible for the violations.

Four big New York banks were fined for currency violations, but corporate officers escaped criminal penalties.

E. F. Hutton & Co., one of the country's largest brokerage firms, pleaded guilty to defrauding banks through a system of calculated overdrafts. Criminal fines totaling $2 million, in addition to other penalties, were imposed on the company. However, the Justice

Department said that it would forgo prosecution of individuals because participation in the scheme was not traced "to the highest levels of the company."

Need for Punishment

Yet punishment of responsible executives—making examples of them, if you will—may be the only real way to get at the problem. After all, you can't lock up a guity corporation; all that you can do is impose financial penalties. In the case of large companies, even multimillion-dollar fines are too small to have much of a deterrent effect. In any event, such penalties are commonly passed on to consumers as just another cost of doing business.

The Pentagon can and does penalize companies that cheat on defense contracts by suspending them from eligibility for future bids. In practice, though, small contractors bear the brunt of such actions because the Defense Department finds it impractical to blacklist large companies whose production and technological capacities are vital to the defense effort.

"Warrington Trently, this court has found you guilty of price-fixing, bribing a government official and conspiring to act in restraint of trade. I sentence you to six months in jail, suspended. You will now step forward for the ceremonial tapping of the wrist."

How could the Pentagon not do business with General Dynamics—the sole supplier of Trident submarines, F-16 fighters, Tomahawk cruise missiles and M-1 battle tanks?

If corporate crimes are to be deterred, action must be taken against the human decision-makers actually responsible. Under our system of justice we shouldn't get into the business of making the legal assumption that, because a corporate president is paid $1 million a year, he knows about everything going on in that company. But where responsibility can be proved and the infraction is serious (such as cheating taxpayers on defense contracts) people should go to jail. The argument that "everybody else is doing it" is no excuse.

Criminal charges against culpable executives are becoming more common, and some legal experts believe that the tough verdict in the Illinois cyanide case may accelerate the trend. To quote a spokesman for the American Prosecutors Research Institute: "When you have that kind of verdict, it's only natural that prosecutors will say, 'Well, maybe times *have* changed.'"

The Need for Deterrence

So far, however, the prosecution of executives remains the exception rather than the rule. And, even when officials of large corporations are convicted, they are more likely to get a fine and a "community service" obligation than go to jail.

One reason is the shortage of jail cells; prisons are bulging with people convicted of violent crimes, leaving little room for anyone else. But that's an argument for building more jail cells, not for winking at corporate crime.

Unquestionably, however, another factor is involved: the reluctance of most judges to put prominent men of their own class behind bars for economic, nonviolent crimes. Many magistrates find it easy to conclude that the corporate executive has learned his lesson, that the humiliation of arrest and trial is punishment enough.

Maybe in some cases it's true, but a major purpose of sentencing is not punishment but deterrence of others who may be similarly tempted. And, even more for people with the personal pride and social standing of business executives than for others, deterrence is much stronger if the miscreant is led away in handcuffs.

"You can't put a corporation in jail, but you can put it on probation."

Companies Should Be Punished for White-Collar Crime

Daniel Farber

Many white-collar crimes are committed on behalf of corporations. In the following viewpoint, Daniel Farber argues that corporations should be punished for crimes by putting them on probation or by imposing stiff fines. Farber is the Henry J. Fletcher Professor of Law at the University of Minnesota in Minneapolis.

As you read, consider the following questions:

1. According to Farber, what is wrong with the current system of punishing corporations?
2. Why does Farber believe fines alone are not enough to fight crime?
3. What are the advantages of putting corporations on probation, according to the author?

Daniel Farber, "Corporate Punishment," *The New Republic*, December 26, 1988.
Reprinted by permission of THE NEW REPUBLIC, © 1988, The New Republic, Inc.

In an unprecedented—some might say zany—decision, a federal judge in Virginia recently imposed a prison sentence on the Allegheny Bottling Company. It's not clear how Judge Doumar expected to imprison an artificial legal entity, and we're unlikely ever to find out, since he suspended the sentence and the case is on appeal. The judge resorted to this extraordinary sentence, he said, because he didn't know how else to impose a meaningful punishment on a corporation that could easily afford to pay the maximum legal fine.

Judge Doumar's frustration has a long and honorable history. Two centuries ago, an English judge lamented that a corporation has "no soul to be damned, and no body to be kicked." In an era of insider trading and Pentagon scandals, the problem is more pressing than ever. When a corporation violates the law, how is it to be punished?

Fines Too Small

The U.S. Sentencing Commission [has been] holding hearings on this subject. One of the first truths it arrived at is that the system for sentencing corporations is in a state of serious disrepair. First of all, corporate fines are inconsistent. Sometimes, the commission found, the fine was two or three times the harm caused by the crime, while in almost identical cases it would be only a fraction of the harm.

Second, the fines are often puny. Half of the convicted corporations are fined $5,000 or less, an amount even most small companies can cover out of petty cash. Third, the fine structure is perverse. The commission found that the penalties for petty crimes were large enough to exceed the corporation's gains, but crimes causing more serious harm received proportionately smaller penalties. On average, a corporate crime that caused a $5,000 loss would result in a $12,000 penalty. This is at least *some* deterrent. But if the crime had caused a $200,000 loss, the penalty would be only about $120,000. Even if Company X were sure of getting caught, its shareholders would profit from the crime. In short: big-time corporate crime pays.

To correct that criminal equation, the commission's staff has proposed an entirely new method of imposing fines. Basically, it would work like this: Step one, determine the amount of harm done. Step two, determine the "multiplier," which is supposed to be the corporation's chances of escaping detection. Step three, multiply the two figures, and there's the fine (with a few other possible adjustments).

Take a case where a corporation has chiseled $20,000 off its taxes, where the fine for doing so is also $20,000, and where the odds of being caught are about 50-50. Half the corporations will get away with tax fraud, while the other half will merely have

174

to pay back the money. This is a winning proposition for the company, so management and shareholders have an incentive to look the other way when the returns are filled out. In fact, low-level employees may feel pressured to commit crimes in order to increase profits. To destroy the profitability of tax fraud, we would have to double the penalty to balance the 50 percent chance of detection. So a $40,000 fine is in order.

The Limits of Fines

The staff's proposal incorporates this principle, but like the current system of fines, it still fails to take the profit out of corporate crimes. Consider a "midnight dumper"—a company that dumps toxic chemicals in the nearest river. It's very hard to estimate a monetary value for the harm done by the dumping. The guidelines arbitrarily assign a value of $10,000 for this offense. The maximum multiplier in the case of all crimes is 3.5, so the *maximum* fine is $35,000—not much of a penalty for intentionally endangering the public health, and hardly deterrent enough when set beside the often high cost of *legally* dumping toxic waste. The 3.5 multiplier is too low. If we detect only ten percent of price fixers, as the Justice Department thinks, we probably catch a similar proportion of midnight dumpers. So the multiplier should be more like ten. And $100,000 doesn't seem like much either. Consider the way we treat the corporate officer who ordered the dumping. Under the sentencing guidelines for individuals, someone who dumps toxic waste without a permit would spend about two years behind bars—but the corporation gets only a slap on the wrist. Something is wrong here.

Probation Can Work

In some instances, putting a corporation on probation will serve the ends of justice to a greater degree than requiring the corporation to serve its sentence. . . .

Judges may also use probation to cure institutional problems within the company. They may, for example, order new management procedures, revise standard operating procedures, and create new channels of communication within the company to ensure compliance with laws.

Russell Mokhiber, *Corporate Crime and Violence*, 1988.

Economist Gary Becker has pointed out that if you impose extremely strict penalties, you can get a lot of deterrence without having to punish very many people, so you can save on law enforcement expenses. In other words, if we were to hang a price fixer now and then, we could probably cut the size of the Antitrust Division and still scare the remaining culprits into obeying the law. At some point, draconian penalties run the risk of becoming unfair or counterproductive, but the commission's proposal hardly reaches that point.

Still, stiffer fines cannot do the job alone. In a world of perfect economic rationality, establishing the correct schedule of fines would automatically lead to the correct behavioral responses. This won't happen in the real world, for two reasons. First, a certain amount of economic irrationality prevails in the business world. Some corporate officers will be willing to gamble on getting away with their crimes; some shareholders won't pay enough attention no matter what incentives we give them. Second, judges probably won't be willing to impose high enough fines in some cases. They'll be leery of punishing "innocent" shareholders, bankrupting companies, or causing plant shutdowns that injure innocent workers. No matter how the commission decides the issues of fines, something more is needed.

Probation

That something more is contained in a report by a group headed by Professor Jack Coffee of Columbia Law School. The Coffee report proposes an intriguing complement to corporate fines. You can't put a corporation in jail, but you *can* put it on probation, a permissible but rarely used alternative for corporations under current law.

Coffee's proposal conjures up the pleasing picture of top executives reporting in to their probation officer once a week. ("Did you stay off drugs? Associate with any felons? Gouge any consumers?") While this is no more than an amusing fantasy, it underscores one purpose of Coffee's proposal—to make a point of treating corporations like "real criminals." Fines, even stiff ones, don't have that effect. In one sense, fines actually legitimize criminal conduct by putting a price on it. They're reduced to yet another one of the costs of doing business. Probation is a reminder that, ultimately, corporate criminals are no better than street punks.

The main purpose of probation, however, is to force the company to set up effective controls to prevent future crimes. This is particularly important because, like street criminals, many corporate criminals are recidivists. The first condition of probation would be a complete investigation into how the crime occurred and why management allowed it. The company might then be required to prepare a "compliance plan" detailing how it intends to prevent future violations. . . . The idea is the same as that behind corporate fines: that it is cheaper for companies to police themselves than for Washington to police them.

"White-collar criminals are . . . getting away with murder."

White-Collar Criminals Should Be Imprisoned

Eric Lewis

Eric Lewis teaches criminal law at the Georgetown University Law Center in Washington, DC. In the following viewpoint, he argues that white-collar criminals are treated too leniently, and that many who deserve imprisonment do not receive it. He asserts that the criminal justice system favors white-collar offenders because they come from the same social class as the lawyers and judges who prosecute crimes and determine punishment.

As you read, consider the following questions:

1. Why are sentences for white-collar crimes lower than for other crimes, according to Lewis?
2. Why does the author believe plea-bargaining favors white-collar criminals?
3. According to Lewis, what are some unspoken reasons why many white-collar criminals receive low prison sentences?

Eric Lewis, "When the Punishment Doesn't Fit the Crime," *The Washington Post Weekly Edition*, January 25-31, 1988. Reprinted with permission.

Ivan Boesky, the rogue arbitrageur who stole upwards of $200 million and may even have contributed to investors' loss of confidence in Wall Street . . . pleaded guilty to a single five-year count, received a three-year sentence from a judge preselected for leniency by agreement between defense lawyers and prosecutors, and will likely serve about a year or two at Lompoc, a "Level-1" minimum-security prison in Southern California that features tennis and gardening opportunities.

All sides greeted the Boesky sentence with approval. Prosecutor Rudolph Giuliani, who is building a political career as a tough prosecutor, termed the penalty "a heavy sentence" and "a very wise decision." Sentencing Judge Morris Lasker believed the sentence would "send a message" to the financial community. Even Boesky himself described the sentence as "fair."

Unequal Justice

In the same week that Boesky received news of his sentence, a local PCP dealer was sentenced to 45 years in prison without parole. One need not downplay the social danger posed by drugs to question whether a small-time dealer's wrongdoing is 15 times worse than that of Boesky, the Nicky Barnes of insider traders.

At a time when the United States puts more people in jail and for longer periods of time than any developed nation except South Africa, white-collar criminals are, relatively speaking, getting away with murder. At the same time, blue-collar criminals, the violent or drug-related offenders, are punished with savage rage.

The debate about this dual system of punishment has gone out of intellectual fashion. Although rates of violent crime have actually declined, the Justice Department continues to focus its efforts on drugs and crime in the streets.

There appears to be little anxiety about having behind bars a country within a country, a burgeoning prison population of more than half a million overwhelmingly poor, overwhelmingly black people. Yet no moral panic has greeted a simultaneous crime wave of virtually unparalleled scope and effect: the wave of white-collar crime.

Easy Treatment

A rational and fair system of criminal justice must operate under a principle of proportionality. Criminal sentences are administered in a single currency—terms of years—and those terms should reflect the relative social harms imposed by each offender.

Our current system of criminal sentencing blatantly violates this principle of proportionality. At every step in the process the system is geared to vent its fury on the poor, the uneducated and the non-white. The white-collar criminal, no matter how substantial or how damaging his actions, will receive easy treatment.

This outcome is not accidental. The people who design and administer this system have constructed it so that the criminals most like them will—relatively—prosper in that system and the criminals least like them will bear its brunt.

Different Sentences

The disparity begins with statutory sentences. Boesky, for example, was convicted on counts that provide for a maximum sentence of five years. A dealer sentenced under the new drug laws can receive a 45-year sentence. What this differential reflects is a judgment that the undermining of public confidence in the marketplace or in democratic institutions is trivial when compared with violent or drug-related crime.

Violence and drugs are special. The outrage felt by victims of violent crime is real and deserving of sympathy and respect. And some, though not all, violent criminals pose a real threat to future victims.

Prison and Deterrence

Opponents of jailing first-time business felons . . . point out that the public shame of a conviction makes it highly unlikely a culpable executive would engage in economic crime again, or that jail could have any conceivable rehabilitative effect. Those critics fail to distinguish between specific deterrence (will *this* offender do it again?) and general deterrence (will *other* potential offenders do it?). A more rational approach would be to incarcerate those guilty of serious economic offenses for short sentences, since deterrence works adequately if jail terms are brief but certain; to punish responsible individuals as well as guilty companies; and to prohibit felons convicted of offenses that threatened widespread injury from ever holding high positions in business again.

Mark Green and John F. Berry, *The Nation*, June 15, 1985.

Yet what seems most to stir the public reaction to violence is a collective sense that the victim or any of us *could* have been killed by the assailant. It is this aftershock that drives victims, prosecutors and, most significant, legislators who launch their election-year wars on crime by raising yet again the penalties for violent offenses. The punishment for what might have been but wasn't is unique in the criminal law.

Drugs are also treated with a severity that borders on the hysterical. Yet the penalty structure has always made sharp divisions between the urban ethnic dealers and their ultimate consumers, who are more widely dispersed across the social spectrum. When marijuana use was confined to beatniks and jazz musicians in the '50s, the penalties for possession were draconian.

When it became the recreational drug of choice for a later generation of middle-class youth, its use was decriminalized, although large-scale dealing continued to be punished. Similarly, the migration of cocaine from the inner city to the suburbs wrought a major change in the treatment of possession crimes.

Working the System

These disparities in statutory penalties are exacerbated by our system of criminal prosecution. It is an axiom of white-collar criminal practice that you always want to be the first one into the U.S. attorney's office. The interests of prosecutor and defense lawyer converge once it is clear the government has the goods on the client. For the defendant who "turns" early, the rewards can be great, not because prosecutors reward contrition—the client has already been caught—but because a cooperating witness eliminates the need to continue an investigation or prepare for a complex jury trial.

In addition, the cooperating witness can set off a chain reaction as each smaller fish implicates the larger fish up to the kingpin of the criminal venture. The prosecutor trades leniency in exchange for less work and more convictions.

As the Boesky plea illustrates, this imperative of accumulating convictions may be achieved at the expense of equity. Boesky did not come in from the cold because of a guilty conscience. He had been fingered by Dennis Levine; his records had been subpoenaed. His lawyers, themselves both former high officials at the Securities and Exchange Commission, knew the time had come to make their best deal. Boesky agreed to tell all and to wear a wire. The great white shark would implicate the tuna in exchange for concessions. The prosecution showed its gratitude in its plea agreement.

Plea bargaining is an endemic feature of all criminal courts. Blue-collar criminals, however, have far less to offer and consequently are offered far less by prosecutors. It does not require a long and complex investigation or close inspection of millions of documents to obtain an indictment or conviction in a robbery or drug case.

In addition, most blue-collar cases do not involve criminal networks. Often the blue-collar offender has no one to turn in but himself. Finally, the blue-collar offender will not have a former SEC general counsel to deal with the SEC. Unlike Ivan Boesky, his plea bargain is a take-it-or-leave-it deal, not a customized one.

Having obtained a great plea bargain to a single five-year count, why did Ivan Boesky then get only three years, 40 percent off what was already a fire-sale price? The explanation rests in part on penal policy and in part on an unarticulated premise about the differential nature of suffering.

Ivan Boesky did not need to be locked up to deter him from doing the same thing again. Nor does he need to be kept off the streets to put at least a temporary halt to his criminal career. Nor does Boesky need a long jail term for rehabilitation.

But these penological principles cannot fully explain why white-collar offenders like Boesky are on a different tariff. Judge Lasker noted that "there is no doubt that Boesky has been humiliated, vilified and cut down to size in a degree rarely heard of in the life of a person who was once regarded favorably as a celebrity." Boesky's sentencing memo spoke of the "devastating price" he has paid, the humiliation of his children, his bar from the securities industry or legal practice, the loss of wealth, his rejection by friends and the philanthropies he supported (probably with stolen money). . . .

The premise, apparently accepted by Judge Lasker, is that the fall from a lofty position is so devastating that the addition of a long prison term would be cruel or inhumane. White-collar offenders also speak of the stigma and strain of prison life.

The unspoken corollaries to these propositions are that those who do not begin with power and position have not really suffered until they are sentenced and that imprisonment is not as devastating given the modesty of their circumstances. These unarticulated premises are pervasive and pernicious. A powerful individual who abuses his advantages should be subject to greater punishment rather than mercy. That many ghetto-dwellers live in prison-like surroundings should lend less, rather than more, moral comfort to their jailers.

Social Advantages

White-collar criminals are more like prosecutors and judges than blue-collar criminals. They look respectable in court and have been coached to say the right things. Powerful people will write letters and testify on their behalf. Judges can empathize with their fall and be touched by the brave support of well-turned-out wives and families.

Most blue-collar criminals will strike no such chords. They'll wear the wrong clothes and will not be able to articulate their remorse in the argot of lawyers and judges. There will be no stretch limousines lost or supportive character witnesses. There will be no ostracism at the racquet club or lost seats on the stock exchange or long-suffering spouses. There will be no anxiety that this person lacks the constitution to cope with incarceration. For all of these things, the blue-collar criminal will be additionally punished.

A humane system of criminal justice must be chary in administering suffering. Our current two-tiered system has empathy with the fallen only when those who administer the system can identify with the plight of the offender. Jail sentences are in the main already far too long. But equity requires that in every case there is inflicted a proportional, just measure of pain.

"House detention in lieu of a prison sentence is highly cost effective."

White-Collar Criminals Should Be Sentenced to House Arrest

Jack B. Weinstein and the Probation Department of the United States District Court, Eastern District of New York.

The following viewpoint has two parts. Part I is by Jack B. Weinstein, Chief Judge of the United States District Court in the Eastern District of New York. Part II is by the probation department of the same court. The authors argue that house arrest can serve as a more appropriate punishment for white-collar criminals than imprisonment.

As you read, consider the following questions:

1. What does Weinstein list to be the goals of punishment?
2. Which criminals should be eligible for home detention, according to the authors?
3. What are some economic advantages of home detention, according to the authors?

Jack B. Weinstein, sentencing opinion from *United States v. Murphy*, No. 108 Federal Rules Decisions 437 (1985). Probation Department, "Protocol on Home Detention," appendix to *United States v. Murphy*, No. 108 Federal Rules Decisions 437 (1985).

I

The prison population in this country is approaching one-half million. Cost estimates of $30,000 a year and upward per prisoner are common. The direct costs are thus in the order of $15 billion a year.

All agree that longer prison terms, and imprisonment for more and more persons cannot be borne indefinitely. Other controls to prevent crime, social policies to avoid criminality and alternative punishments are essential.

Goals of Punishment

The goals of punishment are incapacitation, rehabilitation, specific deterrence of the individual defendant, general deterrence of those who might commit crimes without the threat of punishment and, finally, the related goals of providing an outlet for the expression of strong disapproval of unacceptable conduct together with the catharsis of a specific statement of public condemnation together with punishment.

Incapacitation of those who are dangerous must, of course, continue to be our policy.

Rehabilitation in general takes place more effectively outside prison walls. Federal probation officers in this District have the resources and skill to exercise strict control, supply training and help with jobs. Cutting the person off from family, friends and jobs during this process is counterproductive.

Deterrence

Specific deterrence is important, but where it does not require incapacitation, particularly among non-professional criminals, it can be accomplished without long incarceration. A taste of jail may be enough under such circumstances.

General deterrence is a factor we know little about. For most crimes of white-collar corruption it may not be necessary to provide substantial prison terms. Heavy fines, disgrace and loss of licenses to practice professions will help deter. More important is vigilance of those who should be apprehending and prosecuting the white-collar criminals. Putting our money in swift and sure prosecution rather than in prison terms appears to be cost effective. . . .

In many respects the colonial use of stocks and equivalent punishment in other societies served a useful goal in providing swift social disapproval as a deterrent. It is obvious that some form of this disapproval is required under modern conditions. How it can be accomplished is not clear. Obviously we will not tolerate branding and the carrying of signs. The matter is a difficult one and will require experimentation and modification of procedures in the light of experience.

II

House detention is intended to be used as an alternative to imprisonment. It involves a more restrictive sentence than a sentence of straight probation. It is admittedly less restrictive than actual imprisonment. House detention should not be used in place of a straight probation sentence. The emphasis on this sentencing procedure is its use as an *alternative to imprisonment*.

Selectivity

House detention should be used very selectively. It should never be used for defendants involved in crimes of violence or crimes using firearms. It would not be suitable for defendants with a history of current heroin or cocaine usage. It would be inappropriate for drug sellers. In general, house detention should not be used with any defendant who could be considered a danger to the community, i.e. one offering a substantial risk of further criminal activity.

Less Costly

Such alternative sentences as periodic imprisonment in the local jail, home detention or work release would enable criminals to work and support their families, thereby reducing the tax-burden fostered by welfare. They could also open up additional avenues for restitution to the victims of crime.

Latique A. Jamel, *The Wall Street Journal*, April 2, 1987.

On the other hand, the sentencing alternative of house detention should not be restricted to white-collar crime, although this type of offender is an obvious choice for house detention. In the Eastern District of New York about 55% of defendants appearing before the Court and the Magistrates receive sentences of probation. The remaining 45% receive jail sentences. It is from among this latter 45% of defendants that house detention might be used in selective cases. In actuality, with the Eastern District of New York's heavy concentration of large scale drug smugglers and armed bank robbers, we would estimate that 5% or less of the 45% of defendants destined for jail terms might be considered for house detention sentences. Based on the average of 900 to 1,000 presentence reports yearly, this would amount to somewhere between 35 and 45 feasible house detention sentences over a year's time; nevertheless this can add up to substantial savings nationwide.

House detention in lieu of a prison sentence is highly cost effective from the perspective of government expenditures for incarceration. The Bureau of Prisons estimated for fiscal year 1986 the average cost of imprisoning one person is $15,468.70 a year. The Probation Division of the Administrative Office of the U.S. Courts estimates the (fiscal 1986) annual cost of a probation officer position to be approximately $50,000. It is estimated that one probation officer could monitor a specialized caseload of 25 house detainees. For every 25 house detainees who truly represent 25 persons who would otherwise be imprisoned, the Bureau of Prisons would save $386,717 per year, less the probation officer's salary and expenses ($50,000) for a net saving of $336,717 per year on costs to the government. Even though this sentencing alternative of house detention would be used in highly selective cases, it is obvious that its use as a general option in federal criminal cases would result in savings of several million dollars yearly.

Additional savings of a substantial nature would be realized by the community when the breadwinner is allowed to continue his employment, thereby preventing members of his family from becoming public welfare charges. Further, he would remain on the tax rolls. He would also be in a position to pay restitution or damages if appropriate. More difficult to measure but no less obvious, house detention would prevent the breakup of defendants' families and family networks, with consequent psychological and physical disruption that cause trauma, even to subsequent generations through their wives and children. The defendant's own traumatization in prison will also be avoided. This latter factor over and above the punishment of deprivation of liberty, although not intended by the law's sanction is, unfortunately, a concomitant effect in our prisons today. Imprisonment returns a man to society with a scared psyche, unpaid debts and financial losses, a highly disrupted if not irreparably broken family; children who lose respect for their parent; no job, and a gap in his life history that is hard to explain when he seeks a new job.

A Taste of Prison

It is our feeling that persons being considered for a house detention type sentence should be sentenced to at least a two year jail term. No mention should be made by the Court of the house detention option. The defendant should be taken to the Metropolitan Correctional Center, and allowed to serve five to ten days incarceration on this sentence. The Court would, at the end of a short jail term, sua sponte or on the recommendation of the Probation Department, reconsider the sentence, suspend the execution of the original (two year) sentence imposed, at the same time placing the person on probation for a period of five years with the Special Condition of Probation that the person be confined to his house for a period of from six months to two years.

Another option would be that on the date of sentencing the Court postpone the sentence, remand the defendant to the

185

Metropolitan Correctional Center and after a short period of imprisonment and the defendant's return to the Court for sentence, at that time sentence him to a period of probation with the house detention condition. It is our feeling that the short period of confinement is necessary to impart a shock effect on the individual and will forestall a great deal of later testing of limits on the probationer's part which would result in the Probation Department involving the Court's time again.

Conclusion

All the usual conditions of probation will apply in these cases plus the Special Condition of house detention. The actual monitoring of those restricted to house detention will be done by specially assigned probation officers who will use frequent unannounced daily phone checks and frequent unscheduled home visits, 24 hours a day, seven days a week. It will be made clear to house restricted probationers that violation of the Special Condition (as well as other conditions) will result in a return to court as a violator. *Exceptions*—It will be explained and emphasized to the house detainee that he or she will be allowed out of his house only to go to work; obtain medical or dental care; attend religious services and if no one else in the family can do it, the detainee may go out to shop for food necessities. All of these with the advance permission of the probation officer and with monitoring for conformity. This is not a jail sentence and there is no earning of good time off or furloughs. It is hoped that the Court will impose the original suspended sentence in cases of proven violation, otherwise this alternative procedure will be a waste of the considerable investment of time called for by the Probation Department.

The many advantages to this alternative to prison are obvious if judiciously used and carefully monitored.

Understanding Words in Context

Readers occasionally come across words which they do not recognize. And frequently, because they do not know a word or words, they will not fully understand the passage being read. Obviously, the reader can look up an unfamiliar word in a dictionary. However, by carefully examining the word in the context in which it is used, the word's meaning can often be determined. A careful reader may find clues to the meaning of the word in surrounding words, ideas, and attitudes.

Below are sentences adapted from the viewpoints in this chapter. In each excerpt, one of the words is printed in italics. Try to determine the meaning of each word by reading the excerpt. Under each excerpt you will find four definitions for the italicized word. Choose the one that is closest to your understanding of the word.

Finally, use a dictionary to see how well you have understood the words in context. It will be helpful to discuss with others the clues which helped you decide on each word's meaning.

1. There is a welcome trend toward holding *CULPABLE* executives responsible for criminal acts that are committed by their companies with their knowledge or permission.

    CULPABLE means:

    a) famous   c) guilty
    b) innocent   d) foolish

2. A major purpose of sentencing is to deter others, and deterrence is much stronger if the *MISCREANT* is led away in handcuffs.

    MISCREANT means:

    a) judge   c) public
    b) criminal   d) police

3. When marijuana use was confined to beatniks, jazz musicians, and social outcasts in the '50s, the penalties for possession were *DRACONIAN*. When it became the drug of choice for middle-class youth, its use was decriminalized.

DRACONIAN means:

a) harsh
b) lenient
c) fair
d) uneven

4. A humane system of criminal justice must be *CHARY* in administering suffering.

CHARY means:

a) merciless
b) cautious
c) eager
d) generous

5. The main purpose of probation is to force the company to set up effective controls to prevent future crimes. This is important because, like street criminals, many corporate criminals are *RECIDIVISTS*.

RECIDIVISTS means:

a) harmless jokers
b) innocent victims
c) one-time offenders
d) habitual criminals

6. The total cost of corporate crime will *FLUCTUATE* wildly depending on the methods used to calculate it.

FLUCTUATE means:

a) spin
b) multiply
c) vary
d) remain

7. To call the whole nation criminal *DEBASES* any sensible definition of crime.

DEBASES means:

a) supports
b) cheapens
c) refutes
d) creates

Periodical Bibliography

The following articles have been selected to supplement the diverse views presented in this chapter.

Jay S. Albanese	"Tomorrow's Thieves," *The Futurist*, September/October 1988.
Steve Coll and David A. Vise	"Drexel's Resounding Guilty Plea," *The Washington Post National Weekly Edition*, January 2/8, 1989.
A. Craig Copetas	"White-Collar Manhunt," *The New York Times Magazine*, June 8, 1986.
David Gelman	"White-Collar Shame," *Newsweek*, November 28, 1988.
William Jackson	"Suite Crimes," *Multinational Monitor*, October 1988.
Steven Koepp	"Fraud, Fraud, Fraud," *Time*, August 15, 1988.
Donald Lambro	"Raiders of Wall Street," *The World & I*, May 1987.
Michael McMenamin	"Witchhunt," *Reason*, October 1988.
Myron Magnet	"The Decline & Fall of Business Ethics," *Fortune*, December 8, 1986.
Russell Mokhiber	"Why Do We Let Corporations Get Away with Murder?" *New Age Journal*, September/October 1988.
Mark S. Pestal	"Be Tough on Corporate Criminals— But Justify It," *The Wall Street Journal*, December 12, 1988.
Larry Reibstein	"Nailing the Junk Kings," *Newsweek*, January 2, 1989.
Gonzalo San Segundo	"The Cost of Computer Crime," *World Press Review*, June 1988.
Daniel Seligman	"And Now, a Kind Word for White-Collar Crime," *Fortune*, June 10, 1985.
Robert Sherrill	"White-Collar Thuggery," *The Nation*, November 28, 1988.
Lawrence J. Tell	"Making Punishment Fit White-Collar Crime," *Business Week*, June 15, 1987.

Would Gun Control Reduce Crime?

CRIME AND CRIMINALS

Chapter Preface

Laws limiting individuals' access to guns have been a perennial topic of controversy, attracting passionate and politically active adherents on both sides. One of the many disagreements in the gun-control debate concerns the role of guns in the causes and control of crime.

Proponents of strict gun-control laws argue that the widespread availability of guns is at least partially responsible for the high rate of violent crime in the US. They state that national laws limiting access to firearms would save lives. Murders arising from family disputes would be prevented, they argue, as well as incidents such as John Hinckley's 1981 attempted assassination of President Ronald Reagan.

Opponents of gun control flatly reject the proposition that stricter gun-control laws would reduce crime. They argue that many law-abiding citizens use guns to defend themselves against criminals. Gun-control laws, opponents argue, would leave such people disarmed and helpless.

The viewpoints in this chapter examine several key areas of the gun-control debate.

"If handguns, the weapon most frequently used in murder, were less available . . . fewer attempts at murder would be successful and thousands of lives would be saved."

Gun Control Would Reduce Crime

Irvin Block

Irvin Block has written many books for young people in addition to working in public relations. In the following viewpoint, he argues that the large number of privately-owned handguns is partially responsible for the large number of people killed in the US. He compares the US with other countries and concludes that strict gun control laws reduce crime rates.

As you read, consider the following questions:

1. Why does the author believe handguns should not be bought for self-defense?
2. How does Block respond to the argument that people, not guns, kill people?
3. What evidence does the author use to argue that gun control laws reduce crime?

Irvin Block, *Gun Control: Points of View,* Public Affairs Pamphlet No. 536A, 1986. Reprinted with the author's permission.

A 10-year review of guns as weapons of homicide reveals good news and bad news. The good news is that the magnitude of our annual killing of one another by guns seems to have passed a peak in the early 1980s. The bad news is that new technologic developments in gun manufacture and marketing, together with weakened governmental regulations, may yet reverse this trend and boost our gun death rate to unprecedented highs.

The FBI reports 18,976 homicides in 1985, a drop of almost 11 percent from the 1975 figure of 21,310. (The 1985 homicides represented a 1.5 percent increase over the 1984 incidents, after several years of decrease.) In 1985, guns of various types accounted for 10,296 murders, of which the largest portion—7,548 victims—were killed with handguns. Before celebrating the figure of 18,976 for the significant decline it is, compared with 1975, it would be wise to reflect that it still represents an alarming casualty toll even for a sizable war. In fact, in the decade of our involvement in Vietnam, more than twice as many Americans were killed with guns in their own country as died in combat.

How do we explain it? Is murder only human? People have been killing one another ever since Cain and Abel. Indeed, a popular slogan used by gun enthusiasts declares that "Guns don't kill people; people kill people." But that hardly explains why the American gun homicide rate leads the world.

In the United States, a tremendously large number of firearms, particularly handguns (revolvers and pistols), are owned by civilians. We are a heavily armed citizenry and our capacity for wasting each other has risen alarmingly. Before peaking in 1981, the number of firearms in civilian households nearly tripled in a decade—and the greatest increase by far was in handguns, which are mainly intended for use against other civilians. . . .

Why Handguns Are Popular

Handguns are not efficient or effective hunting weapons. They are designed and bought chiefly for the purpose for which they were invented: possible use against people. Their advantage is that they can be concealed and used with surprise effect, which makes them the prime tool of the criminal. They are personal, close-range weapons, an extension of the owner's aggressions or fears. With a flick of the wrist, a handgun—"the great equalizer"—can make a big man out of a small one, or so it is believed. With the compact comfort of a handgun in his pocket, an impressionable American believes he can dare any challenger.

The criminal obtains a handgun for aggression. The law-abiding citizen buys a handgun primarily for what he believes to be self-defense. Gun stores have reported sharp rises in handgun sales after race riots and news reports of crime waves. Gun manufacturers and gun dealers know very well why people buy handguns:

The advertising and editorial content of handgun hobbyist journals emphasizes the self-defense aspects of the handgun, its portability, its ability to be concealed, the ease with which it can be brought into action, and its ability to stop a human attacker. In surveys, about three-quarters of handgun owners readily admit self-defense as their principal motive. . . .

How Effective Are Handguns?

How effective are handguns? The effectiveness of the handgun in a criminal's hands is obvious enough not to need documentation: There is no answer to the business end of a handgun at close range. But there is good reason to debate the effectiveness of a handgun for defense. . . .

Many gun proponents say that the protective purpose of gun ownership is served even when the gun is not brandished or used—that is, the knowledge that a household owns a gun may of itself keep felons away. There is some evidence from small communities that this is so, at least for a while after a public campaign for more gun ownership. However, the effect is usually short-lived.

The More Guns, the More Violence

The more guns with which our society equips itself, the greater the likelihood for accidents or violent acts involving firearms. Each year, 1,200 people are killed in accidents involving handguns, and someone is injured by a handgun every two and a half minutes. More than 200,000 privately owned handguns are stolen annually. More guns in more hands will serve only to produce a false sense of security and an even more dangerous sense of power.

Ursula Schwerin, *The New York Times*, September 15, 1986.

Weary police departments, in daily touch with reality, know that the real circumstances of crime are quite different. Burglars, who account for the vast majority of assaults on property, rely on stealth. They perform their work when nobody is home. They are after your jewels, your cameras, your VCR, your television set— not your life. When cornered or surprised, they can be dangerous and have the advantage of experience and desperation in nearly every case.

A burglar is delighted when you own a gun. A gun is a good thing to steal—in fact, that is how most burglars get their guns. At least 200,000 weapons are stolen from individuals every year, according to a 1977 study made by the Police Foundation. Steven Brill, author of that report, writes: ''Although the numbers are not clear, the [estimated] volume of thefts . . . indicates that the number of stolen firearms probably equals the *total* number of firearms involved in all reported violent crimes." A Houston, Texas, study of burglaries estimated that a firearm was stolen in one out of 10 burglaries. When you keep a gun in the house for self-protection it may end up in the hands of a criminal.

The robber and the rapist also have the advantage. They depend on speed and surprise. By the time you realize what they are up to, it is too late to find your gun and use it effectively. Should you try, anyway, or should you have a gun on you, your chances of getting killed are vastly increased. Instead of protecting you, the gun may end up killing you or a member of your family. . . .

Tom Bradley, mayor of Los Angeles, said it best a decade ago:

> The public has to be convinced that hand-held guns don't provide the kind of safety and security their owners hope for. On the contrary, chances are that when the family gun is fired, it becomes an instrument of personal family tragedy, not protection from an intruder. . . .
>
> We local officials live with the carnage and tragedies of indiscriminate handgun ownership on a daily basis. We know from personal experience that guns add immeasurably to the climate of violence in the country. We know from experience that guns are dangerous even in the hands of competent, responsible people.

What is the best way to protect yourself? If life and family responsibility are your chief objectives, your best protection is *not* to own a handgun. The overwhelming majority of police officials, testifying before government agencies considering gun control legislation, make precisely that point. . . .

Guns and Murder

Before discussing the relationship of guns to murder, it is instructive to examine who kills whom. It turns out that the crime of murder is not particularly related to other types of crimes. The FBI's crime statistics show that nearly 60 percent of murders in 1985 were "crimes of passion," committed against husbands, wives, parents, children, lovers, love rivals, friends, and argumentative drinking partners. Most killings are the result of quarrels between people who know each other. It is quite true, of course, that such murders are more commonly committed by people more prone to violence. But no group is exempt and no class line protects against the tragedy of the victims and their families.

Murder in real life is rarely planned as in the movies. Most judges have never dealt with a case of coldly planned murder. Murder is usually a spontaneous outburst of unreasoning rage in which the murderer goes for the most readily available weapon.

Given a choice, the potential murderer is likely to reach for a pistol if one is available. Although the handgun is inefficient for hunting and sport, it is the most efficient weapon for murder at close range between people who know one another. It is convenient, concealable, readily put into action.

How the murderers of 1985 chose their weapons is shown in the following chart.

MURDER WEAPONS, 1985

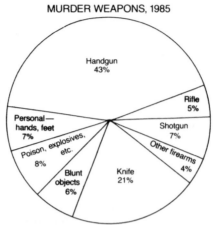

Because figures are rounded off, they add up to more than 100%.
Source: Federal Bureau of Investigation. *Crime in the United States*, annual.

Year after year, the percentages have remained close. In 1985, roughly 60 percent of murders were committed with firearms—with handguns the choice over long guns more than 3 to 1.

Would banning handguns reduce the number of violent arguments and attempts at murder? Most likely not. There will always be a certain proportion of people with enough rage to seek the lives of others.

However, the availability of a handgun may well determine how successful a spontaneous act of aggression will be. Some indication of this may be seen in comparing the statistics of murder with those of aggravated assault. In most instances, aggravated assault—defined as an attack with a weapon—is a murder attempt that does *not* result in death. In 1985, the proportion of guns employed in aggravated assault was more than a third that employed in murder. In other words, attempted murder is more successful with guns.

If handguns were less readily available, a rather large proportion of attempted murders might instead end as aggravated assault and both parties to the dispute might have another chance at life.

How does gun availability affect the murder rate? The overall murder rate and gun death rate are highest in the South, which has the highest rate of gun ownership and the weakest gun control laws. The lowest overall murder and gun death rates are in the Northeast, which has the lowest gun ownership and the strictest gun control laws.

The argument that people, not guns, kill people collapses before such data. People *try* to kill people. Guns kill people best. . . .

If it cannot be shown that guns cause crime any more than they cause attempted murder, it surely can be shown that guns—handguns in particular—are the cutting edge of both. Effective control of guns may not of itself stop attempted murder and felony, but it will help.

If handguns, the weapon most frequently used in murder, were less available to ordinary citizens (the persons most frequently involved in murder), fewer attempts at murder would be successful and thousands of lives would be saved. Fewer attempts at suicide would be successful. To this would be added the further saving of thousands of innocent lives now lost in home gun accidents. Ordinary citizens are gunned down by each other much more frequently than by criminals. These are reasons enough for sterner gun control measures.

If effective gun controls are instituted, would criminals give up their guns? Of course not. They obtain guns illegally now and would continue to do so. But if the private possession and sale of handguns were under tighter regulation nationwide, it would become more difficult for felons to obtain the tools of their trade. A major source of supply, stolen guns, would dry up. Handguns would be smuggled in or obtained in some way by criminals, of course. But the difficulty would make the guns scarcer and more expensive, out of reach of the street felon who gets the notion to rob a gas station. . . .

An important part of that process is to turn back from attitudes that advocate and romanticize violence. The willing surrender of "self-protective" firearms would be a giant step toward a commitment to a rule of law and a denial of the medieval notion that every home is an armed fortress. We cannot live safely or happily with that notion.

Other Nations

Consider the experiences of other industrialized nations. Switzerland provides an illuminating example despite the fact that that country may have the most heavily armed citizenry in the world. Every Swiss male is required by law to serve in the militia and have his own rifle. Indeed, the rifle, ammunition, and training are provided by the government. Each rifle is registered and each round of ammunition must be strictly accounted for. Handguns, too, are rigidly controlled—every applicant to buy a handgun must undergo a careful background check, possess a permit, and register the handgun if the application is approved. The Swiss have a low crime and homicide rate. Their overall homicide rate as well as their handgun homicide rate is about a thirteenth of ours.

In Britain, without a police certificate no one may own any kind of firearm, with the exception of some antiques and air guns. The certificate is given only to those "with a good reason," usually membership in a gun or hunting club. The clubs have a six-month probationary period to determine an applicant's true interest in sport shooting. Illegal possession carries a stiff sentence: Even the use of a fake gun in a crime is punishable by a sentence of up to 14 years in prison. The United Kingdom's overall homicide rate in 1978 was 1.2 per 100,000, compared to 9.4 in the U.S. A comparison based on recent handgun homicides is even more startling.

No One Should Own Guns

Abolishing the private sale of handguns in America would not keep criminals from having their concealed weapons, though they might find it more difficult to get ammunition or replacements. And we would still have an armed police to deal with them. But that's not the point of abolishing handguns for private use, just to keep criminals from owning them. It's rather to keep the rest of us from becoming criminals as well. No one should own handguns, since none of us can trust ourselves to use them properly—and even if we could, they are more likely to harm than do good.

David Glidden, *Los Angeles Times*, November 29, 1987.

Most British police, significantly, do not carry guns except on special assignment. Most people in Britain, including officials of Britain's National Rifle Association, are bewildered by the concept of the "right to bear arms." They consider the idea absurd in modern society, emphasizing that protection is the job of police. In Japan the private ownership of handguns is forbidden to everyone except police, military, and a few competitive marksmen. Their handgun homicide rate is low. . . .

What Can Be Done?

Some proponents of gun control, such as Handgun Control, Inc., say that the emphasis of handgun laws should be on licensing, registration, waiting periods, background checks, and education. Others, like the United States Conference of Mayors and the National Coalition to Ban Handguns, believe the only way to make a real dent in the problem is to completely ban the manufacture, sale, and private possession of handguns unless they are kept and used in an authorized shooting range where their sports features can be safely enjoyed. Rifles and shotguns should be registered and their owners licensed—which should not diminish the pleasures of any true hunting sportsman. . . .

The emphasis is on handguns, for all the reasons cited previously. The only way that sharp restriction and control over the purchase and ownership of handguns can be effective is on a nationwide, shore-to-shore basis. The halfway, piecemeal measures we now have will not do the job. It is unreasonable to point to isolated cities where handguns have already been banned or to the few states that require handgun licenses and scoff at their failures. No one city or state is safe when guns can be bought like chocolate bars a few miles away in the next town or state. New York City has the strictest gun control in the nation; more than 90 percent of handguns seized there after they were used in a crime were found to have been bought outside the state.

The problem was not even partially solved by the 1968 Gun Control Act. The act stopped the importation of foreign military surplus weapons and commercial weapons "not suitable for sporting purposes" (which meant the importation of the cheap handgun called the Saturday Night Special was barred). It forbade interstate and mail order sales between non-dealers and it forbade over-the-counter gun sales and intrastate mail order sales to state residents under 21. It also forbade the sale of guns to felons, fugitives from justice, drug addicts, and those committed to a mental institution or judged to be "mentally defective."

Boom for Gun Dealers

Because of its restrictions on imports, the major impact of this sketchily enforced law was to create a boom for domestic gun manufacturers and dealers. While the act forced dealers to record the identity and addresses of gun buyers, such credentials are easily faked—and, of course, nothing prohibited resale without credentials. Moreover, while the act stopped the importation of Saturday Night Specials, nothing prohibited the importation of parts that could be assembled here. Such a Saturday Night Special, assembled in Miami from parts imported from Germany, was used by John W. Hinckley, Jr. in the shooting of President Reagan and three others in March 1981.

═══════════════════════════════

"A compelling case for 'stricter gun control'
cannot be made."

═══════════════════════════════

Gun Control Would Not Reduce Crime

James D. Wright

James D. Wright is a professor of sociology at the University of
Massachusetts, Amherst. In the following viewpoint, he questions
arguments for stronger gun control laws. He argues that gun laws
will not prevent criminals from acquiring guns. Wright concludes
that people often victimized by crime, including women and the
poor, are justified in relying on guns to protect themselves.

As you read, consider the following questions:

1. How does the author define gun control?
2. What does Wright argue about the use of guns in crimes of
   passion?
3. According to the author, why should "Saturday Night
   Specials" not be banned?

James D. Wright, "Second Thoughts About Gun Control." Reprinted with permission of
the author from: THE PUBLIC INTEREST, No. 91 (Spring, 1988), pp. 23-29. © 1988 by
National Affairs, Inc.

At one time, it seemed evident to me, we needed to mount a campaign to resolve the crisis of handgun proliferation. Guns are employed in an enormous number of crimes in this country. In other countries with stricter gun laws, gun crime is rare. Many of the firearms involved in crime are cheap handguns, so-called Saturday Night Specials, for which no legitimate use or need exists. Many families buy these guns because they feel the need to protect themselves; eventually, they end up shooting one another. If there were fewer guns around, there would also be less crime and less violence. . . .

When I first began research on the topic of private firearms, in the mid-1970s, I shared this conventional and widely held view of the issue. Indeed, much of it struck me as self-evidently true. . . .

In the course of my research, however, I have come to question nearly every element of the conventional wisdom about guns, crime, and violence. Indeed, I am now of the opinion that a compelling case for "stricter gun control" *cannot be made*, at least not on empirical grounds. I have nothing but respect for the various pro-gun-control advocates with whom I have come into contact over the past years. They are, for the most part, sensitive, humane, and intelligent people, and their ultimate aim, to reduce death and violence in our society, is one that every civilized person must share. I have, however, come to be convinced that they are barking up the wrong tree. . . .

What Is Gun Control?

It is critical to stress that "gun control" is an exceedingly nebulous concept. To say that one favors gun control, or opposes it, is to speak in ambiguities. In the present-day American political context, "stricter gun control" can mean anything from federal registration of firearms, to mandatory sentences for gun use in crime, to outright bans on the manufacture, sale, or possession of certain types of firearms. One can control the manufacturers of firearms, the wholesalers, the retailers, or the purchasers; one can control the firearms themselves, the ammunition they require, or the uses to which they are put. And one can likewise control their purchase, their carrying, or their mere possession. "Gun control" thus covers a wide range of specific interventions, and it would be useful indeed if the people who say they favor or oppose gun control were explicit about what, exactly, they are for and against. . . .

There are approximately 20,000 gun laws of various sorts already on the books in the United States. A few of these are federal laws (such as the Gun Control Act of 1968), but most are state and local regulations. It is a misstatement to say, as pro-gun-control advocates sometimes do, that the United States has "no meaningful

ANOTHER GUN-CONTROL ADVOCATE.

Mike Shelton, *The Orange County Register*. Distributed by King Features Syndicate. Reprinted with permission.

gun control legislation.'' The problem is not that laws do not exist but that the regulations in force vary enormously from one place to the next, or, in some cases, that the regulations carried on the books are not or cannot be enforced.

Much of the gun legislation now in force, whether enacted by federal, state, or local statutes, falls into the category of reasonable social precaution, being neither more nor less stringent than measures taken to safeguard against abuses of other potentially life-threatening objects, such as automobiles. It seems reasonable, for example, that people should be required to obtain a permit to carry a concealed weapon, as they are virtually everywhere in the United States. It is likewise reasonable that people not be allowed to own automatic weapons without special permission, and that felons, drug addicts, and other sociopaths be prevented from legally acquiring guns. Both these restrictions are in force everywhere in the United States, because they are elements of federal law. About three-fourths of the American population lives in jurisdictions where the registration of firearms purchases is required. It is thus apparent that many states and localities also find this to be a useful precaution against something. And many jurisdictions also require "waiting periods" or "cooling off" periods between application and actual possession of a new firearms purchase. These too seem reasonable, since there are very few legitimate purposes to which a firearm might be put that would be thwarted if the user had to wait a few days, or even a few weeks, to get the gun.

Thus, when I state that "a compelling case for 'stricter gun control' cannot be made," I do not refer to the sorts of obvious and reasonable precautions discussed above, or to related precautionary measures. I refer, rather, to measures substantially more strict than "reasonable precaution," and more specifically, to measures that would deny or seriously restrict the right of the general population to own a firearm, or that would ban the sale or possession of certain kinds of firearms, such as handguns or even the small, cheap handguns known colloquially as "Saturday Night Specials."

One wonders, with some 20,000 firearms regulations now on the books, why the clamor continues for even more laws. The answer is obvious: none of the laws so far enacted has significantly reduced the rate of criminal violence. [I] reviewed several dozen research studies that had attempted to measure the effects of gun laws in reducing crime; none of them showed any conclusive long-term benefits. . . .

Outlaws and Guns

One of the favorite aphorisms of the pro-gun forces is that "if guns are outlawed, only outlaws will have guns." Sophisticated liberals laugh at this point, but they shouldn't. No matter what laws we enact, they will be obeyed only by the law-abiding—this follows by definition. If we were to outlaw, say, the ownership of handguns, millions of law-abiding handgun owners would no doubt turn theirs in. But why should we expect the average armed robber or street thug to do likewise? Why should we expect felons to comply with a gun law when they readily violate laws against robbery, assault, and murder?

For the average criminal, a firearm is an income-producing tool with a consequent value that is several times its initial cost. According to data published by Phillip Cook of Duke University, the average "take" in a robbery committed with a firearm is more than $150 (in 1976 dollars) and is three times the take for a robbery committed with any other weapon; the major reason for the difference is that criminals with guns rob more lucrative targets. Right now, one can acquire a handgun in any major American city in a matter of a few hours for roughly $100. Even if the street price of handguns tripled, a robber armed with a handgun could (on the average) recoup his entire capital outlay in the first two or three transactions.

As long as there are *any* handguns around (and even "ban handgun" advocates make an exception for police or military handguns), they will obviously be available to anyone *at some price*. Given Cook's data, the average street thug would come out well ahead even if he spent several hundred—perhaps even a few thousand—on a suitable weapon. At those prices, demand will always create its own supply: just as there will always be cocaine available to anyone willing to pay $200 a gram for it, so too will handguns always be available to anyone willing to pay a thousand dollars to obtain one.

Guns Don't Kill

The slogan, "Guns don't kill people, people kill people," may be simplistic, but it is basically accurate. The one out of 400 gun owners who abuses his weapon should be punished, not the other law-abiding 399.

Indeed, cars kill 50,000 people a year: should they be outlawed? Alcohol is actually involved in more homicides than are pistols. The solution, of course, is to hold drunks accountable for their crimes, not to renew Prohibition.

Doug Bandow, *The Union Leader*, April 21, 1988.

The more militant "ban handgun" advocates urge what is easily recognized as the handgun equivalent of Prohibition. Why would we expect the outcome of "handgun prohibition" to differ from its 1920s predecessor? A black market in guns, run by organized crime, would almost certainly spring up to service the demand. It is, after all, no more difficult to manufacture a serviceable fire-arm in one's basement than to brew up a batch of home-made gin. Afghani tribesmen, using wood fires and metal-working equipment much inferior to what can be ordered from a Sears catalogue, hand-manufacture rifles that fire the Russian AK-47 cartridge. Do we ascribe less ability to the Mafia or the average do-it-yourselfer?

A recent poll of the U.S. adult population asked people to agree or disagree with this proposition: "Gun control laws affect only law-abiding citizens; criminals will always be able to find guns." Seventy-eight percent agreed. There is no reasonable doubt that the majority, in this case, is right.

Crimes of Passion

Sophisticated advocates on both sides by now grant most of the preceding points. No one still expects "stricter gun control" to solve the problem of hard-core criminal violence, or even make a dent in it. Much of the argument has thus shifted toward violence perpetrated not for economic gain, or for any other good reason, but rather in the "heat of the moment"—the so-called "crimes of passion" that turn injurious or lethal not so much because anyone intended them to, but because, in a moment of rage, a firearm was at hand. Certainly, we could expect incidents of this sort to decline if we could somehow reduce the availability of firearms for the purpose. Or could we?

Crimes of passion certainly occur, but how often? Are "heat of the moment" homicides common or rare? The fact is, nobody knows. The assumption that they are very common, characteristic of the pro-control world view, is derived from the well-known fact that most homicides involve persons known to one another before the event—typically family members, friends, or other acquaintances. But ordinarily, the only people one would ever have any good reason to kill would be people known intimately to oneself. Contrary to the common assumption, prior acquaintance definitely does *not* rule out willful, murderous intent.

The "crime of passion" most often discussed is that of family members killing one another. One pertinent study, conducted in Kansas City, looked into every family homicide that occurred in a single year. In 85 percent of the cases examined, the police had previously (within the prior five years) been called to the family residence to break up a domestic quarrel; in half the cases, the police had been there five or more times. It would therefore be misleading to see these homicides as isolated and unfortunate outbursts occurring among normally placid and loving individuals. They are, rather, the culminating episodes of an extended history of violence and abuse among the parties.

Analysis of the family homicide data reveals an interesting pattern. When women kill men, they often use a gun. When men kill women, they usually do it in some more degrading or brutalizing way—such as strangulation or knifing. The reason for the difference seems obvious: although the world is full of potentially lethal objects, almost all of them are better suited to male than to female use. The gun is the single exception: all else held constant, it is equally deadly in anyone's hands. Firearms equalize the means of physical terror between men and women. In denying the wife of an abusive man the right to have a firearm, we may only be guaranteeing her husband the right to beat her at his pleasure. One argument against "stricter gun control" is thus that a woman should have as much right to kill her husband as a man has to kill his wife.

International Comparisons

Some will gasp at this statement; no one, after all, has a "right" to kill anyone. But this, of course, is false: every jurisdiction in the United States recognizes justifiable homicides in at least some extenuating circumstances, and increasingly a persistent and long-standing pattern of physical abuse is acknowledged to be one of them. True, in the best of all possible worlds, we would simply do away with whatever gives rise to murderous rage. This is not, regrettably, the world in which we live.

Comparing the United States with other civilized nations in terms of guns, crime, and violence is the "service revolver" in the pro-control armament, the first line of defense against all disputation. The essentials are well-known: there are, in the United States, no strict federal controls over civilian arms, vast numbers of firearms in private hands, and an enormous amount of gun crime and violence. In other nations (England and Japan, for example), there are strict national controls, few guns, and little or no gun crime. Is this not conclusive evidence that strong gun laws reduce gun violence? One would be hard-pressed to find a single example of pro-control writing in which these points are not featured prominently.

Gun Laws Might Increase Crime

By definition, laws are most likely to be obeyed by the law-abiding, and gun laws are no different. Therefore, measures applying equally to criminals and noncriminals are almost certain to reduce gun possession more among the latter than the former. Because very little serious violent crime is committed by persons without previous records of serious violence, there would be little direct crime control benefit to be gained by reductions in gun possession among noncriminals, although even marginal reductions in gun possession among criminals could have crime-reducing effects. Consequently, one has to take seriously the possibility that "across-the-board" gun control measures could decrease the crime-control effects of noncriminal gun ownership more than they decreased the crime-causing effects of criminal gun ownership.

Gary Kleck, *Social Problems*, February 1988.

It does not take advanced training in research methods to see that in the absence of more detailed analyses, such comparisons are vacuous. Any two nations will differ along many dimensions—history, culture, social structure, and legal precedent, to name a few—and any of these differences (no less than the difference in gun laws or in the number of guns available) might well account for the difference in violent crime rates. Without some examination of these other potentially relevant factors, attributing the crime difference to the gun-law or gun-availability difference begs the question.

The English case is commonly cited. It is quite clear, however, that the rates of firearm ownership and violent crime were both extremely low in England for decades *before* that nation's strict gun law was passed, and also that the gun laws have not prevented a very sharp increase in gun crime in England in the past decade. Japan is also commonly cited. In fact, the rate of *non-gun* homicide in the United States is many times higher than the total homicide rate of Japan, so there is also much more to the U.S.-Japan difference than meets the eye. . . .

The Saturday Night Special

The notorious Saturday Night Special has received a great deal of attention. The term is used loosely: it can refer to a gun of low price, inferior quality, small caliber, short barrel length, or some combination of these. The attention is typically justified on two grounds: first, these guns have no legitimate sport or recreational use, and secondly, they are the firearms preferred by criminals. Thus, the argument goes, we could just ban them altogether; in doing so, we would directly reduce the number of guns available to criminals without restricting anyone's legitimate ownership rights.

The idea that the Saturday Night Special is the criminal's gun of choice turns out to be wrong. Our felon survey showed, overwhelmingly, that serious criminals both prefer to carry and actually do carry relatively large, big-bore, well-made handguns. Indeed, not more than about one in seven of these criminals' handguns would qualify as small and cheap. Most of the felons wanted to be and actually were at least as well armed as their most likely adversaries, the police. There may well be good reason to ban Saturday Night Specials, but the criminal interest in such weapons is not one of them. Most serious felons look on the Saturday Night Special with considerable contempt. . . .

Legitimate Use

What about the other side of the argument—that these guns have no legitimate use? It is amazing how easily people who know little about guns render such judgments. When I commenced my own research, it occurred to me that I ought to find out what gun owners themselves had to say on some of these matters. So I picked up the latest issues of about a half-dozen gun magazines. It is remarkable how informative this simple exercise turned out to be. . . .

In my journey through this alien turf, I came upon what are called "trail guns" or "pack guns." These are handguns carried outdoors, in the woods or the wilds, for no particular reason except to have a gun available "just in case" one encounters unfriendly fauna, or gets lost and needs small game for food, or is injured and needs to signal for help. The more I read about trail guns, the more it seemed that people who spend a lot of time alone in the wilds, in isolated and out-of-the-way places, are probably being pretty sensible in carrying these weapons.

One discussion went on in some detail about the characteristics to look for in a trail gun. It ought to be small and light, of course, for the same reason that serious backpackers carry nylon rather than canvas tents. "Small and light" implies small caliber (a .22 or .25), a short barrel, and a stainless-steel frame (to afford greater protection from the elements). The article mentioned that some of the finest weapons of this sort were being manufactured in Europe, and at very reasonable prices. And suddenly it dawned on me: the small, low-caliber, short-barreled, imported, not-too-expensive guns the article was describing were what are otherwise known as Saturday Night Specials. And thus I came to learn that we cannot say that Saturday Night Specials have "no legitimate sport or recreational use."

It would be sophistic to claim that most Saturday Night Specials are purchased for use as trail guns; my point is only that some are. Most small, cheap handguns are probably purchased by persons of modest means to protect themselves against crime. It is arguable whether protection against crime is a "legitimate" or "illegitimate" use; the issues involved are too complex to treat fairly in this article. It is worth stressing, however, that poor, black, central-city residents are by far the most likely potential victims of crime; if self-protection justifies owning a gun, then a ban on small, cheap handguns would effectively deny the means of self-protection to those most evidently in need of it.

Substitute Weapons

There is another argument against banning small, cheap handguns: a ban on Saturday Night Specials would leave heavy-duty handguns available as substitute weapons. It is convenient to suppose that in the absence of small, cheap handguns, most people would just give up and not use guns for whatever they had in mind. But certainly some of them, and perhaps many of them, would move up to bigger and better handguns instead. We would do well to remember that the most commonly owned handgun in America today is a .38 caliber double-action revolver, the so-called Police Special that functions as the service revolver for about 90 percent of American police. If we somehow got rid of all the junk handguns, how many thugs, assailants, and assassins would choose to use this gun, or other guns like it, instead? And what consequences might we then anticipate?

The handgun used by John Hinckley in his attack on President Reagan was a .22 caliber revolver, a Saturday Night Special. Some have supported banning the Saturday Night Special so as to thwart psychopaths in search of weapons. But would a psychopath intent on assassinating a President simply give up in the absence of a cheap handgun? Or would he, in that event, naturally pick up some other gun instead? . . . One can readily imagine at least three deaths, including the President's, had Hinckley fired a more powerful weapon.

"Handguns are particularly well-suited for self-defense."

Guns Are Necessary for Self-Defense

David B. Kopel

Many people believe that gun control laws would deprive people of the means of self-defense against crime. In the following viewpoint, David B. Kopel argues handguns are necessary because the police cannot always be depended upon for protection and crime prevention. He cites several studies which conclude that guns can be used successfully to fight crime. Kopel was an assistant district attorney in Manhattan, New York, and currently is a lawyer in Colorado.

As you read, consider the following questions:

1. What lesson does Kopel draw from the case of syndicated columnist Carl Rowan?
2. According to the author, why should people not depend on the police?
3. Why do few burglaries occur when someone is at home, according to Kopel?

David B. Kopel, "Rowan Case and the Need to Bear Arms," *The Wall Street Journal*, June 24, 1988. Reprinted with permission of The Wall Street Journal © 1989 Dow Jones & Company, Inc. All rights reserved.

Syndicated columnist Carl Rowan, who wounded an intruder who had taken a dip in his swimming pool, said he was forced to shoot the young man in self-defense before the police arrived. The U.S. Attorney's Office said that Mr. Rowan will not be charged with assault. Instead, prosecutors reinstated charges of unlawful entry against two of the intruders. The U.S. Attorney's Office said it would let the District of Columbia authorities decide whether Mr. Rowan should be charged with possession of an unregistered firearm.

Many people charged Mr. Rowan with hypocrisy because he has been a longtime advocate of strict gun control. In a 1981 column he advocated "a law that says anyone found in possession of a handgun except a legitimate officer of the law goes to jail—period." In 1985 he called for "a complete and universal federal ban on the sale, manufacture, importation and possession of a handgun (except for authorized police and military personnel)."

Police Undependable

But Mr. Rowan's middle-of-the-night experience appears to have taught him what many Americans already know: You can't always count on the police to be there to protect you. Many ordinary citizens have had the experience of calling "the authorities" for help—and having that help arrive too late or not at all.

In April [1988], Brooklyn residents phoned 911 to report that a man outside their apartment building was screaming for help because robbers were stabbing him to death. When notifying the police, however, 911 relayed only a message that the man was unconscious. The police, thinking that the man was just drunk, stopped on their way to the scene in order to issue a reckless-driving ticket.

One of the callers to 911 told a reporter, "They kept asking me stupid questions—what race the victim was, what race I was—can you imagine that? A man's outside hurt and they're asking me things like that." The patrol car took 20 minutes to arrive, and the man died.

As a mob of whites in Howard Beach beat Cedric Sandiford, Theresa Fisher called 911 to report that a crime was in progress right outside her window, at 156th Avenue and 86th Street. Said the 911 operator, "Ma'am, that location is not in the computer." Ms. Fisher and her sister simplified the address, telling the operator that it was 86th Street in Howard Beach. After being given the simplified address, the operator asked, "Beach 86th Street?" Police reports state that 911 ultimately gave the police an address on the wrong side of the Belt Parkway.

As courts in Washington, D.C., and New York City have ruled, a government cannot be held liable for having failed to protect people from crime, even when it is found to have been negligent.

Don Eckelkamp/The New American.

It should hardly be surprising that so many people arm for self-defense.

Peter D. Hart Research Associates found in 1981 that in 4% of American households, someone had used a handgun to protect himself from another person within the previous five years. Prof. Gary Kleck at Florida State University School of Criminology estimates that if each of those people used a gun for that purpose only once during the five-year period, handguns were used in self-defense 645,000 times a year. That's once every 48 seconds.

Handguns are particularly well-suited for self-defense because they are smaller and hence more maneuverable than long guns. They are also harder for an attacker to take away, and their lesser recoil makes them easier for women and the elderly to handle.

According to a 1979-85 study by the National Crime Survey, when a robbery victim does not defend himself, the robber succeeds 88% of the time, and the victim is injured 25% of the time. When a victim resists with a gun, the robbery success rate falls to 30%, and the victim injury rate falls to 17%. No other response to a robbery—from drawing a knife to shouting for help to fleeing—produces such low rates of victim injury and robbery success.

Further, guns prevent many crimes from even being attempted. A 1982-83 study of prison inmates by the National Institute of Justice showed that two-fifths of them had decided not to attack a victim when they found out that he or she was armed. In the 1960s the Orlando police responded to a rape epidemic by training 2,500 women to use guns. The next year rape fell 88% and burglary by 25%.

Guns Reduce Crime

Widespread gun ownership is the most important reason that so few burglaries take place when someone is at home. If a burglar commits a crime at an occupied residence, his chance of being shot is equal to his chance of going to jail.

Guns reduce crime; gun control causes crime. In 1986 the National Association of Chiefs of Police and the American Federation of Police sent a questionnaire to every chief of police and sheriff in the country. More than 90% of the respondents agreed that a federal gun ban such as the one Mr. Rowan has repeatedly proposed would not deter criminals. Instead, said the officers, a handgun ban would result in more citizens being the target of armed violence.

But when people are armed for self-defense, aren't they likely to accidentally shoot innocent bystanders? Aren't people shooting a gun so panicky and impulsive that they're dangerous? Apparently not; the most common defensive use of a gun is merely to brandish it.

When civilians do shoot, they are far less likely to hit an innocent person than the police are when they shoot (in part because the police have to intervene in situations that citizens can avoid). . . .

Anti-gun columnists live in a bizarre world where guns are objects of terror and where American citizens are too mentally unstable or clumsy to be entrusted with them. Perhaps the incident at Mr. Rowan's swimming pool will remind such columnists—and their readers—that in the real world, one cannot always count on the police to come to one's aid. For that reason, many American households choose to own guns, and virtually all of them do so responsibly.

VIEWPOINT

"The handgun in your house is more likely to kill you or a member of your family than to save your life."

Guns Should Not Be Used for Self-Defense

Franklin E. Zimring and Gordon Hawkins

Whether guns are effective for self-defense is one of the key issues of the gun control debate. In the following viewpoint, Franklin E. Zimring and Gordon Hawkins argue that the protection guns provide is illusory. They argue that guns are more likely to injure or kill innocent victims rather than to deter criminals. Zimring is a professor of law and Hawkins a senior fellow at the Earl Warren Legal Institute at the University of California at Berkeley.

As you read, consider the following questions:

1. According to the authors, why is the issue of self-defense a focal point in the gun control debate?
2. Why do people feel the need to buy handguns, according to Zimring and Hawkins?
3. Do the authors believe that statistical studies are convincing to gun owners? Why or why not?

One of the principal focal points of the gun control debate relates to the ownership and use of guns for self-protection, particularly in urban areas. There are good reasons for this. The guns that are owned for self-defense in cities are mainly handguns. At the same time, the handgun is the criminal's primary firearm, and handguns have become the pivotal issue in the current debate about gun control. . . .

Some years ago, a national sample of people with some shooting experience was asked what were good reasons for owning guns. Seventy-one percent of the shooters mentioned self-defense as a good reason for owning a handgun—far more than gave one other good reason. Only 16 percent gave hunting as a good reason for owning a handgun. . . .

Another poll found that 66 percent of householders with any guns listed "protection" as one reason for having them. More recently, a survey of all U.S. adults found the 71 percent of those owning a handgun said that they owned it only for protection or self-defense.

Illusory Protection

Those who support restrictive handgun policies argue that self-defense handguns are a very poor investment and that the protection they provide is illusory. Even though the great majority of handguns are kept for household self-defense, it is absolutely clear that the handgun in your house is more likely to kill you or a member of your family than to save your life. In Detroit, Michigan, for example, more people died in one year from handgun accidents than were killed by home-invading robbers or burglars in four and a half years. And it is rare indeed that a household handgun actually stops the burglar who tries to elude the homeowner, or the home robber who counts on surprise and a weapon of his own. So the gun that will not save your life, more than 99 times out of 100, will not save your color television either.

It would be foolish to think that millions of American families keep handguns merely because they have not read the statistics or to suppose that sending them a copy of the latest gun control article will change their minds. The risk of accidental or homicidal death from a gun in one's home—though far greater than the chances that the gun will save life—is nevertheless small. In the great majority of gun-owning homes, the only real use of the gun is to make its owner feel less uneasy about the possibility that a hostile stranger will invade his home.

This feeling of well-being, although a statistical illusion, is an emotional reality. People will resist the statistics that show otherwise because, if their guns do not give them any real measure of protection, they have no other way to deal with their fears. In addition, everything that makes the handgun a special problem in

America also makes it hard to understand that the handgun is not effective against the home-invading criminal. How can something so deadly be so ineffective? Trying to persuade someone that the gun in his house is not really protecting him is like trying to persuade a nervous friend that flying in a jet plane—seven miles above the ground at 600 miles an hour—is really safer than driving the family car to Florida. . . .

Handguns: A Deterrent?

It is also argued that the most important deterrent effect of private weaponry is likely to be the *generalized* deterrence that results from the high overall possession rate of firearms among U.S. households. In other words, there may be large numbers of *potential* criminals who do not commit crimes because they know that many citizens are armed and they fear the possibility of getting shot. It is argued that the crime rates might be still higher were it not for firearms, and that the widespread ownership of guns keeps crime and violence below the level it might otherwise reach.

Guns Difficult To Use

Guns alone are not the crime-proofing insurance the NRA [National Rifle Association] suggests. The police, from their own experience in dealing with guns, crime and criminals, know the sheer lunacy of the proposition. Guns aren't used quickly, easily or without consequence.

I've worked with highly skilled and trained police officers who have failed to use deadly force when it was more than justified and appropriate. People tend to hesitate, even freeze up, in a life-threatening, traumatic situation. When an attacker sees a victim lift and aim a handgun, he is hardly going to wait to see whether there is any hesitation about using it—he will most assuredly use his own weapon quickly. The police experience is that the consequences of such confrontations are often more serious than if the victim had no weapon.

Jerry Vaughn, *The Washington Post National Weekly Edition*, November 30, 1987.

There is no evidence to support this hypothesis, and its proponents acknowledge that this effect could never be detected even in the largest and most sophisticated research effort. It is therefore possible to examine critically only the more specific assertions made by those who claim that private firearms are an effective crime deterrent and means of self-defense.

In the first place, although some crimes are thwarted or foiled by the victim shooting at the offender, the risk to the offender is very small indeed. For example, the Violence Commission Task

Force on Firearms reported that in Detroit over the period 1964-1968, at the most no more than two in 1,000 burglaries were foiled by shooting the burglar. Similarly, only about 2 percent at most of all robberies result in the firearms injury or death of the robber. Moreover, the risk to the homeowner's life from burglars is very small.

The situation may be different in regard to business robberies and burglaries. Of all crimes against businesses, robbery is the primary threat to life. In Detroit in five years, fifty persons were killed during robberies of businesses (and six died in business burglaries). The evidence suggests that "protective" firearms might be reducing robbery rates of commercial establishments in high crime areas. Moreover, the *known* possession of firearms may well deter robbers when businesses of a particular kind—such as bars—are known to have firearms for protection. It is not known whether, when, or how much guns protect businessmen, but the possession of firearms by businessmen appears to entail less risk of accident, homicide, and suicide than firearms in the home.

Thus guns may be of some utility in defending businesses, whereas they are very rarely an effective means of protecting the home against either the burglar or the robber. Moreover, this largely illusory defense is purchased at the high price of increased accidents and homicides, and more widespread illegal use of guns.

Thwarted Thieves

The argument made by James D. Wright, Peter H. Rossi, and Kathleen Daly to the effect that there are at least as many if not more crimes "thwarted" by the victim actually shooting at the offender than there are offenders who are apprehended and imprisoned for their offense is simply mistaken. The argument begins with the assertion that "the burglary of an unoccupied residence, the most common type of home burglary, is clearly not deterrable by any firearms kept in the home, since there is no one home to use them." But this fact, it is said, has no bearing "on whether private weapons are useful deterrents to crimes that occur in a situation or area where they would be potentially deterrable, which is the more important empirical issue."

The argument then runs as follows: 90 percent of all home burglaries occur when no one is at home. If two in 1,000 of all burglaries are foiled by the victim's use of a firearm and 900 in 1,000 occur with no one home, then the actual prevention rate for burglaries committed with a person in the home is roughly 2 percent. This seems a relatively low risk, but it exceeds the risk to a burglar of being apprehended, charged, prosecuted, convicted, and sentenced for the crime. For in 1976 "the overall risk of a burglar being arrested and convicted was only about 1.8% for any given burglary. If half . . . received a prison sentence then the risk

216

of imprisonment was 0.9%."

This conclusion, however, is a statistical illusion. The *overall* risk to the burglar of being foiled is not 2 percent but two in 1,000, even in the optimistic best-case guess by George D. Newton and Zimring, the origin of this figure. The overall risk of imprisonment is nine in 1,000. In other words, the risk of imprisonment is four and a half times the prevention-by-shooting estimate cited. And the burglary "thwarted" under this measure by a gun need not incapacitate the burglar at all, whereas prison for those who serve time may prevent further crimes.

Too Great a Risk

The preventive effects of gun ownership and use on household crime are not measurable and probably small. It almost never pays to confront an armed criminal, because the extra risk to the victim's life is more important than the chance of saving property.

Yet, the need to see guns as effective is based on the feeling of helplessness that citizens encounter because of the threat of household crime. Even though putting burglars in prison is much more important than homeowners using guns, the low rates for catching and convicting burglars are the reason why people grasp at guns and other ephemeral solutions. Greater confidence in law enforcement would doubtless remove the emotive foundation for self-defense guns, and no statistics on cost and benefit will provide emotional comfort without that confidence.

With all the controversy over the costs and benefits of guns for household self-defense, there is one aspect of the matter—on which experts are in unanimous agreement—that has not achieved the recognition we think it deserves: Almost all authorities from gun-control advocates to the National Rifle Association counsel that the loaded gun easily accessible in the bedroom dresser is an invitation to disaster. The risks, from children playing or showing off, from adults who are drunk or frightened or both, or from burglars themselves, are just too great.

"The right to keep and bear arms guarantees the right to keep arms, such as pistols and revolvers, for self-defense."

Gun Control
Violates the Constitution

National Rifle Association

One of the key controversies in the gun control debate is whether gun control laws violate the Second Amendment to the US Constitution, which states people have a right "to keep and bear arms." The following viewpoint, an analysis of the Second Amendment by the National Rifle Association, argues that the freedom to possess firearms is a right of all US citizens. The NRA is an independent, nonprofit organization that sponsors firearms education and competition, and is best known for its political lobbying against gun control laws.

As you read, consider the following questions:

1. How should the "militia" be defined, according to the NRA?
2. Why does the NRA believe the right to bear arms is important?
3. What problems does the NRA see with the Supreme Court case of *US v. Miller*?

The National Rifle Association Institute for Legislative Action, *The Right to Keep and Bear Arms . . . an Analysis of the Second Amendment*. Washington, DC: NRA Institute for Legislative Action, 1988. Reprinted with permission.

"A well regulated Militia, being necessary to the security of a free State, the right of the people to keep and bear Arms, shall not be infringed."

—Amendment II
The Constitution of the United States

Those words, of late, have been used both in defense of, and as an argument against, the individual American's right to keep and bear arms.

Some argue that the use of the term "Militia" in the Second amendment limits the rights protected by the Second Amendment to members of organized State military bodies. They claim the right to keep and bear arms is a "collective" not "individual" right and that the U.S. Supreme Court has affirmed that "collective" interpretation in four decisions.

That contention, however, cannot be historically or legally substantiated. And glib references to Supreme Court decisions in defense of that position also fall flat when closely examined. . . .

Making the Constitution

At the time the Constitution was being considered for ratification, a majority of Americans, conscious of their common law heritage and desirous of ensuring the existence of their natural and common law rights, objected that the proposed Constitution provided few express guarantees of individual rights. In addition, there was concern on the part of the Antifederalists (those opposed to the Constitution as then written) that the proposed Constitution gave Congress power in areas which had traditionally been concerns of the states; they were also concerned that Congress could, by way of its power to raise armies, establish a standing army with which to deprive the people of their liberties.

Among the natural and Common Law rights which were sought to be preserved was the right to self-defense. And among the latter concerns about the powers of Congress was the concern that Congress had been given too much power over the militia. As expressed by George Mason, the power to "provide for . . . arming . . . the Militia" might, particularly if viewed as an exclusive power of Congress, purposefully be neglected by Congress to "render the militia useless . . . [and] have a pretence of establishing a standing army" with which to deprive citizens of their freedoms. To prevent such an occurrence, Mason and other Antifederalists wished the proposed Constitution amended to remove from Congress what they were concerned would be viewed as an exclusive power to provide for arming the militia.

By the time the Constitution had been ratified, it was clear, because of tremendous public support, to Federalists (those who supported the Constitution as then written) and Antifederalists alike, that guarantees of individual rights would have to be added

219

to the Constitution. Thus, when the First Congress met, the Federalists agreed to give up their objections to the addition of a Bill of Rights if the Antifederalists would give up their attempts to restructure the federal-state division of power.

The Militia

In the course of reaching this great compromise, a number of comments were made concerning the right to keep and bear arms, the militia, and the standing army. For example, Representative Elbridge Gerry of Massachusetts stated: "What, Sir, is the use of a militia? It is to prevent the establishment of a standing army, the bane of liberty." Thus, Gerry saw the existence of the militia as making unnecessary a standing army, a tool easily manipulated by a tyrannical federal government attempting to deprive citizens of their liberty. The militia, on the other hand, which maintained the character of the "citizen soldier"—men from every walk of life—would resist any efforts by a despotic federal government to erode individual liberties.

An Individual Right

The framers of the second and fourteenth amendments intended to guarantee an individual right to carry firearms and other common hand-carried arms. It is inconceivable that they would have tolerated the suggestion that a free person has no right to bear arms without the permission of a state authority, much less the federal government, or that a person could be imprisoned for doing so. As the Founding Fathers realized, every right has its costs, but the alternatives are often more costly.

Stephen P. Halbrook, *Law and Contemporary Problems*, Winter 1986.

Men like Gerry, therefore, staunchly believed in and defended the individual's right to keep and bear arms since they believed that an armed citizenry was the best defense against maladministration by government, a sentiment which had been expressed by Alexander Hamilton and James Madison in the Federalist Papers.

Plainly evidencing their belief in an armed citizenry being the safest and natural means of defending a nation of freemen is the fact that the term "well regulated" was used to modify the word "militia" in the Second Amendment. The use of that term demonstrates the Framers' intent that the militia, consisting of all able-bodied persons, be proficient and experienced in the use of firearms, a condition that could most effectively be arrived at if every person owned and was familiar with firearms. . . .

On January 21, 1903, Congress passed a law providing that the "organized militia, to be known as the National Guard of the State,

Territory or District of Columbia," is under the command of the Nation's Chief Executive, who, as Commander-in-Chief, may "federalize" it at any time. Secondly, through the Secretary of the Army, all National Guard weapons are owned and controlled by the Federal government.

The United States Code states:

"The militia of the United States consists of all able-bodied males at least 17 years of age and . . . under 45 years of age.". . .

Most importantly, the U.S. Code divides the militia into two classes: "(1) the organized militia, which consists of the National Guard and the Naval Militia; and (2) the unorganized militia, which consists of the members of the militia who are not members of the National Guard or the Naval Militia."

Under the theory of government by which the United States was established, the final check against an unjust Federal government was and is the armed whole body of the people—the "unorganized militia" which has always existed under the law. It is obvious that the National Guard—whose every member, whose every weapon, whose every move is subject to the authority of the President—cannot be the militia protected by the Second Amendment. Otherwise, there could be no checks on the abuse of power by a President, discredited by Congress and disgraced in the eyes of the people, using the Army and National Guard to prevent successful impeachment. . . .

The guardians of our basic liberties are not formal bodies of police or military. They are not mercenaries hired to preserve and defend the rights of free men and women. The guardians of civil liberty are those, each individual, who would enjoy that liberty.

Supreme Court Rulings

Since the first ten Amendments, collectively known as the Bill of Rights, were penned, the U.S. Supreme Court has decided only four cases involving the Second Amendment. The Court has touched on the individual right to keep and bear arms in three cases, but only briefly, without outlining the full scope of the guarantee.

The first three cases, (*United States* v. *Cruikshank*, heard in 1876, *Presser* v. *Illinois*, in 1886, and *Miller* v. *Texas*, in 1894), cases involving infringements by either private individuals or by a state, held only that the right to keep and bear arms "shall not be infringed by Congress.". . .

Similar Supreme Court decisions holding that the guarantees of the Bill of Rights were limitations solely upon the Congress, and not the States, were reversed in a series of decisions beginning more than thirty years later. Those decisions, based upon the Fourteenth Amendment, held that various of the provisions of the Bill of Rights limited not only the Congress, but the states as well. It should be borne in mind that three of the four decisions on the Second Amendment—*Cruikshank, Presser,* and the first *Miller* case—dealt only with its *applicability* to the States, not to its *meaning.* Not until much later did the Supreme Court hold that *any* of the provisions of the Bill of Rights—including the First Amendment freedoms of speech and press—were individual rights limiting both the Congress and the States.

A Definitive Ruling

The case continually cited by "gun control" advocates as the Supreme Court's definitive ruling against the *individual's* right to keep and bear arms is *U.S.* v. *Miller,* 307 U.S. 174 (1939).

While such a decision was sought by the Justice Department, which was the *only* party presenting an argument in the case, the Court decided only that the National Firearms Act of 1934 was constitutional *absent the presentation of evidence to the contrary.*

The major flaw in the process which led to the *Miller* decision was the fact that the defendants—Miller and Layton—did not appear and were not represented by counsel before the Supreme Court. A lower federal court had released them from custody and they had disappeared.

A Wrong Interpretation

Anti-gunners like to argue that because the Second Amendment talks about "a well-regulated militia" its provisions apply only to the state governments. In other words, the states have the right to arm a military force (like the National Guard) without interference from the federal government.

But this interpretation is, quite simply, ridiculous. It would make the Founding Fathers roll over in their graves. It has no basis in either constitutional history or in American jurisprudence.

Alan M. Gottlieb, *Gun Rights Fact Book,* 1988.

In his study, *"Restoring the Balance: The Second Amendment Revisited,"* attorney David I. Caplan reasoned, "The Court did not benefit from the vigorous presentation of conflicting views which is considered a basic advantage of our adversary system of justice. The case was argued solely by the government attorneys who failed to alert the Court to the existence of several holdings clearly in favor of the individual's right to keep and bear arms."

Despite a one-sided presentation, the actual decision in the case involved only the narrow issue of whether a specific type of firearm—a sawed-off shotgun—had been proven suitable for militia use and was thus protected by the Second Amendment. The court ruled only that:

"In the absence of [the presentation of] *any evidence* tending to show that possession of or use of a 'shotgun having a barrel of less than eighteen inches in length' at this time has some reasonable relationship to the preservation of efficiency of a well regulated militia, we cannot say that the Second Amendment guarantees the right to keep and bear *such an instrument*. Certainly it is not within judicial notice that this weapon is any part of the ordinary military equipment or that its use could contribute to the common defense." (Emphasis added.). . . .

More importantly, however, the Supreme Court implicitly recognized that the rights guaranteed by the Second Amendment protected *all* individuals and not merely those who are members of the militia since it was completely unconcerned with whether Miller or Layton were members of the militia.

Issue Not Settled

One of the shortcomings of the Supreme Court's decision in *Miller* can be seen in the Court's use of precedent. The Court cited but one case, *Aymette* v. *State* (1840), in support of its position that Second Amendment protection was limited to weapons of ordinary warfare or whose use could contribute to the common defense. That case involved Tennessee's constitution where the protection of the citizens' right to arms was specifically "for their common defense." Not mentioned by the Court was the fact that the "common defense" clause was condemned by the first U.S. Senate when it was suggested that the limit be placed on the proposal for what became the Second Amendment. And even with the "common defense" restriction, the broad *Aymette* case findings were rejected by later Tennessee State court decisions as too restrictive of the individual right to keep and bear arms.

In more recent years, state courts, . . . in interpreting state constitutional provisions similar to the Second Amendment, have concluded that the right to keep and bear arms guarantees the right to keep arms, such as pistols and revolvers, for self-defense.

Caplan adds, "As a consequence of the failure of government counsel to direct the Supreme Court's attention to the subsequent treatment of the right to keep and bear arms in Tennessee, and the failure of the Court to consider the legislative history of the Second Amendment, the *Miller* case should be narrowly read, even assuming that the Court decided it correctly. . . . In any event, contrary to the widespread popular belief that the Supreme Court of the United States has definitively spoken on the issue of the constitutionality of gun-control legislation, the issue remains far from settled."

"No gun control measure has ever been struck down as unconstitutional under the Second Amendment."

Gun Control Does Not Violate the Constitution

Michael K. Beard and Kristin M. Rand

Michael K. Beard is the executive director of the National Coalition to Ban Handguns, a Washington-based organization that lobbies for strict gun control laws. Kristin M. Rand is an attorney with the same organization. In the following viewpoint, they argue that the right "to keep and bear arms" in the Second Amendment of the US Constitution does not refer to an individual's right to possess a gun, but rather a collective right of states to form their own militias. They argue that the federal courts, including the Supreme Court, have clearly ruled that gun control laws do not violate the Constitution.

As you read, consider the following questions:

1. What has the Supreme Court determined about the Second Amendment, according to the authors?
2. Why do people still believe the Second Amendment guarantees a right to own a handgun, according to Beard and Rand?
3. What significance do the authors see in the 1986 law forbidding the sale of machine guns to private citizens?

Michael K. Beard and Kristin M. Rand, "Article II," *The Bill of Rights Journal*, December 1987. Published by the National Emergency Civil Liberties Committee. Reprinted with permission.

The National Rifle Association is the only lobbying organization in Washington with half an amendment emblazoned across the front of its building. The NRA systematically deletes the phrase "A well regulated militia being necessary to the security of a free state," from the oft quoted second phrase, "the right of the people to keep and bear arms shall not be infringed."

The Second Amendment is the most misunderstood of the amendments to the United States Constitution. There exists an extensive body of authority supporting the interpretation that the amendment protects a collective right of the states rather than an individual right to own guns. However, the gun lobby, particularly the NRA, persists in propagating the myth that the amendment guarantees an individual right.

A review of the history and decisions relating to the Second Amendment will explain why those who benefit from the current misinterpretation will not likely choose to make their arguments in court.

The Second Amendment was included in the U.S. Constitution to enable the states to maintain a militia composed of civilians who would become soldiers should the security of the nation be threatened. The amendment was generated by a deep distrust of standing armies and not out of any desire to protect the right of an individual to own a firearm for self defense or other proper purpose.

Supreme Court Rulings

The U.S. Supreme Court has addressed the issue in several cases. In 1886, the court ruled in *Presser v. Illinois* that the Second Amendment does not apply to the states and acts only as a check on the power of the federal government. The argument that the Second Amendment is incorporated against the states through the 14th Amendment has been rejected repeatedly. States therefore are free to regulate private ownership of handguns and other firearms in any way they see fit. The issue then becomes to what extent the federal government may regulate the ownership of firearms by private citizens.

The U.S. Supreme Court dealt directly with the scope of the Second Amendment in a 1939 decision. In *United States v. Miller*, the court upheld a federal law making it a crime to ship a sawed-off shotgun in interstate commerce. The court refused to strike down the law as violative of the Second Amendment because there was no evidence that a sawed-off shotgun had "some reasonable relationship to the preservation or efficiency of a well regulated militia." The court held that the Second Amendment "must be interpreted and applied" keeping in mind the obvious intention of the continuation and effectiveness of a militia.

The Supreme Court has not recently had occasion to speak directly on the Second Amendment. However, Justice Douglas addressed the subject in a powerful dissent, joined by Justice Marshall, in a case extending police ability to stop and frisk suspects. Justice Douglas pointed out that part of the damage wrought by popular misinterpretation of the Second Amendment is a diminution in Fourth Amendment protections against search and seizure. Disagreeing with the majority opinion expanding police power he argued, "The police problem is an acute one not because of the Fourth Amendment, but because of the ease with which anyone can acquire a pistol. A powerful lobby dins into the ears of our citizenry that these gun purchases are constitutional rights protected by the Second Amendment. . . . There is no reason why all pistols should not be barred to everyone except the police."

A Collective Right

From 17th-century Britain, through the framing of the U.S. Constitution, and thence through constitutional adjudication to the present, the right to bear arms has been recognized as a collective right for a collective purpose: to enable organized bodies of citizens to resist central government tyranny.

It has not been recognized as establishing a general right of private citizens to own weapons.

For present-day gun owners, the Second Amendment is hardly more than an emotional symbol.

Thomas Seess, *The San Diego Tribune*, April 30, 1986.

The federal courts, in accordance with the Supreme Court precedents, consistently hold that there is no individual right to own a firearm.

In *United States v. Warin*, the Sixth Circuit Court of Appeals expressed exasperation with the misguided arguments made by the defendant in attempting to persuade the court that a federal law prohibiting the possession of an unregistered machine gun violated his Second Amendment rights. In upholding the defendant's conviction under the federal law, the court stated, "It would unduly extend this opinion to attempt to deal with every argument made by defendant and amicus curiae, Second Amendment Foundation, all of which are based on the erroneous supposition that the Second Amendment is concerned with the rights of individuals rather than those of the States."

In a decision upholding a ban on the possession of handguns in the Illinois town of Morton Grove, the Seventh Circuit stated flatly, "possession of handguns by individuals is not part of the right to keep and bear arms." The U.S. Supreme Court refused to review this decision.

The same court upheld an ordinance freezing the number of handguns in Chicago when it was challenged as a violation of the equal protection clause. The court ruled that the ordinance need only be rationally related to a legitimate state interest. Since the legislation did "not impinge upon the exercise of a fundamental personal right," a higher level of scrutiny was not mandated.

A Collective Right

In short, every federal court decision that has considered the issue has given the Second Amendment a collective, militia interpretation. Moreover, no gun control measure has ever been struck down as unconstitutional under the Second Amendment. Clearly, the federal government is free to regulate or prohibit the possession and transfer of firearms in order to promote the general welfare of the public.

Despite the volume of evidence to the contrary, Americans continue to believe the Second Amendment is concerned with individual rights. The extent of the confusion is apparent from the results of a recent Hearst Corp. poll which found that half of those surveyed believed the Constitution guarantees every citizen the right to own a handgun. Why the misinterpretation?

NRA Propaganda

It is primarily the result of an extremely successful propaganda campaign carried out by the gun lobby. At the forefront of the disinformation effort is the NRA. The NRA, and other pro-gun groups, regularly mobilize members' ingrained fear of infringement of a perceived individual right to bear arms for fundraising purposes and constantly reinforce the idea that the Constitution guarantees all Americans the right to keep and bear firearms for home and self protection. An NRA ad campaign admonishes, "Don't own a firearm if you choose not to. But never let anyone deny or delay your constitutional freedom to make that choice." Implicit in this message is the suggestion that even a waiting period imposed before a firearm purchase somehow would impinge on rights guaranteed by the Second Amendment.

The NRA and other pro-gun groups get a lot of mileage out of the Second Amendment and have succeeded in convincing most Americans that banning individual ownership of firearms would be unconstitutional. The problem is, the gun lobby doesn't believe their own argument.

The firearm lobby has been presented with the perfect opportunity to prove the Second Amendment was intended to guarantee an individual right. In 1986, Congress passed the first federal ban on any type of firearm when it banned the sale to private persons of machine guns manufactured after May 19, 1986. This new law represents the first opportunity to challenge the concept of a federally imposed ban on a class of firearm.

If the gun lobby had confidence in the arguments they offer in support of their interpretation of the Second Amendment they would have filed suit on May 20, 1986 challenging the ban as a direct violation of individual Second Amendment rights. The gun control movement realizes that there could be no greater public relations coup than a modern U.S. Supreme Court decision affirming the fact that the Second Amendment guarantees not an individual right to have firearms but a right of the states to arm a militia for the collective defense of the nation. Unfortunately, the gun lobby knows that this indeed would be the result if the Supreme Court were to consider the Second Amendment. They therefore are not anxious to pursue such a case.

The Need for Gun Control

It is time the gun lobby be forced to address the issue of gun control on the merits. Handguns are undoubtedly the murder weapon of choice, accounting for nearly half of all homicides in this country. Almost half of those 9,000 were simply a quick end to an argument. Another 12,000 people commit suicide with handguns each year. Mental health professionals agree that up to 60 percent of handgun suicides would not have occurred were it not for the immediate presence of a lethal weapon. Finally, there is little argument that the 1,000 unintentional fatal injuries would not have happened if a handgun had not been accessible.

However, measures of handgun control, registration, licensing, and even mandatory sentencing may have limited success reducing felony related incidents. Nothing short of a total ban on private possession can make a dramatic impact on the enormous toll this one class of weapon has taken on the citizens of this country. There is certainly no constitutional barrier to laws designed to end the slaughter.

Distinguishing Between Fact and Opinion

This activity is designed to help develop the basic reading and thinking skill of distinguishing between fact and opinion. Consider the following statement: "In 1988 there were over 10,000 homicides committed with handguns in the US." This is a fact which can be verified by checking US government crime statistics. But consider this statement: "We must enact strict gun control laws to prevent killings." This statement expresses an opinion about the positive effects of gun control. Many people would disagree that gun control laws can lower the number of homicides, and some might argue that such laws are so bad they should be avoided regardless of this consideration.

When investigating controversial issues it is important that one be able to distinguish beween statements of fact and statements of opinion. It is also important to recognize that not all statements of fact are true. They may appear to be true, but some are based on inaccurate or false information. For this activity, however, we are concerned with understanding the difference between those statements which appear to be factual and those which appear to be based primarily on opinion.

The following statements are related to topics covered in this chapter. Consider each statement carefully. *Mark O for any statement you believe is an opinion or interpretation of facts. Mark F for any statement you consider a fact. Mark U if you are uncertain.*

If you are doing this activity as a member of a class or group, compare your answer to those of other class or group members. Be able to defend your answers. You may discover that others come to different conclusions than you. Listening to the reasons others present for their answers may give you valuable insights in distinguishing between fact and opinion.

> O = *opinion*
> F = *fact*
> U = *uncertain*

1. During the Vietnam War, more than twice as many Americans were killed with guns in their own country as died in combat in Vietnam.

2. Buying a handgun for self-defense is a foolish idea.

3. Most burglars obtain their guns by stealing them.

4. Saturday night specials have no legitimate function.

5. Gun control is an ambiguous term that can mean many things.

6. There are approximately 20,000 gun laws of various sorts already on the books in the United States.

7. The right to keep and bear arms is found in the Second Amendment to the US Constitution.

8. Even if handguns were banned, they would always be available to anyone willing to pay a thousand dollars to obtain one.

9. Many people own guns because they cannot count on the police to protect them.

10. Handguns are used only for killing other people.

11. Gun control laws violate the essence of liberty for which America stands.

12. State and local gun laws are of little use because criminals can obtain guns elsewhere.

13. A loaded gun in the bedroom dresser is an invitation to disaster.

14. The US Constitution guarantees everyone the right to own a gun.

15. Widespread gun ownership is the most important reason burglaries do not take place when someone is at home.

16. Only one gun owner in 3,000 commits homicide.

17. In Detroit, more people died in one year from handgun accidents than were killed in four years by home-invading burglars.

Periodical Bibliography

The following articles have been selected to supplement the diverse views presented in this chapter.

American Rifleman	"Medical Journal's Article Seriously Flawed, NRA Says," January 1989.
Sarah Kemp Brady	"Handguns Must Be Kept Away from the John Hinckleys of the World," *Glamour*, May 1986.
Gail Buchhalter	"Why I Own a Gun," *Parade Magazine*, February 21, 1988.
Joe D. Casey	"Whose Side Is the NRA On?" *The Washington Post National Weekly Edition*, August 15/21, 1988.
William B. Couch	"The Great Debate Continues . . ." *Guns & Ammo*, February 1989.
Christopher Elias	"Handgun Industry Gets Fired Up," *Insight*, November 30, 1987.
Stephen P. Halbrook	"What the Framers Intended: A Linguistic Analysis of the Right To 'Bear Arms,'" *Law and Contemporary Problems*, Winter 1986.
Holly Hazard	"Bearing Arms: The Right That Isn't," *The Animals' Agenda*, November 1988.
James J. Kilpatrick	"Gun Control Is an Exercise in Futility," *Conservative Chronicle*, October 26, 1988. Available from Box 29, Hampton, IA 50441.
David B. Kopel	"Trust the People: The Case Against Gun Control," *Cato Policy Analysis*, July 11, 1988. Available from the Cato Institute, 224 Second St. SE, Washington, DC 20003.
Matthew Maranz	"Guns 'R' Us," *The New Republic*, January 23, 1989.
William Saletan	"Sons of Guns," *The New Republic*, March 2, 1987.
John Henry Sloan et al.	"Handgun Regulations, Crime, Assaults, and Homicide: A Tale of Two Cities," *The New England Journal of Medicine*, November 10, 1988.

Organizations To Contact

The editors have compiled the following list of organizations which are concerned with the issues debated in this book. All of them have information or publications available for interested readers. The descriptions are derived from materials provided by the organizations themselves. This list was compiled upon the date of publication. Names and phone numbers of organizations are subject to change.

American Civil Liberties Union (ACLU)
132 W. 43rd St.
New York, NY 10036
(212) 944-9800

Founded in 1920, the ACLU champions the rights set forth in the Declaration of Independence and the Constitution. It provides legal defense, research, and education. It publishes the quarterly newspaper *Civil Liberties* and various pamphlets, books, and position papers.

American Correctional Association (ACA)
8025 Laurel Lakes Court
Laurel, MD 20707
(301) 206-5061

The ACA is an organization of practitioners and academicians in the corrections field. It works to improve prison and correctional standards by providing timely materials on theoretical and practical aspects of criminal justice. The Association publishes books and the periodical *Corrections Today*.

Crime Stoppers International (CSI)
3736 Eubank NE, Suite B4
Albuquerque, NM 87111
(505) 294-2300

CSI works to increase citizen action in crime prevention. It assists in organizing programs that offer anonymous rewards for information leading to the resolution of serious crimes. It has produced a documentary video, and publishes *The Caller*, a monthly magazine.

Delancey Street Foundation
2563 Divisadero St.
San Francisco, CA 94115
(415) 563-5326

The Foundation is a residential treatment center that has become renowned for its success in rehabilitating criminals. It distributes a variety of informational materials, including reprints of articles from *The Washington Post, San Francisco Chronicle,* and other publications.

Figgie International, Inc.
4420 Sherwin Road
Willoughby, OH 44094
(216) 953-2811

Figgie International is a diversified Fortune 500 corporation which has sponsored and published a series of research reports on crime in America. The book-length studies are available on request.

Handgun Control, Inc.
1225 Eye St. NW, Suite 1100
Washington, DC 20005
(202) 898-0792

Handgun Control, Inc. is a public citizen's lobby which works for stricter laws and regulations on the manufacture, importation, and possession of handguns. It compiles information on gun control, and publishes books, reports, and pamphlets, including *Handgun Facts.*

National Association of Chiefs of Police (NACOP)
1000 Connecticut Ave. NW, Suite 9
Washington, DC 20036
(202) 293-9088

The NACOP is a professional organization of chief law-enforcement officers. It regularly surveys its members on criminal-justice matters including gun control and drug laws, and publishes books and the periodicals *Chiefs of Police Magazine* and *Criminal Investigator.*

National Center on Institutions and Alternatives
635 Slaters Lane, Suite G-100
Alexandria, VA 22314
(703) 684-0373

The Center is a private non-profit agency that promotes alternatives to prisons. It sponsors the Client Specific Planning Program which develops alternative sentences for criminals. The Center publishes books, pamphlets, and *Augustus,* a monthly journal.

National Coalition To Ban Handguns
100 Maryland Ave. NE
Washington, DC 20002
(202) 544-7190

This coalition of educational, professional, and religious organizations works to ban the sale of handguns in the US by supporting gun-control laws at the national, state, and local levels. The organization compiles statistics and information on handguns, develops educational materials, and publishes reports and *The Banner,* a quarterly newsletter.

National Council on Crime and Delinquency (NCCD)
77 Maiden Lane, 4th Floor
San Francisco, CA 94108
(415) 956-5651

The NCCD consists of corrections specialists and others interested in crime prevention. It conducts research and initiates policies to reduce crime and delinquency. The Council supports community-based programs for crime prevention and citizen involvement in crime-control efforts. The Council publishes booklets and the quarterly journal *Crime and Delinquency.*

National Crime Prevention Council
733 15th St. NW, Suite 540
Washington, DC 20005
(202) 393-7141

The Council works with businesses, citizen groups, law enforcement agencies, and other organizations to gather and disseminate information on crime-prevention programs. It seeks to educate the public in crime prevention and building safer communities. The Council publishes books, pamphlets, and other materials.

National Criminal Justice Association (NCJA)
444 N. Capitol St. NW, Suite 608
Washington, DC 20001
(202) 347-4900

The NCJA works to improve state criminal-justice systems. It publishes and distributes information on criminal-justice administration. The NCJA's publications include several reports and the monthly *Justice Bulletin*.

National Institute of Justice (NIJ)
US Department of Justice
Box 6000
Rockville, MD 20850
(800) 851-3420

The NIJ supports research into crime, criminal behavior, and crime prevention. It publishes and distributes numerous reports and books through the National Criminal Justice Reference Service, an international clearinghouse of criminal-justice information for researchers and other interested individuals and organizations.

National Rifle Assocation of America (NRA)
Institute for Legislative Action
1600 Rhode Island Ave. NW
Washington, DC 20036
(202) 828-6330

The NRA is an organization of target shooters, hunters, gun collectors, and others interested in firearms. It has lobbied against gun-control laws, and has published *A Question of Self-Defense* as well as numerous other pamphlets, position papers, and articles on gun control.

Second Amendment Foundation
James Madison Building
12500 NE 10th Place
Bellevue, WA 98005
(206) 454-7012

The Foundation believes the US Constitution guarantees individuals the right to possess firearms. It organizes many educational and legal-action programs against gun-control laws, and publishes numerous monographs and pamphlets, including *The Battle over Gun Control*.

The Sentencing Project
1156 15th St. NW, Suite 520
Washington, DC 20005
(202) 463-8348

The Project provides information on alternative-sentencing programs to public defenders and other government officials. It promotes public understanding of the sentencing process. The Project publishes the *National Directory of Felony Sentencing Services* and other materials.

Bibliography of Books

Malin Åkerström	*Crooks and Squares*. New Brunswick, NJ: Transaction Press, 1985.
David C. Anderson	*Crimes of Justice*. New York: Times Books, 1988.
Robert M. Baird and Stuart E. Rosenbaum, eds.	*Philosophy of Punishment*. Buffalo, NY: Prometheus Books, 1988.
Georgette Bennett	*Crimewarps: The Future of Crime in America*. Garden City, NY: Anchor Books, 1987.
John Braithwaite	*Corporate Crime in the Pharmaceutical Industry*. Boston: Routledge & Kegan Paul, 1984.
Michael Castleman	*Crime Free*. New York: Simon and Schuster, 1984.
Elliott Currie	*Confronting Crime*. New York: Pantheon Books, 1985.
Ralph Adam Fine	*Escape of the Guilty*. New York: Dodd, Mead & Company, 1986.
Brent Fisse and Peter A. French, eds.	*Corrigible Corporations & Unruly Law*. San Antonio, TX: Trinity University Press, 1985.
Alan M. Gottlieb	*Gun Rights Fact Book*. Bellevue, WA: Merril Press, 1988.
Jean Harris	*They Always Call Us Ladies*. New York: Charles Scribner's Sons, 1988.
Barbara Hudson	*Justice Through Punishment*. London: Macmillan Education, 1987.
James A. Inciardi	*Criminal Justice*. San Diego: Harcourt Brace Jovanovich, 1987.
Elmer H. Johnson, ed.	*Handbook on Crime and Delinquency Prevention*. Westport, CT: Greenwood Press, 1987.
Don B. Kates Jr., ed.	*Firearms and Violence*. Cambridge, MA: Ballinger Publishing Company, 1984.
Jack Katz	*Seductions of Crime*. New York: Basic Books, 1988.
Philip Kropatkin and Richard P. Kusserow	*Management Principles for Asset Protection*. New York: John Wiley & Sons, 1986.
Michael Levi	*Regulating Fraud: White-Collar Crime and the Criminal Process*. New York: Tavistock Publications, 1987.
Jack Levin and James Lan Fox	*Mass Murder: America's Growing Menace*. New York: Plenum Press, 1985.
Patrick B. McGuigan and Jon S. Pascale, eds.	*Crime and Punishment in Modern America*. Washington, DC: Free Congress Research and Education Foundation, 1986.
Terrie E. Moffitt and Sarnoff A. Mednick, eds.	*Biological Contributions to Crime Causation*. Dordrecht, The Netherlands: Martinus Nijhoff Publishers, 1988.
Russell Mokhiber	*Corporate Crime and Violence*. San Francisco: Sierra Club Books, 1988.

National Crime Prevention Institute	*Understanding Crime Prevention.* Boston: Butterworths, 1986.
Harold E. Pepinsky and Paul Jesilow	*Myths that Cause Crime.* Cabin John, MD: Seven Locks Press, 1984.
Morgan O. Reynolds	*Crime by Choice: An Economic Analysis.* Dallas, TX: The Fisher Institute, 1985.
Dennis P. Rosenbaum	*Community Crime Prevention.* Newbury Park, CA: Sage Publications, 1986.
Warren J. Samuels and Arthur S. Miller, eds.	*Corporations and Society.* Westport, CT: Greenwood Press, 1987.
Parviz Saney	*Crime and Culture in America.* Westport, CT: Greenwood Press, 1986.
Joseph F. Sheley	*Exploring Crime.* Belmont, CA: Wadsworth, 1987.
Pete Shields	*Guns Don't Die—People Do.* New York: Arbor House, 1981.
Mark Stevens	*The Insiders.* New York: G.P. Putnam's Sons, 1987.
Edwin H. Sutherland	*White Collar Crime.* New Haven, CT: Yale University Press, 1983.
C.L. Ten	*Crime, Guilt, and Punishment.* Oxford, England: Clarendon Press, 1987.
Charles W. Thomas	*Corrections in America.* Newbury Park, CA: Sage Publications, 1987.
William Tucker	*Vigilante: The Backlash Against Crime in America.* New York: Stein and Day, 1985.
James Q. Wilson and Richard J. Herrnstein	*Crime & Human Nature.* New York: Simon and Schuster, 1985.
Lord Windlesham	*Responses to Crime.* Oxford, England: Clarendon Press, 1987.
Franklin E. Zimring and Gordon Hawkins	*The Citizen's Guide to Gun Control.* New York: Macmillan Publishing Company, 1987.

Index

239

240